Advance Praise for *Mantle of Mercy*

"Applause for *Mantle of Mercy*. This extraordinary compilation of personal essays provides insight into Muslim chaplains' experiences and contributions to the field of chaplaincy in the United States. Readers gain a glimpse of the foundational Islamic principles and values that undergird the writers' ministry and leadership within the diverse institutions they serve. *Mantle of Mercy* is a must-have resource for theological schools, Clinical Pastoral Education (CPE) Centers, and students pursuing a career in chaplaincy."

— CHAPLAIN TAHARA AKMAL, MA, BCC, Association for Clinical
    Pastoral Education Certified Educator

"*Mantle of Mercy* fills an important void within the emerging body of research and writing about the field of chaplaincy. While chaplaincy may be unfamiliar to many Muslims, the writers in this volume generously engage with both the educational formation processes and spiritual practices of chaplaincy while thoroughly and authentically integrating them with the Islamic faith. Careful, scholarly attention is paid throughout the text to the core principles of Islam, demonstrating through story and reflection how a chaplaincy is an ideal form of practice for the faithful Muslim leader. The result is a beautiful witness to the many ways that Islamic chaplaincy embodies the kind of compassion that is at the heart of professional spiritual care. This text is an incredible resource to chaplaincy educators, professional chaplains, and those Muslims seeking to serve as professional spiritual care providers."

— TRACE HAYTHORN, PHD, executive director & CEO, Association
    for Clinical Pastoral Education

"Islamic chaplaincy, a relatively new field of inquiry and practice, has been skillfully outlined in this first volume of its kind, *Mantle of Mercy*. The editors have done a wonderful job in assembling a chorus of diverse voices of practitioners from the field. Critical perspectives from chaplains serving in universities, the healthcare sector, the military, and underrepresented communities provide fascinating insight into the world of fostering human souls. In a world where cynicism, distrust, and division have impaired our collective ability to engage with one another, this volume offers a reprieve, and perhaps even a way forward to reacquaint ourselves with our inherent humanity."

—SHAYKH WALEAD MOSAAD, PHD, Chair and Resident Scholar, Sabeel Community

"In this superbly curated collection of essays, trailblazing Muslim chaplains provide intimate portraits of their professional lives and how they arrived at their vocational calling; how they create healing spaces through the Prophetic example; and how they provide pastoral care by drawing upon Islamic theology. As readers amble into this garden of stories, they will surely feel the hearts of these chaplains speaking to their own. And by taking in the vista, they will come to recognize the value Islamic chaplaincy adds within hospitals, prisons, college campuses, the armed forces, and, indeed, even within mosques and third spaces."

—AASIM I. PADELA, MD, MSc, chairperson and director of the Initiative on Islam & Medicine, and professor of Emergency Medicine, Bioethics, and the Medical Humanities at the Medical College of Wisconsin

"I really loved this book. Muslim chaplains do amazing work for religious identity, pastoral care, and civic pluralism. This volume captures the complexity and range of such work remarkably well."

—EBOO PATEL, author of *Acts of Faith* and president of Interfaith Youth Core

"In the last few decades, Muslim chaplains have emerged as a profoundly important model of spiritual accompaniment. *Mantle of Mercy* brings together most of the leading Muslim chaplains in North America who bring a tradition-centered approach to healing in their various settings. The chapters are as spiritually rich as they are accessible. It is lovely to see how they advance the concept of healing and care beyond the Western obsession with 'self' care to the heart-community-Divine level. Particularly poignant and bittersweet are the chapter and the farewell from the departed and much beloved Imam Sohaib N. Sultan. I commend Ali, Bajwa, Kholaki, and Starr for this urgently needed volume and enthusiastically recommend this book to all who work with the Muslim community and in pastoral care in the context of universities, hospitals, and beyond."

— OMID SAFI, PHD, professor of Islamic Studies at Duke University and director of Illuminated Courses and Tours

"Ali, Bajwa, Kholaki, and Starr have created a watershed moment with the publication of *Mantle of Mercy*. By assembling North America's leading lights in Islamic chaplaincy, the editorial team has provided an essential resource not just for Muslim chaplains but for all spiritual care providers who are rightly attentive to contemporary spiritual and religious diversity. Students, educators, and chaplains in the field will benefit from *Mantle of Mercy*. This essential addition to the literature makes it definitely clear that North American spiritual care cannot develop further without taking Islamic chaplaincy into much greater account."

— MICHAEL SKAGGS, PHD, director of programs, Chaplaincy Innovation Lab

"This is an important and much-needed scholarly contribution to the literature on chaplaincy in general and, more specifically, Islamic chaplaincy. It gives insight into how far the field has come and how Islam is establishing itself into the fabric of North American life in such a beautiful way. The contributors and the topics they write beautifully demonstrate how diverse the Islamic tradition is and how interesting and wonderful such diversity can be. This compilation is a moving and inspiring book and a must-have for anyone interested in chaplaincy, pastoral care, the healing arts, Islam, Islam in North America, and many other related fields."

— CARRIE M. YORK, PHD, president, The Alkaram Institute

THANK YOU FOR ALL OF YOUR
WORK TO MAKE WESTY AWESOME FOR ALL!
AS WE SAY: JAZAK ALLAH KHAYRUN —
MAY GOD REWARD YOU,

Jaye

MANTLE OF MERCY

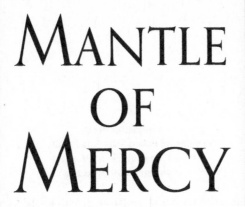

MANTLE
OF
MERCY

Islamic Chaplaincy
in North America

Editors

Muhammad A. Ali, Omer Bajwa,
Sondos Kholaki, *and* Jaye Starr

TEMPLETON PRESS

Templeton Press
300 Conshohocken State Road, Suite 500
West Conshohocken, PA 19428
www.templetonpress.org

This paper meets the requirements of ANSI/NISO Z39.48-1992
(Permanence of Paper).

ISBN: 978-1-59947-593-6 (cloth)
ISBN: 978-1-59947-594-3 (ebook)

Library of Congress Control Number: 2021943236

A catalogue record for this book is available
from the Library of Congress.

Printed in the United States of America.

22 23 24 25 26   10 9 8 7 6 5 4 3 2 1

Bismillah al-Rahmân al-Rahîm
We begin in the name of God, the Compassionate, the Merciful

This book is dedicated with the deepest gratitude to
Dr. Ingrid Mattson, whose tireless pioneering efforts
planted the seeds for our training, and to the late
Chaplain Sohaib Sultan, who helped nurture those
seeds by building joyful communities.

CONTENTS

A NOTE ON CONVENTIONS

LANGUAGE CAN FALL SHORT IN translation. We have therefore chosen to use Arabic terms and provide close English equivalents in parentheses. In doing so, we honor the richness of our own tradition while giving non-Muslim readers an opportunity to experience the challenges and insights involved in translating a term in a way that resonates with our being and practice.

The medallion (ﷺ) placed after the name of the Prophet Muhammad at the first mention in each paragraph serves as a reminder to Muslim readers to utter the pious blessing "*salla llâhu 'alayhi wa-sallam,*" which translates to "God, send blessings and peace upon Muhammad."

Qur'anic references are cited by surah (chapter) name and number, colon, and verse number; for example, al-Baqarah/2:163. Unless otherwise noted, all translations are from *The Study Quran* (HarperOne, 2015).

Hadiths are reports of the Prophet Muhammad's ﷺ actions, statements, and practices. They are cited here by collection name and number.

We use a simplified transliteration for Arabic words, where circumflexes represent long vowels. Familiar terms and names are spelled according to English convention.

FOREWORD

Dr. Ingrid Mattson

ISLAMIC CHAPLAINCY IN ITS MODERN form is the fruit of hard-fought battles waged by Black American Muslims for religious freedom and dignity. The sinister structures of anti-Black racism guarantee that disproportionate numbers of Black folks populate American prisons. When incarcerated Black American Muslims and their communities on the "outside" began advocating for religious accommodations and freedom decades ago, they demonstrated their commitment to their faith, resistance to oppression, and knowledge of how American legal and political systems, while deeply biased against them, could nevertheless be used to fight for their rights. The first Islamic chaplains in American prisons owed their positions to the advocacy and litigious activity of mostly incarcerated Black Muslims.

Black Muslims in the United States military were the next significant group to fight for their rights to religious accommodation. Like incarcerated Americans, although usually to a lesser extent, those in the military are restricted in their movements, even hour to hour, often can only eat the food provided to them, and wear uniforms provided by the state. Religious accommodations in the form of lawful food, the ability to fast and break the fast, to perform the daily *salat* and attend Jummah prayer, and to meet the requirements of modest dress are necessary to meet the constitutionally protected religious rights of Muslims. While Muslims have served in the U.S. military since the founding of America,[1] it was not until 1993, in the wake of large numbers of Black Americans who converted to Islam during the "First Gulf War" (Operation Desert Storm), that the U.S. military hired an active-duty Muslim chaplain. Who could have anticipated such a development, except perhaps a believer who trusts that Allah can bring good out of bad, light out of darkness: "Allah knows and you do not know."[2]

When I started my PhD, Islam was not taught in any seminary, divinity school, or theology faculty in the United States; it was only taught in departments of Middle East, Near East, or Oriental Studies. I was fortunate to supplement my academic program by studying with Muslim religious scholars. I stayed involved in Muslim communities on the South Side of Chicago because I had a husband and children—an ivory tower life was neither possible nor desirable.

In 1998, Hartford Seminary, which had a few years earlier made history as the first American seminary to hire a Muslim to teach Islam (Ibrahim Abu-Rabi), hired me to teach Islamic Studies and to develop "some kind of leadership program" for Muslims. Community leaders such as Imam Qasim Sharif of Masjid Muhammad and Dr. Saleem Bajwa, a Hartford Seminary board member, had advocated for such a program and were key advisors. To develop this program, I employed the same methodology I had used two years earlier when I was hired by a Canadian Muslim relief organization to develop some kind of support program for Afghan women living in Pakistani refugee camps: understand the context, study other programs with similar goals, consult widely with Muslim leadership, and find the people already stepping forward to serve their communities and support them.

What I learned about the context of Hartford Seminary was that religious communities were respected and valued. Students could study Islam and be Muslims without being presented with a false choice between academia and faith. What struck me most, however, was Hartford's emphasis on offering academic study and credentialing to believers for whom the standard program for religious leadership (an MDiv) was unattainable due to the students' social, economic, or political marginalization in the broader society, or because their own religious communities did not deem them worthy of leadership. I was in awe at the respect and support given to students in the Black Ministries Program, Women's Leadership Institute, and Programa de Ministerios Hispanos. I wanted a program like this for Muslims, where those who served their communities, even when they had no resources, could have access to quality education and training.

When I looked for other initiatives for Muslim religious leadership, and consulted with academic and organizational leaders in the American Muslim community, it became clear that other programs had failed or not flourished for some similar reasons: they were centered around one scholar, they were isolated from the broader academic and faith community, and they did not take the American context seriously.

Imam Qasim and Dr. Bajwa connected me with local and regional Muslim leaders; I attended meetings and consultations, and I listened. I met many men and women, almost exclusively Black Muslims, who had been volunteering or working as prison chaplains. They told me about the challenges they faced doing their work due to racism, anti-Muslim discrimination, and marginalization, often justified by the administration because they lacked the credentials and academic degrees of the Christian chaplains.

Before the end of my first year of research and consultation, we were approached by some Muslims who were seeking an MDiv equivalency program so they could serve as military chaplains. The path had become clear: our Muslim leadership program would be an Islamic chaplaincy program, with Islamic studies, pastoral care, and interfaith and intercultural engagement as key components.

In designing the original program, there was one major reason I chose to make it an MA plus graduate certificate (GC) program. I wanted to ensure that the original Muslim chaplains, specifically the Black Muslim men and women who struggled as volunteers and marginalized employees in American prisons, would not be deemed unqualified once our graduates entered society. The GC gave credits for "relevant life experience," did not require the student to write a thesis, and could be completed in a relatively short time.

I was not trained as a chaplain, but it has been my honor to train chaplains. My confidence has been in the Qur'an and the example of the blessed Prophet ﷺ as sufficient for giving Muslims the theological, spiritual, and ethical teachings we need for chaplaincy. Allah, Who is Exalted, destined that my beloved daughter Soumayya, may Allah have mercy on her soul, would be struck with a terrible illness while I was in the early years of the program. For a dozen years she was my teacher in Islamic pastoral care; she taught me not to judge her reactions, not to give her cheap advice, not to offer answers to unanswerable questions, but to be present, to see her, to listen to her, to affirm her beauty despite her wrecked body, to affirm that her life was meaningful, despite being confined to a bed in a room—a room that became my *ribât*.

Islamic chaplaincy is not a magical space where ideological, political, and social disparities do not exist; we will not agree on all approaches to this service. But I have always believed that sincere Muslims could uncover and discover how to manifest the sacred teachings of Islam in this work. This volume is a witness to the truth of this belief.

Notes

1. Shareda Hosein, "Muslims in the US Military: Revolutionary War to Civil War," Hartford Seminary MA thesis, 2007.

2. al-Baqarah/2:216.

MANTLE
OF
MERCY

Editors' Introduction

MUHAMMAD A. ALI, OMER BAJWA,
SONDOS KHOLAKI, AND JAYE STARR

AT ITS ROOT, the word "chaplain" derives from the Latin word for "cloak" or "mantle," representing security, comfort, protection, and warmth—qualities that a chaplain aims to bring to the careseeker. The symbol of the mantle appears in connection with the Prophet Muhammad ﷺ in myriad ways in the Islamic tradition, each demonstrating the mercy he embodied, such as when he laid his cloak on the ground for Halîmah (his former wet nurse) as a gesture of love and respect when she visited. He also gathered his cousin Ali, his grandsons Hasan and Husayn, and his daughter Fatimah under his cloak as a declaration of their status as his beloved family. Imam al-Busîrî, the author of the *Qasîdat al-Burdah*, or "Ode of the Mantle," composed this oft-recited poem following a dream in which the Prophet used his cloak to cover the ailing poet, who awoke completely and mysteriously healed of his illness. In a display of compassionate care some Muslim chaplains point, as a source of inspiration, to the Prophet's wife, Lady Khadîjah, lovingly wrapping the Prophet in a *dithâr*, or cloak, to provide comfort immediately following his jarring experience of receiving his first revelation. In his time of doubt, she affirmed his beautiful qualities and gently accompanied him to her cousin, the monk Waraqah, for additional support. Lady Khadîjah—through her compassionate presence, affirmation and validation, and "referral," demonstrated what chaplains strive to provide.

This connection between the cloak or mantle and chaplaincy proves significant for Muslim chaplains, for whom the Prophet Muhammad ﷺ remains the foremost model and example of compassionate spiritual care. The pastoral way he used questions in lieu of direct advice, the full presence and deep listening he provided in conversation with careseekers, and his emphasis on community all inform the ministry of Muslim chaplains. According to the Spiritual Assessment and Intervention Model (Spiritual AIM),[1] a chaplain strives to embody three roles as part of their intervention: valuer, guide, and truth-teller. As a valuer, the Prophet communicated to a careseeker their innate worth and belonging when he turned his entire body toward the person he was speaking to, such that the person felt like they were the most important person.[2] As a guide, the Prophet asked meaningful questions to help the care-seeker discern their way forward.[3] As a truth-teller, the Prophet tolerated the anger of others, understood the deeper emotions beneath the anger, and addressed brokenness and tension in relationships.[4] Muslims remember the Prophet as a gentle, loving, and merciful example who embodied the Qur'an's teachings of spiritual advancement, which appropriately fits the characteristics of a spiritual guide and caregiver.

To inform their ministry, most Muslim chaplains draw on two main sources: the Qur'an, the scriptural text, considered the revealed word of God, and the Sunnah, the example and practice of the Prophet Muhammad ﷺ. Both the Qur'an and the Sunnah emphasize one key characteristic: *rahmah*, a term which encapsulates mercy, love, and compassion. All but one of the Qur'an's 114 chapters begin with *Bismillah al-Rahmân al-Rahîm*—In the name of God, the Compassionate, the Merciful—an invocation that reminds the reader of these central attributes of the Divine. What is more, God refers in the Qur'an to the Prophet Muhammad as *rahmatan lil-'âlamîn*,[5] "a mercy to all of creation."

A more nuanced definition of *rahmah* emerges when we break it down into its constituent Arabic root letters *r-h-m*, the same root letters from which comes the word *rahm*, or womb. This feminine attribute of God, *rahmah*, is a direct link to the cushioned home of the growing fetus nestled safely within the mother, underscoring this similarly protective, nurturing, and loving nature of the Divine. God—every created soul's First Guardian—protects, nurtures, and remains present with us before our own parents protect, nurture, and love us. Notably, many hospital chaplains share that patients coming out of surgery or in the active death phase will call out for their mother, suggesting that the comfort of a guardian's love is perhaps the closest thing we have in this terrestrial life to understanding God's love for us.[6]

As *rahmatan lil-âlamîn*, the Prophet ﷺ served everybody around him, from the most vulnerable to the most powerful, whether a follower or not. In the essays gathered here, readers will learn how the mantle of mercy, as demonstrated by the Prophet Muhammad and his wife Lady Khadîjah, is brought to life in the compassionate spiritual care provided by Muslim chaplains. The diverse collection of contributors use storytelling to demonstrate the work of professional chaplaincy, the teachings and doctrines that inspire it, and the obstacles they have overcome entering into this predominantly Christian field. Notably, while chaplaincy has its roots in Christianity, traditions we recognize now as pastoral care have existed throughout Muslim history. These essays present contemporary North American manifestations and offer vibrant contributions toward the field of professional chaplaincy. Muslim chaplains, through their service to careseekers of all belief systems in colleges, hospitals, correctional facilities, community organizations, and the armed forces, offer a vision of their lived service in the way of God.[7]

Islamic Chaplaincy—Muslim Chaplains

As we developed the idea for this book, we struggled with a topic that has long been a point of discussion: is it properly Muslim chaplaincy or Islamic chaplaincy? One reason not to use "Islamic chaplaincy" is that it suggests a normative guide to *one* form of correct chaplaincy rooted in a specific praxis of the *dîn* (religion). "Muslim chaplaincy," on the other hand, implies that we only care for Muslims when, as chaplains, we are often called to serve non-Muslims in the institutions where we work. Since we are examining a multiplicity of understandings of chaplaincy—informed by Islam through engagement with the Qur'an, Sunnah, religious scholarship, and *'urf* (custom)—we have chosen "Islamic chaplaincy" to characterize our work and "Muslim chaplain" to describe who we are.

"Chaplain" itself is a title that many Muslims have questioned using, pointing out that Muslim careseekers are often not familiar with the title, particularly international students and immigrants. Unlike Christian and Jewish chaplains who are also clergy holding titles such as "minister" or "rabbi," Muslims do not necessarily have another title given the lack of ordination in most forms of Islam. For a variety of reasons, including a desire on the part of hiring institutions to consolidate their authority[8] and/or showcase their diversity in ways "chaplain" alone does not convey, many males and some women have also embraced the title "imam,"[9] while some others use *ustâdh/ah* (teacher) or *shaykh/ah* (elder, or scholar).[10] Yet many excellent and otherwise well-trained chaplains do not possess the depth of formal Islamic knowledge these titles suggest. Any understanding of the term "chaplain" is further complicated by the fact that the term "imam" itself is not clearly defined nor is the training standardized.[11] We hold that, ultimately, the work of chaplaincy often extends beyond the roles these titles imply and requires specialty in pastoral care; as such, we believe chaplain to be the most appropriate title for our North American context.

Drs. Nancy Khalil and Celene Ibrahim identify three primary characteristics of chaplains: an absence of any perceived gender restrictions; a focus on pastoral care as the central skill set; and employment within institutions that are either typically interreligious or secular, where they are called to serve *everyone* regardless of their faith affiliation (though we see an exception in Ch. Dr. Joshua Salaam's essay about chaplaincy in a masjid [mosque] context).[12] There have been various attempts to distinguish the two roles such as the idea that "imams preach, chaplains listen," or that imams are the holders of the faith while chaplains are the holders of the faithful.

While the role of a chaplain is unique, chaplains are often a collaborative complement to masjid imams as Ch. Kaiser Aslam shares in his essay. Some male chaplains (and at least one female, Ch. Sondos Kholaki) are also members of their local imams' council, which provides opportunities to offer their pastoral care expertise during tragedies as well as their interfaith skills (as seen in Ch. Samsiah Abdul-Majid's essay), while providing access to scholars when religio-ethical cases surface in chaplains' institutions.

The professional nature of chaplaincy with its more consistent hours, work-life boundaries, and reliable paycheck with benefits has appealed to many masjid imams and scholars. However, their hire by institutions (e.g., prisons) without chaplaincy-specific training has resulted in confused expectations for the "chaplain," the institution, and the careseekers, as well as the broader Muslim community. Meanwhile, many masjid imams have found that they have benefited from one or two units of Clinical Pastoral Education (CPE) or from a weekend course on compassionate care, a core part of chaplaincy training. Does that make them chaplains? Not necessarily, but it may help to bring some of the best skills of chaplaincy into their work as imams.

Our goal in understanding and parsing out the difference between chaplains and imams is not to undermine one profession or prefer one over the other; rather, we aim to develop an understanding of the diversity of religious leadership styles and roles. Ultimately, much of the difference and similarity between the roles of chaplain and imam, irrespective of the title adopted, depends largely on the individuals themselves—what they are called to do in their chaplaincy work, for whom, and in what their training consists of. As has been said, when people contact someone as a *muftî* (jurist), his job is to give his interpretation of their shari'ah obligation; when he is preaching at the masjid as an imam, his job is to uphold the faith as he understands it; and when he visits people in the hospital as a chaplain, his job is to accompany them with compassion.

Islamic Chaplaincy in North America

Islamic chaplaincy has manifested uniquely in the different national contexts where chaplains serve. There is increasing interest in pastoral care professionals in Muslim majority contexts responding to the contemporary displacement and fragmentation of communities as seen in Ch. Dr. Kamal Abu-Shamsieh's essay. The foundations of Islamic chaplaincy in the United States were, in fact, overwhelmingly laid by African Americans, many of whom began as dedicated volunteers during the second half of the twentieth century[13] at a time when training and paychecks did not yet exist. The earliest chaplains were predominantly men, with varying degrees of training as imams. Many early hires occurred in correctional institutions beginning in the 1970s and 1980s. Some were hired while affiliated with the Nation of Islam and subsequently the community led by W. D. Muhammad.

There has been a distinct theme of professionalization within Islamic chaplaincy in the United States.[14] In addition to the groundbreaking work of Hartford Seminary, which established the first graduate training program under the leadership of Dr. Ingrid Mattson in 2000, the efforts of three chaplains to professionalize the field cannot be overlooked: Dr. James (Jimmy) Jones, Matiniah Yahya, and Abdul-Malik Negedu. Through a decade of organizing an annual conference and establishing an endorsement agency, a professional association, and an educational foundation, they built the institutions that significantly advanced the professionalization of the field of Islamic chaplaincy.[15] A profession is typically defined by having an established training process, an association with a code of ethics, and credentialing criteria. For Muslim chaplains in the United States, this consists of a combination of study of Islamic sciences (such as *tafsīr* or Qur'anic exegesis, aqeedah, doctrine, and history of the early community), relevant graduate-level studies, clinical training, endorsement, and membership in a professional association.

In contrast to England,[16] where the majority of Muslim chaplains are South Asian, trained in Islamic schools affiliated with the Deoband Madrasa movement from India, and have no graduate education, in the United States the majority now hold a Master of Divinity (MDiv) degree in Islamic Chaplaincy (or the equivalent)[17] and come from a variety of cultures and traditions. MDiv programs typically consist of a combination of Islamic studies, interfaith studies, and pastoral care, including counseling.[18] Unlike modern psychology, which comes out of a secular framework, chaplaincy developed from the field of sociology.[19] Islamic studies, as a subset of religious studies, focuses on the study of belief and the ways in which believers engage with their faith through fields such as history, sociology, and anthropology. For example, in learning about the sciences of *aqeedah* (creed), *kalam* (theology), and *hadith*, students look to understand how Muslim engagement with these subjects has been impacted by the socio-political milieu. Through the Islamic studies component of chaplaincy training, students develop an appreciation for the different ways in which Muslims have connected with their faith and draw inspiration from pastoral examples in scripture and the Sunnah. As they progress into chaplaincy work, this appreciation allows them to ask careseekers how their faith informs their decision-making rather than instructing them in how their faith *should be* informing their decision-making. Both academic Islamic studies and traditional Islamic sciences are important fields of knowledge and training for a chaplain and, as Ch. Dr. Bilal Ansari articulates in his essay, critical for developing the skill of theological reflection.

Similarly, interfaith studies are a core component of chaplaincy preparation, as chaplains are called to provide spiritual accompaniment for all those in their institution's purview, regardless of what faith (if any) a careseeker practices. To do this, chaplains require foundational knowledge of the major religious and spiritual traditions, as well as an ability to engage in interfaith dialogue with curiosity, respect, and appreciation.

Pastoral care classes make up the final critical component of the education of chaplains. These include courses on mental health, pastoral counseling, professional ethics, and other coursework specific to different experiences such as addiction, gender-based violence, and trauma. Many chaplains report that what they learn in these classes is what they employ the most in their daily work.[20]

Clinical Pastoral Education (CPE)

Clinical Pastoral Education (CPE) provides clinical field training, ideally in an interfaith cohort, where students provide direct chaplaincy services under a supervisor. Through a reflective process, students come to recognize how their own lived experiences impact the care they provide. This self-awareness is critical for limiting malpractice. Hospitals, where most CPE placements occur, offer an ideal setting for pulling students out of their comfort zones. In the midst of difficult emergency department cases, the aspiring chaplain may not be able to consult a religious scholar and must sometimes develop their own practical theology in the moment, a process Ch. Ibrahim Long calls *ijti-hâd* (exertion) of the heart.

The various CPE curricular components provide an opportunity to authentically self-evaluate with the help of peers, similar to the Muslim practice of *tazkiyah*, or refinement of oneself, with the aim of recognizing how one's lived experiences, triggers, and biases impact one's caregiving. In CPE, students engage in an exercise aptly named the Verbatim, which nicely mirrors the Islamic spiritual processes of *murâqabah* (self-observation) and *muhâsabah* (self-assessment) through the reflective process that it calls students to partake in as they examine their encounters, as discussed by Ch. Jawad Bayat in his essay. Current MDiv programs focused on Islamic chaplaincy require students to complete a unit of CPE, recognizing that students benefit from practicing what they've studied under supervision.

Professional Association, Endorsement, and Certification

Contemporary professions have associations responsible for maintaining standards while providing accountability, advocacy, and continuing professional development. In the United States, the Association of Muslim Chaplains (AMC) has emerged at the forefront of several efforts. Established in 2011 for all chaplaincy sectors, AMC's commitment to developing professionalism (including a code of conduct), advocacy, and *suhbah* (companionship) has made significant contributions to enriching the field of Islamic chaplaincy.[21]

Endorsement provides secular institutions with a means of evaluating a candidate as a competent, representative member of a specific faith tradition. Importantly, endorsement allows government agencies to stay within the boundaries of the First Amendment of the U.S. Constitution. While mosques have precipitously provided letters of endorsement, chaplaincy-specific endorsing agencies look to evaluate a person's practice and knowledge of their own tradition as well as their mastery of the foundational chaplaincy competencies.[22]

The concept of endorsement and certification, through which the professional practitioner is held accountable, has long existed in Muslim spaces, according to Ch. Abdul-Malik Negedu of the Muslim Endorsement Council. When an individual masters a topic or subject, an *ijâzah* (license) is conferred. Through established initiation processes, Sufi orders elevate apprentices to full membership.[23] Scholars have, at different points in time, organized themselves into guild-like organizations.[24] In many Muslim majority countries today, the government undertakes the oversight and licensure of imams.

Board certification, typically only required for healthcare chaplains, does not certify a person's religious convictions and practices but rather their ability to apply them to the work of chaplaincy and their mastery of an identified chaplaincy skills set.[25] In addition to the competencies, for board certification by the Association of Professional Chaplains, a chaplain must hold a Master of Divinity degree and have completed four units of Clinical Pastoral Education as well as 2,000 supervised hours of care.[26]

Why This Book

Professional chaplains augment the spiritual caregiving of the Muslim community through their specialized training in trauma response, healing, and compassionate presence. Chaplains excel as first responders, in part because they are adept at facilitating referrals to longer-term care—particularly important given the stigma around mental health in many Muslim cultures. Muslim chaplains have emerged as key figures in the American Muslim landscape, particularly as leaders able to engage with the North American cultural context, yet many Muslims do not understand the role and function of chaplains. Indeed, as one example, many assume that chaplains are agents of da'wah (proselytization) despite the fact this is clearly prohibited by chaplaincy codes of ethics. This lack of understanding often manifests as the underutilization and underfunding of chaplains by Muslims.

Additionally, institutions have often hired well-intending Muslims without chaplaincy training, such as social workers, imams, academics, and religious scholars, resulting in confused expectations. While many have provided valuable care, chaplaincy-specific training would enhance the ability of these individuals to provide appropriate pastoral care and to reduce burnout, boundary crossing, and the risk of spiritual malpractice, which can manifest as spiritual bypassing to spiritual abuse.[27]

Finally, aspiring and current chaplains, regardless of their faith affiliation, have had few resources to turn to as they try to understand what pastoral care by and/or for Muslims looks like. This dearth of resources contributes to feelings of isolation and inadequacy among Muslims in CPE and undermines the richness of what Islam and Muslims offer the profession. We hope that this book will enrich the discourse by adding to the earlier foundations developed through theoretical contributions,[28] personal reflections,[29] important theological works pertaining to pastoral care,[30] as well as the work of our colleagues in the Islamically integrated psychology and Muslim mental health fields.[31]

How This Book Came to Be

This book has come into being only through the mercy of God and the assistance of many along the way. We began by putting out a call for proposals. To our delight, and to our heartbreak, we received many more abstracts than could be accommodated, and many we have not included would have been enriching additions. While the essays do not necessarily represent our own views, we recognize chaplaincy as a discursive community. We have sought to create a diverse collection of voices representing the different areas of chaplaincy; we do, however, acknowledge the absence of several important topics, including care for converts, refugees, those struggling with substance abuse, domestic violence, infertility, spiritual abuse, as well as disaster chaplaincy, the role of art in healing, and the development of Islamic chaplaincy in Canada. We are also acutely aware that the voices of the pioneers without whom we would not have this profession are largely missing from this anthology. We compiled this book entirely during the COVID-19 pandemic and, accordingly, rely on our readers' spirit of generosity. These have been challenging times for chaplains; we pray that this will not be the last such collection of essays and that the depth and breadth of such publications will only grow from here.

How to Read This Book

We compiled this book to give readers a glimpse into the work and practical theologies of Muslim chaplains, a *Muslim theology of engagement* to use Dr. Martin Nguyen's term—that is to say, how we engage religious teachings and practices in relationship to the work of chaplaincy.[32] Depending on what brings you to this collection, some essays may be of greater interest to you than others: if your attention drifts, skip ahead. Remember that for the profession and the individual contributors, you are seeing only a glimpse of a moment in time. This is a profession still in its infancy, our views and understandings of things are in constant evolution, but we believe by risking the vulnerability to share honestly where chaplains are in this moment, we create a foundation for delving deeper into conversation that we might grow together.

Anything beneficial herein comes from God; the shortcomings remain ours alone.

Notes

1. Michele Shields, Allison Kestenbaum, and Laura B. Dunn, "Spiritual AIM and the Work of the Chaplain: A Model for Assessing Spiritual Needs and Outcomes in Relationship," *Palliative Support Care* 13, no. 1 (2015): 75–89.

2. Martin Lings, *Muhammad: His Life Based on the Earliest Sources* (Inner Traditions, 2006), 221.

3. Consider the hadith where the Prophet advised Muʿādh ibn Jabal by asking him a series of questions. See *Sunan al-Tirmidhi* 1327.

4. A Bedouin came to the Prophet ﷺ complaining angrily that he owed him a camel, and the Prophet responded to the man's abrasiveness with utter gentleness and generosity. See *Sahîh al-Bukhârî* 578 and *Sahîh Muslim* 3898.

5. al-Anbiyâ'/21:207.

6. The Prophet ﷺ said to his companions, "Do you think this woman nursing the infant would throw her baby into the fire?" We said, "No, not if she was able to stop it." The Prophet said, "God is more merciful to His servants than this mother is to her child." See *Sahîh al-Bukhârî* 5999 and *Sahîh Muslim* 2754.

7. Sophie Gilliat-Ray, Mansur Ali, and Stephen Pattison, *Understanding Islamic Chaplaincy* (Routledge, 2016) provides an exploration of the ways Muslims have held pastoral care roles throughout history.

8. Corrections departments have generally required staff (including some women) to use "imam" for the purposes of consolidating their authority over inmates; see more in Ch. Dr. Fiazuddin Shuayb's essay in this collection.

9. "Imam" may be used to denote the leader of prayer, as an honorific title regardless of gender, or—as commonly used in a North American context—as the leader of a masjid or community. For more on chaplains using the title imam, see Timur Yuskaev and Harvey Stark's "The American *'Ulama* and the Public Sphere," in *Routledge Handbook of Islam in the West*, ed. Roberto Tottoli (Routledge, 2021).

10. See more in Ch. Tricia Pethic's "Chaplains Are Not Imams," *Illume*, http://www.illumemag.com/articleDetail.php?Muslim-Chaplains-Are-Not-Imams-Tricia-Pethic-14195 (accessed July 2021).

11. Nancy Khalil and Celene Ibrahim, "From the Madrassa to the Seminary: Training Programs for Aspiring American Muslim Professionals," *Maydan*, August 8, 2018, https://themaydan.com/2018/08/madrassa-seminary-training-programs-aspiring-american-muslim-professionals/ (accessed September 2021).

12. Khalil and Ibrahim, "From the Madrassa to the Seminary."

13. Ibrahim J. Long and Bilal Ansari, "Islamic Pastoral Care and the Development of Muslim Chaplaincy," *Journal of Muslim Mental Health* 12, no. 1 (2018): 111.

14. See Wendy Cadge's *Paging God* (University of Chicago Press, 2013) about the general professionalization of healthcare chaplaincy.

15. See B. Mumina Kowalski, "A New Profession: Muslim Chaplains in American Public Life" (unpublished master's thesis, Hartford Seminary, 2011) for more on the development of Islamic chaplaincy in the United States. Available at the Association of Muslim Chaplains website, https://associationofmuslimchaplains.org/.

16. For a rich and detailed look at Muslim chaplains in England and Wales, see Sophie Gilliat-Ray, Mansur Ali, and Stephen Pattison, *Understanding Muslim Chaplaincy* (Routledge, 2013). The Association of Muslim Chaplains has been collaborating with Boston University to conduct similar research in the United States.

17. From 2000 to 2020, Hartford Seminary's Islamic Chaplaincy Program consisted of an MDiv equivalency furnished through an MA in Islamic Studies and Christian-Muslim Relations and a graduate certificate in Islamic Chaplaincy. Current degree programs are described in note 18 below.

18. Currently, there are three Association of Theological Schools' accredited programs: Bayan Islamic Graduate School (MDiv in Islamic Chaplaincy, conferred through Chicago Theological Seminary); Hartford Seminary (MA in Interreligious Studies and MA in Chaplaincy, both with Islamic concentrations); and the Islamic Seminary of America (MDiv in Islamic Chaplaincy, conferred through Unity Theological Seminary). Additionally, American Islamic College (MDiv in Islamic Studies, with chaplaincy focus) holds candidacy status for accreditation with the Higher Learning Commission.

19. Kowalski, "A New Profession," 8.

20. Data provided by the Association of Muslim Chaplains from its 2021 Employment Survey.

21. For more on the impact of AMC, see Long and Ansari, "Islamic Pastoral Care," 111.

22. Nationally in the United States, endorsement is provided by the Islamic Society of North America, the Muslim Endorsement Council, and Muslims for Progressive Values.

23. Ingrid Mattson, Association of Muslim Chaplains conference, March 2019.

24. Gabriel Baer, "The Administrative, Economic and Social Functions of Turkish Guilds," *International Journal of Middle East Studies* 1, no. 1 (January 1970): 28–50.

25. See Board of Chaplaincy Certification Inc., "BCCI Competency Essay Writing Guide," https://bcci.professionalchaplains.org/files/application_materials/competencies_writing_guide.doc (accessed July 2021).

26. Muslims apply for board certification through the Association of Professional Chaplains or the Spiritual Care Association as there is not yet a Muslim certifying body.

27. "Using religion to manipulate, control, and bully through the guise of religion, religious principles, or claims to spirituality. This includes using religion for personal gain, such as sexual or financial" (HEART, https://hearttogrow.org/wp-content/uploads/2020/05/Important-Definitions-Sexual-Violence.pdf). Dr. Ingrid Mattson addresses this abuse as a violation of one's *hurmah* (sacred inviolability) through her work with the Hurma Project.

28. See publications by Bilal Ansari, Ibrahim Long, and Nazila Isgandrova.

29. Almost all the available published personal reflections appeared in the journal *Reflective Practice: Formation and Supervision in Ministry* 29 (2009), ed. Herbert

Anderson, "Forming Religious Leaders in and for a Diverse World," with contributions from S.E. Jihad Levine, Mary Lahaj, Rabia Terri Harris, Bilal Ansari, and Mumina Kowalski. The two other pieces of note are Sondos Kholaki, *Musings of a Muslim Chaplain* (self-published, 2020); and Sohaib Sultan, "A Muslim Chaplain on Finding His Way," in *College & University Chaplaincy in the 21st Century*, ed. Lucy A. Forster-Smith (SkyLight Paths, 2013).

30. See publications by Ingrid Mattson.

31. Such as Carrie York Al-Karam, Hooman Keshavarzi, Hamada Hamid Altalib, and Rania Awaad.

32. Martin Nguyen, *Modern Muslim Theology* (Rowman & Littlefield, 2019).

A Source of Strength

IBRAHIM J. LONG

"CODE BLUE, MAIN entrance. Code blue, main entrance," rings out from a shaking speaker above me. My chest tightens as I exchange glances with Marilyn, a staff chaplain working diligently at her desk in our small spiritual care office. She does not have to say a word. We both know what I have to do. Someone in the hospital is experiencing a medical emergency. They may have gone into cardiac arrest, fallen down, or stopped breathing. Specialists from across the hospital are expected to rush to the site of the code blue to assess and support—even the chaplain.

Unlike Marilyn and the other staff and resident chaplains working today at the St. Charles Hospital, I am on call. Today, it is my responsibility to answer all emergency requests for a spiritual care provider as well as respond to each of the code blues in the hospital. I am expected to report promptly to the scene and assess for any individuals—perhaps friends or family members of the person in medical distress—who may be in need of emotional support. My heartbeat quickens—what can I, *a chaplain*, really do for a person in medical

Ibrahim J. Long is from California and currently lives with his wife and two children in Edmonton (Alberta, Canada). He holds a BA in Religious Studies and is a graduate of Hartford Seminary's Islamic Chaplaincy Program. Ibrahim has completed four units of Clinical Pastoral Education (CPE) and one unit in Pastoral Counseling Education. He has served in a number of healthcare organizations, as well as in educational and correctional institutions. Presently, Ibrahim is pursuing a master's degree in social work with a specialization in community-informed practice for health and well-being. He loves to read, engage in geeky discussions, and spend time with his family and close friends.

need? My mind races through all the protocols I have just been taught for responding to code blues. As I take a deep breath and step out of our office into the hallway, I hear the sound of a heavy cart rolling at great speed over the linoleum floor. A group of physicians in green scrubs are rushing to the scene that I feel so hesitant to approach, pushing a cabinet full of lifesaving medical devices and medicine. I step out of their way with my back against the wall as they run by.

As a chaplain, I don't wear scrubs or any other uniform. With my beige slacks, black kufi, and blue button-up shirt, I am not immediately recognizable as a staff member. The only difference in my appearance from any friend or family member visiting a patient is a lanyard around my neck with my staff ID, an ID also worn by the team that just ran past me. However, their IDs likely identify them as "Doctor" or "Nurse," while mine doesn't make my purpose within a hospital quite so clear: "Spiritual Care Provider."

I hurry to follow the team to the code blue, feeling for a moment a sense of self-importance and authority as people in the long hallway make way for us. Any confidence drains from my face as we arrive at the scene. Near the main entrance of the hospital, a man, perhaps in his late fifties, is lying unconscious on the ground. Two of the doctors check his vitals with quick, precise movements, while a third stands ready next to their open cabinet of medical instruments. Onlookers watch with tight lips and wide eyes as the physicians work. I don't see any hints that anyone here knows the man. They simply seem concerned for his well-being and interested in watching the doctors respond. I recognize that I am like them: a caring spectator. In a few minutes, the man opens his eyes, staring back at the crowd in confusion. He replies to the doctors' questions in a low, scratchy voice. All I can make out are the words "dizzy," "just visiting," and "thank you." The onlookers are slowly dispersing. The man in distress is now being cared for by these three doctors, and I find myself wondering what, if anything, my presence offered at the scene.

What Led Me Here?

Four years earlier—when I began my chaplaincy education—I started with a great deal of hope yet little knowledge about what Clinical Pastoral Education (CPE) was and what it would it entail. I had no idea that one day I would be responding to code blues or emergency calls in a hospital. Like many of my classmates at the Hartford Seminary, I entered the Islamic Chaplaincy Program out of a desire to learn how to draw upon Islamic scripture, history, theology, and law to help me better understand and support fellow North American Muslims. I did not quite understand how CPE could help me do this or how it would help me grow. Moreover, the idea of providing spiritual care and counseling to patients of various faiths within a hospital setting was intimidating. As a practicing Muslim man with a beard and kufi, I worried whether I would be welcome at the patient's bedside. Would I be able to act in accordance with my faith when serving others? And how could I, a chaplain, truly help?

GROWING UP

I am white and grew up in a middle-class suburban neighborhood in northern California, the fourth of five children and the youngest son. I had a safe and stable home with two loving parents. My parents held differing Christian beliefs: my father a Mormon and my mother a Roman Catholic. Neither of them ever forced religion on me, yet religion was always present in our home. One day after school, my mother called me to her room and asked me what I thought about God. The question shocked and surprised me—I quickly dodged it and fled. Sometimes I wonder what that conversation might have been like if I had stayed, though I have always been more interested in how my mother lived her faith than the specifics of her theology.

This became especially evident when I was fifteen: my mother was diagnosed with leiomyosarcoma, a rare form of cancer. Then she showed me the strength of her faith while I was still trying to find what I believed in. I was scared. I did everything I could to not be around because I could not stand seeing my mother suffer. I could not accept her mortality. One day, when I came home, I found that a hospital bed had been placed in our living room. My mother could no longer walk up and down stairs. I knew then that I had to accept what seemed increasingly inevitable—my mother would soon be gone. I wanted to talk to her, tell her how much I loved her, but I was still struggling to accept the truth that my mother was dying.

After some time had passed, I finally felt determined to tell my mom how much I loved her and how much I would miss her. My father and sister were in the kitchen, and my mother was alone in her hospital bed. I stood beside her, trying to find the courage to say the words I so painfully wanted to say. They felt stuck in my chest. Saying them would be like admitting a truth that I still did not want to accept. If only my mother could be with me longer. If only she could see me get married and as a grown man. But that would not be the case. As my lips started to form words, they trembled and my eyes filled with tears. Fear rose within me that this might be my only chance. Finally, the words came through: "Mom, I love you." Saying this in this moment was like admitting aloud that I was losing my mother. I felt so weak. Yet my mother truly showed me her strength. Perhaps realizing why I had chosen this time to say those words, she smiled and leaned forward as much as she could. As she lay in what would be her deathbed, she sought to comfort me with what can only be described as a mother's love. Where did she find that strength? There was no naivete in her warm eyes, nor did she try to pretend that she was going to make it. Rather, she comforted me and assured me that I was going to be okay because she trusted God. She wasn't resentful that she would not see all of her children grow up, nor did she lose faith due to her battle with cancer. Though I have found my faith in a religion other than my mother's, the power of her spirituality has remained an inspiration for my own. The way that her faith gave her strength caused me to realize the importance of faith in my own life and in the lives of others. Ultimately, her faith amid her struggles led to my interest in spiritual care. So why am I struggling today? Why do I see myself as inferior to physicians when it was more than mere medicine that gave my mother the strength to face her own mortality?

The Prayer Room

As I head back to the spiritual care office, I stop by our multifaith prayer room. Part of me is stalling to avoid Marilyn, who will ask me about the code blue, and I just want to be alone for a while. I sit down, self-doubts running through my mind. I do not have any lifesaving medical skills or tools. I have been trained in theology, ethics, and the history of Islamic thought and law, but many of the religious studies terms I have learned seem out of place in this environment. Here, I have to get used to hearing discussions around resuscitation, intubation, and the patient's "goals of care." With my lack of knowledge in medicine, it feels like I am somewhere near the bottom of a professional hierarchy in a setting where I feel out of place.

I am not alone in the prayer room for long—or as long as I would have liked—when the door opens. It is my CPE supervisor, Richard. I don't know if Richard realizes he has caught me hiding or simply thinks I have come here to pray, but he greets me cheerfully. He tells me that he plans to make some changes to the prayer room and wanted to take a good look at it. As he shares his ideas for the room, I am conscious of my deep respect for Richard. On previous occasions, he opened up to me about struggles he had faced in his own faith and professional life, and I admired him for his vulnerability. I decide that I also want to be vulnerable. I take a deep breath and proceed to tell Richard that I am struggling to see my place in a healthcare environment. He stands there calmly listening as I share. And his response surprises me.

The professional hierarchy that seems so clear to me is not how Richard sees it. Rather, he explains to me how each care provider in the hospital—including chaplains—is part of an interdisciplinary team working together to support our patients' needs. "Yes, when a person is in physical pain or has a medical concern, they need a physician," he said. "However, who is there to support a person as they grapple with their own mortality? Or as they struggle with guilt or shame because of choices they have made? Who can help family members deal with the loss of a loved one in the moments just after they are gone?" I lean back in my chair, feeling a bit embarrassed. Richard's perspective now seems obvious. Of course, we are here to care for our patients' spirituality. Yet what challenges me the most about what Richard says is the degree of confidence in his voice. It is such a stark contrast to the uncertainty in my own. I have been focusing on what I *can't* offer as a spiritual care provider. I don't carry a stethoscope. I don't know how to resuscitate. But there is value that only I as a chaplain can bring.

Turning a Corner

I am thinking about all of this as I leave the prayer room. I turn a corner and walk down a hallway that is lined with hanging photos on either side that document the original construction and early history of the St. Charles Hospital. My attention is drawn toward a collection of black and white photos depicting Catholic nuns working alongside physicians. With their unique religious attire, the nuns stand out among the doctors and patients. This history seems so far removed from anything I have experienced so far at St. Charles.

This thought is interrupted when my pager emits a series of high-pitched beeps. My heart races as I call the extension shown. "Palliative care unit," says a nurse on the other end. "Hello," I say, "this is spiritual care; I'm responding to a page." "Thank you," she says with noticeable relief. "There is a request for you in room 401." When the elevator doors open on the fourth floor, I hear someone screaming. Hesitantly, I step out of the elevator and into the unit. The screaming is so loud—someone is obviously in some sort of pain. At the unit desk, I inform the clerk that I am the chaplain responding to the page and that I need to find room 401. The unit clerk points. "Follow the screams."

As I walk toward room 401, the screams get louder and more clear. What can I do for someone in so much distress? As I arrive at the patient's door, I see that the room is full of medical personnel—and one lone member of the patient's family. They all look desperate, anxious, and uncertain about what to do. What was *I* going to do if *they* were desperate? Then something strange happens. As several medical personnel turn to look at me in the doorway, the patient also turns and suddenly stops screaming. The abrupt change in the patient's demeanor is immediate and unexpected. Now looking directly at me, the patient holds out his hand and motions for me to come forward. Without thinking, I come in and grasp his hand. He looks at me as if I am the only person in the room. "Thank you for coming," he says. "I did not want to be alone." He was surrounded by people, but I believe I understand what he means. He wanted someone there for the sole purpose of spiritual care. As I continue to hold his hand in mine, he looks at me intently without ever shifting to take note of anyone else in the room. His eyes warm up as he speaks about his faith, his life, and thoughts about death. I say very little, I simply listen to his words. The palliative care team grows quiet. Without looking, I can feel them staring in astonishment at this sudden change in their patient. He then thanks me again for "being here." It was important for him to have a person of faith with him as he faced death. I offer a short prayer and make my way out of the room. One of the doctors stops me in the hallway. "I've never seen something like that before," she says. Her medical team had done everything they could for his physical pain and were struggling to understand what more they could do to help. "I was also surprised," I say. "Yet, it is now clear to me that the patient's pain had been existential and could only be treated with spiritual care."

The Source

Spiritual care is unique among all other forms of caregiving. It supports an innate and essential nature within ourselves (and each other) that we may refer to at various times as the *rûh* (soul), *nafs* (self), *qalb* (heart), or *'aql* (intellect). Whatever name we choose, it is driven by its nature to help us understand the reality of our existence and our place in the world. This deep-seated need for meaning in our lives lies at the root of spirituality, and yet, this need is also the means of our greatest strength—a strength that supports us as we, and others, are confronted with our own mortality and life's challenges.

In the years that followed my mother's death, I have searched, stumbled, and finally fell upon that source of strength for me. While I found it in a faith other than my mother's, the source feels very much the same: the heart. I sometimes wonder what my mom would have said if I could have told her about the patient in room 401. Perhaps she would have told me that it was obvious that no medicine could have helped him. What he needed was spiritual care. Perhaps she would have been proud that her son agreed.

The *Jihâd* of Self-Realization and Human Growth in Clinical Pastoral Education

JAWAD A. BAYAT

I APPRECIATE LEARNING FROM Clinical Pastoral Education (CPE) graduates how CPE improved their ability to care for the human soul, their own included. One Muslim colleague expressed her love and passion for the CPE process and how it has improved her way of *being* a mother to her children. Another remarked upon his ability to lean into vulnerability as a source of relational strength with his wife and children in a way that paralleled his more wholehearted spiritual care. Such expressions by many graduating CPE students are commonly heard as they continue on into their particular spiritual care vocation. What I offer here is a glimpse into the theoretical and practical

Jawad A. Bayat is a first-generation Afghan American, born and raised in New Jersey to parents who sought refuge in the United States. An ACPE certified educator, he serves as manager of pastoral care and Clinical Pastoral Education (CPE) at Penn Medicine Princeton House Behavioral Health in Princeton, New Jersey. Jawad holds a BA degree from William Paterson University, is a graduate of Hartford Seminary's Islamic Chaplaincy Program, earned four units of CPE, and completed the multiyear ACPE educator certification through the Cleveland Clinic. He participated in the Fellowship at Auschwitz for the Study of Professional Ethics, and studied abroad in the Sultanate of Oman and Indonesia. Endorsed by the Islamic Society of North America, he is also a member of the Association of Muslim Chaplains. Jawad enjoys playing action adventure role-playing video games, spending quality time with his family and friends, delighting in flavorful foods, and witnessing the beauty in creation through walks, hikes, and travel. He lives in the Princeton, New Jersey area with his wife and daughter.

writings I have completed as part of my Association for Clinical Pastoral Education (ACPE) educator certification process to become among the first Muslim ACPE certified educators. My writing seeks to reveal part of the process ACPE certified educators have undergone to help enable the transformative learnings and challenges many participants of CPE reflect upon.

I

The story of my life is marked with a *jihâd* (sacred struggle) toward a transformative integration of my identities and experiences. As a first-generation Afghan American Muslim in our diverse yet dominantly white Christian American milieu, my concern has often been one of identity: who am I in relationship to those who are similar and different from me. One of my first memories of this was as a six-year-old when I asked my mother as she was walking me to school whether the kids there would understand me if I were to speak to them in Farsi. My awareness of my difference and similarity as well as the tension between acceptance and rejection had already begun. As I have grown, my re-formation as a human being was inspired by these kinds of multicultural realities. The impetus for the growth in my worldview and for how I relate to others has been my struggle with paradox and the holding of opposing tensions together, which grew when I entered college. Given the Islamic emphasis upon *tawhîd*, which is the unity and oneness of Allah, my struggle has been one of recognizing the unity in diversity and the affirmation that diversity within creation is the wisdom of Allah.

My *jihâd* of integration, especially as it relates to my identity and experiences, has given me special insight into the nuances that allow for connections. In other words, I learned that I may have colleagues who are Afghan or Muslim, but that does not mean that I will feel a strong connection with them. Sometimes I do, but I have also found deep connections with friends and colleagues of other identities around our inner values and things we cherish and mutually aspire toward. To bring about this opening, a vulnerability that allows for connection is required. The recognition of how I am like all others, like some others, and like no other is both what propels me into this work of discovery and what I invite my students into as well. This has served to carry not only me but my students through our sacred relational encounters.

II

The Mulla[1] . . . complained every day at lunch that he was getting sick and tired of cheese sandwiches. His coworkers listened to his complaints for several days, and finally they offered him some advice. "Mulla, tell your wife to make you something different. Be persuasive with her." "But I'm not married," replied the Mulla. "Well, then," they asked, "who makes your lunch?" "I do!" replied the Mulla.[2]

Individuals make their own choices, but it may not always be clear to the person who has not developed enough self-awareness about where their motivation comes from, like this playful story of the Mulla illustrates. Yet choices are manifestations that come forth from the person, so this begs the question of what, like with the Mulla, kept him from realizing that he could make a different sandwich for himself. As human beings, if we only look to the symptoms or choices that have become a pattern to bring about a change, then we miss the person's human development, which is what their choices relate to. As the CPE educator, I seek to address the development of the adult learner and to help nurture their growth in ways that support their individual and relational formation through a process of self-realization that is based within the self and within relationships.

This process of learning about oneself for our growth is a process of *jihâd al-nafs*, a sacred inward struggle with the self. This *jihâd* is a process of self-realization that highlights the effort connected to human growth and the applications of its learning in life, which within an Islamic context, is a striving in the way of and toward Allah.[3] This *jihâd* is about realizing our true nature for self-betterment and within Islamic terms is a spiritual practice allowing me to draw closer to Allah, as the Qur'an says, "and We are nearer to him than his jugular vein."[4] In terms of this, the imagery that al-Ghazâlî (d. 1111) offers is useful here: "Your heart is a polished mirror. You must wipe it clean of the veil of dust that has gathered upon it, because it is destined to reflect the light of divine secrets."[5] This act of polishing our inner self's mirror is the *jihâd* of self-realization. And this self-realization where one's sense of self can be transformed given this knowledge is complete only when we act on what we know. At the same time, to take human development and self-realization *too seriously* is to miss that we are *only* human: only Allah is truly complete and absolute. To make the *jihâd* with a seriousness that, for instance, believes "I should already be there" is to embrace a rigidity that stifles human growth. A playful attitude allows for flexibility and the trying on of different perspectives, which the Mulla's retort "I do!" helps reveal. I have found that approaching my *jihâd* toward self-realization with a playful yet serious mind frame in the demanding learning environment of CPE can support human growth in a way that is akin to children experimenting with building blocks. It allows for flexibility and, hence, is about taking it *seriously enough*.

One of the "cheese sandwich" stories I grew up with in my family has to do with often feeling unworthy when disappointments befell my relationships. A significant part of CPE is learning to identify why one responds the way they do in their relational encounters. In a personal example, my father uneasily shared the decision that he would leave New Jersey to attend a relative's wedding right before my wife and I would leave for hajj (pilgrimage). Previously I would have taken it *too seriously* and chided him, saying he *should* know better than to leave *me* during a significant moment of my life (the hajj). This perspective stems from my earlier sense of unworthiness and shame due to feeling I am not good enough for his love. However, in my growth through my *jihâd*, I have come to witness that I have created these doubts. Therefore, I could change the story. I took it *seriously enough* through a display of vulnerability by expressing my disappointment (that I would miss him) and affirmed his uneasiness due to the awkward timing of events. I now told a story that acknowledged that his decision does not sabotage his love for me and that I am good enough. No one but me could affirm my worthiness, and this helped create the space where I not only felt love and joy, but he did too.

In taking CPE seriously enough, this *jihâd* through the act of polishing the mirror of one's heart is the action–reflection–action educational process. This is because it is demanding us to implement our self-discoveries in relationship to others, be it with one's peers, students, or care receivers. As a result, those engaged with CPE often experience healing if they are faithful to this self-discovery, which is what I have also experienced as meaningful and challenging, yet life-giving. However, this healing is primarily a significant by-product of CPE, since therapy is neither the goal nor the intent of CPE. Thus, through the students' self-realization in light of their formation and often healing, they may come to the goal of better providing spiritual care to their care receivers. This is a reflection of their skills by having the awareness of when they are or are not getting in their own way. CPE provides a life-giving opportunity to those who engage its process of facilitating healing in one's self and, by extension, for the careseeker.

III

I believe that the instinctual impulse humanity is tasked with by Allah is that of growth through the struggle toward realizing our real self, our *fitrah* (innate nature). With regard to this Karen Horney states, "You need not . . . teach an acorn to grow into an oak tree, but when given a chance, its intrinsic potentialities will develop."[6] However, this process of self-realization is hindered when a person's strong inner tensions lead them toward the self-idealization process as a means to resolve the inner tension by actualizing an ideal/false self that responds *too seriously*.[7] This begins when the person abandons their *fitrah*/real self (Horney calls this the alienation from self) by disregarding their authentic feelings, thoughts, and wishes in a reactively protective way. The result is the development of an ideal/false self, which is both unique to the person's life experiences and particular needs, and promises to complete every inner need of the individual uncompromisingly.[8] In this sense, the ideal/false self is compelled to enact high expectations upon itself through the belief that human limitations should not apply to them (Horney calls this the tyranny of shoulds) along with shaming self-judgments for being unable to measure up to these expectations (Horney calls this self-hate). I see this ideal/false self like the dust that gathers upon the mirror of the *fitrah*/real self, which the person has become accustomed to living with over the course of their life until they seek to regularly polish it.

The act of polishing one's mirror to uncover the *fitrah*/real self is a process. It requires specific self-reflections and particular attention to what is preventing the manifestation of self-realization into one's life circumstances. This can be seen as both a form of and application of *murâqabah* (watchfulness or reflection upon the developments within one's heart) and *muhâsabah* (self-observation and/or assessment of one's actions) that I guide students through. The introduction/orientation period, evaluation process, didactics, group processing time, and the clinical presentations like the verbatim (a written account and analysis of a spiritual care encounter with a care receiver) are the structural ways I guide students toward their growth. As a result, the CPE curriculum I set up serves the students' development and growth, which highlights the educational program design's emphasis upon furthering self-awareness and putting it into action in a way that is akin to the exercise of *murâqabah* and *muhâsabah*. This is so that the student may be able to reflect, articulate, and apply their learnings, which highlights the process of struggle that self-realization is.

My role as an educator is to recognize when the inner tension/conflict arises within my students, as it serves as an opportunity for their growth. Through this, I am mindful of the self-judging tendencies of their ideal/false self because of its alienating effects upon their *fitrah*/real self. Therefore, I help to create the favorable conditions that lend themselves toward my students' integration— namely, directness and/or gentleness.[9] For example, throughout the different CPE program components, Lina's *jihâd* in relationship to her main inner tension played out. As a daughter of a pastor, Lina was raised in a household where there was pressure to maintain a tailored image for the community to help look the part. She was also educated in a religious school system that stressed the formation of the ideal/false self with how a woman *should* be, which alienated Lina from her true thoughts, wishes, and emotions. There was an emphasis on appearing rather than being. CPE asked the opposite of her. I felt powerless at times witnessing her struggle as I remained present with her in class and in Individual Supervisory Consultation. However, self-realization is a *jihâd/* struggle, and no one can do it except for oneself. During one of Lina's verbatim presentations, I saw her work diligently on her learning goal of reframing but also recognized her scaling back from seeing the steps she was taking. The main inner tension was at play in that her ideal/false self was resisting the growth of the *fitrah*/real self that could come from her affirming her faithful attempts. My educational concern here was that if Lina did not affirm and realistically observe her progress, then it would be hard for her to notice this with her care receivers. Through highlighting this specific concern for the group, Lina's peers expressed their discomfort with her self-shaming. As a result of the favorable conditions that I helped stimulate, Lina recognized that her self-assessments were unrealistic because her ideal/false self expected her to already be the master of reframing. Due to the specific connections Lina came to make from her past emphasis on looking the part in her present, she came to feel relief in realizing that it was her ideal/false self that was constricting her growth. It was not her *fitrah*/real self. Lina's *jihad* of self-realization has been to name the behaviors, polish the shaming away, and to believe that she *is* good enough.

IV

I remind myself what it was like for me as a CPE intern and resident entering into a simultaneously personal and professional learning experience that was both disruptive and consoling. This *jihâd* of my self-realization and human growth began most directly as a first-unit CPE intern during my final year at Hartford Seminary. One of these realizations came from absorbing the sadness, fears, and powerlessness regarding the various deaths and sufferings I was bearing witness to during the first four weeks of the program. I felt a heaviness upon the mirror of my heart. The sensation felt like a heavily soaked sponge that had not been wrung, which had my body tired and my attention diminished. I made my way into my educator's office after class and her affirmation of the emotional weight she observed provided me the space to cry: to allow my sponge to be wrung. In other words, to allow the water from the sponge to help polish the mirror of my heart. I was amazed by and thankful for her creating the favorable conditions for this courage to lean into my vulnerability and the growth that came from it. I soon saw more clearly the connection between human growth and its impact on providing deeper spiritual care.

This experience increased my intrigue with the CPE process, and I set my *niyyah* (intention) to seek this educator training to gain Allah's pleasure. I did not realize then the vulnerable space I would enter into by pursuing this journey, especially since there was so little precedence for Muslim certified educators. There are limited fully paid educator training opportunities so I knew I would likely have to move away from my family to go wherever an opportunity opened. At the annual Association of Muslim Chaplains 2017 gathering, I gathered the courage to approach the ACPE chair-elect about this vulnerable space I was in, especially since I had a stable state chaplain position already. I was surprised when she sought out my contact information three months later to recruit me to the Cleveland Clinic as their first Muslim chaplain and certified educator candidate. After a hearty conversation with my wife and family, and a visit to the Cleveland Clinic, I accepted the opportunity. Had I not leaned into my vulnerability and engaged in the sacred struggle, the *jihad*, in my relationships with others, I may not have been able to serve Allah and Allah's creation as I am now able to.

Could we say that the *jihâd* can ever be over? I believe that as long as we are living, the *jihâd* of integrating our self-realizations into our lives and relationships will be with us. Rather than recoil from this, I have continued to learn to embrace this *jihâd* of growth and to do so with a playful yet serious mind frame, especially since the absence of playfulness serves as a prediction of the emotional regression present in any relationship or group.[10] The peculiar humanizing humor of the Mulla that I offered earlier conveys that growth often comes with realizations that seem so obvious only after the connections are made. Self-realization can be a humanizing and liberating process if one embraces the vulnerability or emotional exposure that it often yields. It permits one to lean into the vulnerability that Allah has created humans with for the purpose of human growth, which in turn enables one to draw closer to Allah. This has meant seeking integration of my self-realizations into my relationships, both with Allah, myself, and Allah's creation. Through this, as an educator making use of the opportunities Allah makes available to me, I am able to honor the self-realizations that enable both my growth and those of my students: to serve as one of Allah's instruments in this sacred struggle, this *jihâd*, of integration, human growth, and healing.

Notes

1. The Mulla referred to is the wise scholarly fool character named Mulla Nasruddin. He goes by different names based on the cultures that claim him, which are often found throughout the Asian continent with particular emphasis in Central Asian Muslim communities. His stories are often employed with humor and pedagogical intent that is sudden, similar to Zen koans.

2. Jamal Rahman, *Sacred Laughter of the Sufis: Awakening the Soul with the Mullas Comic Teaching Stories and Other Islamic Wisdom* (SkyLight Paths, 2014), 6.

3. Sachiko Murata and William C. Chittick, *The Vision of Islam* (Paragon House, 1996), 42.

4. Qâf/50:16.

5. Robert Frager, *Heart, Self, and Soul: The Sufi Psychology of Growth, Balance, and Harmony* (Quest Books, 1999), 27.

6. Karen Horney, *Neurosis and Human Growth: The Struggle Toward Self-Realization* (Norton, 1991), 17.

7. Horney, *Neurosis and Human Growth*, 13.

8. Horney, *Neurosis and Human Growth*, 21–22.

9. Horney, *Neurosis and Human Growth*, 18.

10. Edwin H. Friedman, *A Failure of Nerve: Leadership in the Age of the Quick Fix* (Seabury Books, 2007), 63–64.

4

Finding My Path

KAISER ASLAM

SITTING ON THE FLOOR of my room in my parents' home in a suburb of Chicago at 2:00 a.m., my face dimly lit by the glow of my laptop, I wonder, *What do I do next?* It was that time in my life when a decision had to be made. I was almost finished with my bachelor's in biology while dabbling in more minors than reasonable (art, chemistry, physics). I had already made the decision that Islamic studies was the next discipline I wanted to gain proficiency in, but which career path?

I had landed on Islamic studies because I felt like it seemed like the right trajectory given my experiences up to that point. I'd undertaken an honest census of what activities consumed most of my time and my interest and found that a cultivation of spiritual identity—mine and that of my community—stood out. Having grown up in Villa Park, Illinois, I was involved in several different spiritual circles from an early age supplemented by public school education. My parents made sure I attended Sunday school from elementary school until I graduated from the weekend program in high school and ended up teaching there. More impactful, however, was my involvement with Young Muslims, a national youth group that I was leading by the time of that fateful

Kaiser Aslam serves at the Center for Islamic Life at Rutgers University. He is a graduate of Hartford Seminary's Islamic Chaplaincy Program where his thesis was on developing a curriculum of Islamic literacy for undergraduate American Muslims. He completed two units of Clinical Pastoral Education (CPE), and previously served at Hartford Hospital, Wesleyan College, and the Farmington Valley Muslim Association. A member of the Association of Muslim Chaplains, Kaiser lives near campus with his wife and two children.

night of decision making. YM gave me the tools to cultivate much of my identity as a young Muslim while simultaneously giving me the language to diagnose what was wrong with it. To this day, I have not found another organization that can compete with its ability to give young Muslims a sense of purpose and passion—not just to think about their own evolving Muslim identities but to motivate them to responsibly serve their community and greater society. My participation with YM planted a seed of interest in continuing to work with Muslim youth.

The connections I maintained to the community blessed me with the opportunity to study Arabic and Qur'an for a summer in Egypt, the dream of any aspiring Islamic studies student. Up to that point, years of weekly social gatherings, intensive book studies, and national leadership workshops led me to feel like the path of spiritual activism was open and available. Eventually, though, I felt myself recognizing a fatal flaw: my own competency. I felt like I was literally reading chapters just to present them in a speech, developing skills just as a means. On the surface, it seemed like I was extremely well put together, but I felt empty and hollow inside with my spiritual education only skin deep. I had just enough to present basic outlines but not enough to hold up to the slightest scrutiny. Communities would reach out asking for me to speak, not realizing that what I presented was not based on true experience or complex study but rather just crammed preparation. It was unfair to those I served and to myself. I remember my mentor, Ch. Omer Mozaffer, telling me one of the greatest obstacles to serious studies is that the second the community recognizes your ability to speak or teach, they never give you time to study again. I had completely fallen into that pitfall and needed to crawl out. Pursuing graduate-level Islamic studies seemed the best option. I had spent the previous months exploring the available paths, narrowing it to three or four major options with hundreds more combinations. Hence the question, *What do I do next?*

There was the path, chosen by many of my close friends, of studying abroad at a "traditional" Islamic seminary to pursue degrees from one of several world-renowned universities. My short list of possibilities included Madina University (Saudia Arabia), Al Azhar (Egypt), Darul Uloom (South Africa), Nadwatul Ulama (India), and IIUM (Malaysia). Each institution, with unique histories and contexts, had strengths and weaknesses and a different approach to Islamic scholarship, but I put them all in the same category because this path would involve leaving my family, my country, and life as I'd known it for almost a decade to immerse myself in what I considered the sacred sciences. There was a romantic appeal to this path—an escape of sorts, time to reinvent myself while running away from the responsibilities of community work to gain some sort of proficiency. While I ultimately decided against the path of traditional scholarship, to this day I dream of a well-established tradition of sabbatical for Muslim chaplains that allows us to spend time studying the Islamic sciences and working on ourselves somewhere far away from the communities that otherwise demand our time.

Ultimately, I decided I wasn't sure I had the necessary discipline, but also because I wasn't sure it was truly what I needed to help foster Muslim identity within America's youth. Additionally, navigating the politics of leaving and returning in a path of service seemed like quite the task. I distinctly remember a conversation I had with another mentor, Shaykh Suhaib Webb, who had studied abroad. He told me one of the biggest challenges he faced after returning was having become an outsider to his own home community, lamenting that it took him almost a year to fully reacclimate to the customs and struggles of American Muslims, during which he found it almost impossible to be effective in the job he'd been hired for. This insight scared me but also shed light on why young Muslims so often find it hard to connect to their spiritual identities: for the most part, their spiritual leaders have literally inherited the tradition in a radically different environment, imbuing a degree of foreignness into their approach. Lastly, I was coming to grips with the grim reality that I was seeing in my own networks and in research: Muslims' interactions with religious leaders and institutions were shrinking. In one self-reported survey, only 10 to 15 percent said they visited a masjid more than twice a year. This made me realize that the typical space and practices found within masjids needed modification to reach broader audiences. I wanted to be a part of the solution that promoted that modification.

The next natural approach then was to look at Islamic studies programs within the United States. However, I had heard horror stories that the academic study of religion is where spirituality goes to die. Another early mentor of mine once said that the way religion is studied in Western institutions is the way cadavers are studied: chopped up and analyzed rather than treated as living breathing communities. It didn't help that the majority of those teaching Islamic studies I was aware of were, at best, not practicing and, at worst, appeared to have an agenda to dismantle Islamic practice in society. Of course, I later learned that this was dangerous hyperbolic exaggeration, and there are many amazing Muslim academics who have done much for the field of Islamic studies and indeed for society's practice. Reading books like *Observing the Observer* by Dr. Sulayman Nyang helped me understand the field a bit more, and conversations with local professors and graduate students eventually corrected some of my misconceptions.

The path of Islamic studies at academic institutions still seemed to have one
major flaw: with the exception of a handful of well-known names like
Dr. Jonathan Brown, Dr. Sherman Jackson, and Dr. Ingrid Mattson, there
seemed to be a disconnect between the mainstream practicing Muslim community I had grown up in and the academics. I wasn't sure if this was a
problem with academia or with my community not being ready for the style
of study being presented at these institutions. Most Muslims I interacted with
learned the religion as one learns cultural identity, over casual rituals and conversations rather than studying through the consumption of reverent and
historic texts in classrooms. Yet, after conversations with local academics, I
thought I had found my mission: being a bridge to raise the minimum education of the average American Muslim by going into Islamic studies while maintaining a solid connection with what I had (then) deemed to be "the Muslim
community." I began the process of getting to know the culture of a few academic institutions by speaking with students currently in their programs. I
attended the famous American Association of Religions conference to get my
feet wet and started graduate applications, really thinking I had found my
space within this complicated field.

During my interviews over the next few months of 2013, I traveled the country and eventually came across a field that was foreign yet familiar to me: Islamic
chaplaincy. I had interacted with a Christian chaplain during my undergraduate
years and very much appreciated the work he did, but I assumed that chaplaincy
was only a Christian discipline. At Muslim conferences, I had seen a few Muslim
chaplains but had not paid too much attention to their title, dismissing it as
some "new age" twist on Muslim leadership. But in mid-April, I was traveling to
the East Coast for a few interviews while also visiting a few communities to fulfill my responsibilities as national coordinator of Young Muslims. En route to an
interview in Boston, I paid a visit to my friend Sami Abdul Aziz, then a student
in Hartford Seminary's Islamic Chaplaincy Program.

I was immediately impressed by the faculty I met and by the atmosphere of
the students' relationship with them. I was particularly taken that historian
and Ibn Taymiyyah specialist Dr. Yahya Michot hosted a weekly poetry night
at his home for students in which he combined a host of different disciplines
ranging from studying the languages of Arabic and Persian, Muslim history,
and myriad random tangents on life. That night, I think I learned more about
the science of Hadith than I had in years of study on the topic, even though
Hadith studies was not even the gathering's focal point. There was a deeply
appealing atmosphere of camaraderie and openness that I had not seen in
other institutions.

This was already making me rethink my dismissal of Islamic chaplaincy, but what really changed my perspective occurred the following morning as I was leaving, and we got news of what would become known as the Boston Marathon bombing. Public transportation to Boston was suspended, and I found myself stuck in Hartford, which allowed me to witness how Hartford Seminary transformed; my heart recognized that "Allah is the best of planners." I witnessed faculty helping students contextualize information and make sense of the news as it was unfolding. Hearing about the Chechnian origins of the bomber, Dr. Michot carefully unpacked the historical context of trauma that the people of Chechnya suffered and explored how that was being used to justify such a heinous and indefensible attack. I saw a structure of Muslim leadership come alive and a model of how to provide support to Muslim communities that would soon face the backlash of yet another so-called Muslim terrorist attack. I realized then what chaplaincy really was: a profession that facilitates safe and confident transition from one part of life to another providing language and methods to process life's complexities. In this case, it was the seminary faculty giving chaplaincy students the proper context to facilitate the processing of this tragic event for themselves *and* the communities they may have already served. I could see the students' learned capacities to maintain and grow their Muslim identities in the face of their constantly changing contexts, whether that was because of a historic event, a life event, a new perspective, a change of location, a change of physical ability, or just the passing of time. At that moment, it all seemed to click. This was really the role I'd found myself in all along yet did not have the training to perform.

A few short days later, I made it back home to Chicago and immediately began my Hartford Seminary application. I would go on to spend the next few years there learning and reinventing myself and my approach to studying Islam surrounded by the full diversity of Muslims—Sunni and Shi'a, of every ethnicity imaginable, but united by a passion for our studies and our dreams for future service. Through my education, I had a chance to study in a few programs abroad and outside the seminary during breaks through domestic organizations like Al-Maghrib and Qalam Institute, as well as in Turkey and Oman. The bulk of my time, however, was gaining practical proficiencies in topics related to counseling, practical theology, sociology, and Islamic studies.

Being exposed to the different contexts that Muslim chaplains practiced in expanded my understanding of chaplaincy. Through a few units of Clinical Pastoral Education (CPE) and subsequent employment as a chaplain at Hartford Hospital, I came to appreciate that a primary role of chaplains anywhere is to facilitate the wholesome transition of people from a state of sickness to one of health—sometimes even as their physical health is failing irrevocably—by allowing them to recognize and work on their emotional and spiritual health. In CPE, I felt like I was experiencing theology rather than reading about it. I came to understand that if medicine can be seen as the practical application of health sciences, pastoral care is the practical application of spiritual traditions. CPE was the space to test my own theological foundations and to practice preventing them from getting in the way of providing care. Years of studying texts, methodologies, and systems were replaced by learning instead how to study and witness each individual heart and appreciate its frameworks and workings.

Volunteering at a local state prison, I found myself doing something similar. While patients in the hospital often spoke of their isolation, isolation in the prison was different. Through conversations, I tried to provide space to help individuals make the best of their time going from freedom to incarceration, from blood family on the outside to needing to make a chosen family on the inside, and oftentimes striving to move from the chaos of instability to peace and acceptance of the decree being experienced. While I didn't get direct exposure to military chaplaincy, I learned from my classmates as they journeyed with the challenges of transitioning from civilian life into military service. I heard echoes of the isolation in the prison and hospital from their own experiences, but also how they were called to address its manifestation in those suffering from war-related trauma, moral injury, and suicidal thoughts. Theirs had a different urgency. I also worked as an imam at two area masjids, functioning as best I could as a chaplain more than an imam, though that distinction is tough to fully articulate. This was where I faced the broadest type of service: supporting people through major milestones like the birth of a child, weddings, and leading the washing, shrouding, and *janâzah* (funeral rites).

I benefited from each of these chaplaincy contexts, but it was my field education as a campus chaplain at Fairfield University that confirmed my sense that education chaplaincy was a good fit that I was uniquely qualified for. Working with students trying to make sense of their spiritual identities in an ever-changing world while they were encountering new possibilities resonated with my earlier dreams. I like the possibility of forming relationships as a chaplain that can be maintained for years. My role was akin to a spiritual first responder, providing tools to navigate all the ways to interact with Islam and Muslim identity. The other natural appeal of campus chaplaincy was its reception in the community: campus chaplains increasingly frequented the conferences and conventions I'd grown up with, enabling their expertise as chaplains to influence the larger Muslim community.

I was blessed to start my first full-time role as a campus chaplain at Rutgers University's Center for Islamic Life (CILRU) in central New Jersey, a region where trailblazing campus chaplains like Sohaib Sultan and Khalid Latif had already done wonders establishing the role of chaplain for the greater Muslim community. People had learned to see chaplains as spiritual guides who were approachable and competent complements to—but not replacements for—the local imams. Those who found themselves without an established community for a multitude of reasons often gravitated toward the chaplaincy programs and spaces—a widening of the tent if you will. Within weeks of starting at CILRU, I plugged into the collaborative working system Ch. Sohaib had so masterfully developed, giving and receiving referrals to imams and mental health providers. His contributions to the field cannot be understated, for he built a vibrant Muslim Life Program at Princeton University that works adjacent to local Islamic centers and masjids, without feeling like a replacement space the way third spaces often become. As the first full-time public university Muslim chaplaincy, much of the methodology of CILRU was an application of the guidance provided by Ch. Sohaib.

I've appreciated the gracious partnership local Muslim leadership has provided me. I often get invited to local masjids, Islamic schools, and Muslim centers to provide pastoral care, talks, and general information for communities on how to better support students. One benefit of being connected in this way is that I've rarely found myself needing to answer questions of *fiqh* (jurisprudence) or advanced theology, as I've established pastoral care as my primary role. The primary difference between a chaplain's perspective and that of a traditional religious leader comes down to the skill set developed through CPE: "ministry of presence," the ability to recognize your own bias and triggers in any given situation so you can be available to the soul in front of you rather than pushing them in a direction that you feel they should go "Islamically."

Everyone is a library of experiences that oftentimes contains within it the guidance needed. A chaplain's role is to provide a non-anxious presence to help organize that library so that an individual can see that themselves. One needs to be well versed in the motivational and foundational human and spiritual texts to track complex ideas appropriately but not be overbearing. This requires constant study and, importantly, continual self-reflection, two essential features of the field that I honestly enjoy.

Having served at Rutgers for five years, I can't express the joys and sense of accomplishment being able to interact with members of the community and being witness to them as they experience some amazing life milestones. There are now a handful of students who embarked on marriage conversations in my office, that have led to my facilitation of premarital counseling, the honor of officiating their *nikâh* (marriage), and subsequently the *ʿaqîqah* (celebration) of their children. I love when excited students share how they finally landed their first job, found their first real community at CILRU, or aced an exam. The sense of fulfillment and joy being present with them through these moments is tough to put into words.

There is also the other side, which is equally as beautiful yet extremely taxing—bearing witness as students navigate some of their darkest moments of grief, loss, and confusion. It is an honor to be present with them but takes a toll of how to process the experiences to maintain competence. A practice I have taken on to help myself let go is to write a sentence of *duʿâ* after each inter-action in my own journal and then each year on CILRU's annual *umrah*, I spend a day in Makkah doing *tawâf* (circumambulations) around the Kaaba and letting go of the 800 to 1,000 stories I witnessed that year. There are times in this role I have been blessed to feel like I provided support. There are others in which I have felt powerless. This practice allows me to recognize there is a way to address that feeling of powerlessness.

There are of course challenges in campus chaplaincy. One of the biggest has been establishing work boundaries. Having been blessed with two children, my wife and I have had to find a way to maintain privacy while still being accessible in times of crisis. Simple things like going for prayer at masjids, tak-ing a walk in a park, or even a meal at a local restaurant often turn into unplanned pastoral care encounters with community members. Finding strong social support was an absolute must as well as planned breaks to be able to re-create ourselves. We had to have nuanced conversations about the role of college students interacting with our children who are often on campus.

There are many more challenges and merits to this field that can be exten-sively described and many more that I have yet to learn about. But I feel like I am finding the answer to that question I asked so many years ago at 2:00 a.m. *This* is what was next. This was the space I was really looking for all along, the path where service and education met in a meaningful way: a vehicle to engage with Islamic studies and provide support as individuals and communities come to terms with the changes happening to their internal worlds and the world around them.

5

Pastoral Care as an Islamic Tradition and Practice

BILAL W. ANSARI

MY JOURNEY IN chaplaincy started with my own experience of having a Christian mother and a Muslim father. My family is Black American. My grandparents lived in a predominantly Jewish neighborhood in New Haven, Connecticut. From elementary school through high school, one of my best friends was Jewish. I wanted to do what he did, so I played on his Jewish Community Center's traveling basketball team. I grew up with firsthand experience of his synagogue and its songs, my mother's Pentecostal church and its hymns, and my father's mosque and its Qur'anic recitation. The multifaith context of my formative years fueled a passion to care for and minister to all as a chaplain.

My first ministry was in a men's prison, and my immediate supervisor, Sister Patricia Cook, was a Catholic nun who held a PhD from Yale. Reverend Laura Etter, the head of prison chaplaincy, was a Protestant pastor trained at New York City's infamous Rikers Island jail. The lessons and narratives of

Dr. Bilal W. Ansari is director of the Islamic Chaplaincy Program at Hartford Seminary and faculty associate for Muslim Pastoral Theology. Bilal began volunteering as a chaplain in 1994 for a naval and marine base in San Diego. He subsequently served from 1997 to 2011 in corrections chaplaincy before completing Hartford Seminary's Islamic Chaplaincy Program in 2011. He received his doctorate degree in Pastoral Theology from the Pacific School of Religion. Bilal served as a chaplain and is now assistant vice president for campus engagement at Williams College, dean of students at Zaytuna College, and was a founding member of the Association of Muslim Chaplains and the Muslim Endorsement Council.

those two pioneering women stay with me: Sister Patty Cook's bold and confident institutional leadership and Reverend Laura Etter's practiced skill in vocational discernment. She asked me a few times, "Are you sure prison ministry is your calling? I think you would excel as a higher education chaplain." Conversing with and learning from these two women, a Catholic nun and a Protestant pastor, at the outset of my prison ministry, encouraged me to think far beyond the position I served in at the time. They motivated me to go beyond the informal education I brought to my ministry and to seek a quality graduate professional education.

After a decade of prison ministry, I discovered Hartford Seminary's Islamic Chaplaincy Program. Though it had prided itself on its nondenominational, multifaith orientation for decades, Hartford Seminary's Christian foundations suffused its curriculum. It offered the perfect challenge for me to wrestle critically with the Christian presuppositions undergirding the prevailing texts in the field of chaplaincy. I learned how to reflect theologically and make meaning from diverse religious texts, meanwhile pondering the intersections of my marginalized interreligious identity and experience as a Black American Muslim. Studying other religions, I was challenged to be actively self-reflective in understanding Muslim behaviors and practices, and analytical in examining texts and contexts. My previous private informal studies with Imam Zaid Shakir and Shaykh Hamza Yusuf had added to my academic knowledge of Islam and provided the firm foundation in the Islamic tradition from which to address the psychosociological issues a chaplain deals with in ministry.

Three core aspects of my studies at Hartford Seminary—the study of other faiths, Islamic theological education with Muslim scholars, and the fostering of introspective self-knowledge and growth essential to compassionate care— developed in me the understanding of what it means to be a shepherd for all regardless of my clients' identities. Now, as the director of the Islamic Chaplaincy Program at Hartford Seminary, I want this for our students as well, irrespective of their religious identities.

Central to the development of my ability to be self-reflective as a professional chaplain was my Clinical Pastoral Education (CPE) experience, where my cohort included a rabbi, a United Church of Christ minister, a Black Southern Seventh Day Adventist, and a Puerto Rican Pentecostal Christian. For my hospital assignment, I was sent to a unit of care for retired Catholic nuns and priests. There I was, a chaplain who was Muslim—with patients calling me "Father." In CPE, I felt like I was being squeezed to own and perfect my own distinct pastoral theology of care; it was unacceptable to blindly follow tropes of *spiritual care* unexamined or untranslated. My Christian CPE supervisor instilled, drilled, and insisted that I uncover and develop for myself and my clients an Islamic pastoral theology of care that demonstrated a working knowledge of applied psychological and sociological disciplines. This formative experience propelled me to realize that the key to the professional practice of *pastoral care* was the integration of the religious sciences such as Islamic legal and theological theory with knowledge of the social sciences.

Just as importantly, my CPE training led me to think about how to integrate the ethical and emotional dimensions of character development into my practice of care as I drew from teachers of the Islamic tradition, such as Imâm al-Ghazâlî, Dr. Tim Winter, and Dr. Ingrid Mattson. CPE became for me the laboratory in which I began to discover what Muslim pastoral theology has been to scholar-practitioners from Imâm Mâlik to Sîdî Ahmad Zarrûq, who dove into our sacred sources to produce pastoral works for their times.

The Abrahamic scriptures, the Qur'an included, charge believers with a responsibility of leadership and care for others, but prophets—and emulating them, religious leaders—are called to acquire the necessary abilities to guide and heal individuals and communities. I learned my peer rabbis, priests, and pastors all had abundant literature distilled over centuries of pastoral leadership that interpreted and reinterpreted the shepherding role for the care of souls. Often these texts based their guidance on an image of care for the flock demonstrating a conceptual understanding of group dynamics and organizational behavior. The interreligious similarities demonstrated that all were based on ethical theories guarding against spiritual, social, or psychological danger zones. What I realized in comparing the current state of chaplaincy literature is that although great Muslim religious authorities such as those mentioned above have offered works of pastoral guidance and care in early and medieval Islam, little pastoral work has been produced in the modern and postmodern periods. There is a dearth of research and thought leadership produced by Muslims in the field of spiritual care. Thus, I suggest that we Muslims in the field start producing—not just for other Muslim chaplains, or those chaplains serving Muslims, but for the field of chaplaincy itself. We have a rich pastoral tradition of care that begs exploration and deserves to be known, but most importantly, we must advance our own contributions to the field for our day and time.

The Abrahamic concept of shepherding, or pastoral care, exists centrally within the Islamic sacred texts: the Qur'an and hadiths. But, unlike in Judaism and Christianity, it has not previously been articulated systematically as a *distinct* body of knowledge. Consequently, Christians have argued that pastoral care is rooted wholly in the Judeo-Christian tradition. Reading Christian pastoral theologians such as Carrie Doehring during my seminary studies, I was surprised to find some go even further, asserting that "pastoral" is not a notion or practice inherent to the Muslim tradition.

An authentic scriptural basis in Islam exists for a notion of pastoral care rooted in a fulfillment of a Qur'anic imperative[1] as Ch. Ibrahim Long and I have written about extensively in our piece "Islamic Pastoral Care and the Development of Muslim Chaplaincy."[2] A corollary to this claim is that Islamic pastoral care requires religious caregivers to provide spiritual care within ethical standards of professional identity and conduct following the lived experience modeled after the Prophet Muhammad's ﷺ compassionate example to be true to its name and to live up to Qur'anic standards and imperatives of the Divine.

In my teaching, I help students identify and listen for the evidence of the pastoral voice in Islamic scripture, law, and theology. I provide guidance in exploring the subtle pastoral allusions and distinct framing in the Qur'an, for example in the story of Moses caring for the women shepherds being prevented from watering their flock by a larger group of male shepherds, and then becoming a shepherd himself before receiving a message from God.[3] I share pastoral care examples from the *sîrah* of Prophet Muhammad ﷺ, such as his ethical development of each of the Four Rightly Guided Caliphs. I demonstrate the interreligious nature of the development of legal and theological scholarship, seen, for example, in Abû Hanîfah's legal theory and practices, which spoke to the complex multifaith, social, and political contexts in which he served. I then lead students to engage with how this can inform the pastoral care they will provide in multifaith environments. Lastly, I show how spiritual caregivers integrated a theory of pastoral care articulated with varying degrees of directness in the Islamic tradition through the centuries through our studies of texts such as Imâm al-Shâfi'î's *Kîtab ar-Risâla fî Usûl al-Fiqh* and the *Risâle-i Nur Collection* of Said Nursi.

One example I gleaned from Dr. Tim Winter that I share with my own students is how al-Ghazâlî's *Revival of the Religious Sciences* is one of Islam's greatest pastoral theological manuals. In this magnum opus, al-Ghazâlî serves as pastoral theologian teaching how to provide care firmly rooted in the eternal scripture. My father introduced me to al-Ghazâlî; he also introduced me to Imam Warith Deen Muhammad, whom I credit with teaching me an interreligious hermeneutic of engagement.[4] This hermeneutic provided me with a culturally comfortable approach to Muslim pastoral care using primary textual resources centering our American context.[5] It gave me the confidence to believe that, despite the complexity and often psychologically distant medieval framing, al-Ghazâlî's pastoral theology was meant to be implemented in my ministry. This hermeneutic of engagement informed my belief that my scripture and tradition required that I begin to frame my professional conduct and identity as a shepherd of others because I am meant to care for all as a *khalîfah* or pastoral leader on earth.

In presenting Islamic sources that are foundational to chaplaincy, I seek to demonstrate that Islamic pastoral care is a process whose aim is spiritual wellness, resulting in what the Qur'an terms a *qalbun salîm* (a sound heart).[6] Thus, I contend that the Muslim chaplain's pastoral care can and should be grounded in Islamic faith and practice, and when it is, it is capable of helping any client establish a healthier spiritual state regardless of whether they identify with a faith tradition or whether their belief system is theistic or not. The form of care articulated in the Qur'an is described as "shepherding one's trusts and covenants" in both personal and public responsibilities.[7] The exemplar and model of the most excellent inner and outward caregiver is the Prophet Muhammad ﷺ. Muslim chaplains also need to see their caregiving as a dimension of Islamic theological ethics which must be integrated with scientific knowledge so that it is possible to chaplain atheists or agnostics: the pastoral vision of being just a shepherd, guiding the soul before me, where they are and in whatever state they are in.[8]

But before the integration of religious and scientific knowledge can happen, Muslim chaplains must engage deeply with the pastoral theology in the Islamic tradition. This requires that those Muslims who pursue chaplaincy work be deeply rooted in not just the practice of Islam but also knowledge of the tradition so they can develop from their faith their own theologies of pastoral care, grief, anger, and spiritual resources. Additionally, Muslim chaplains need to understand how Islam guides people effectively in the cultivation of virtue and away from vice—in other words, how Islam promotes the highest and best development of the human being. The Muslim chaplain must understand that the first principle of "do no harm" in Islamic pastoral theology begins with being a shepherd of one's trusts and covenant with God. Indeed, the merit of Islamic pastoral theology is that it leads to a noble discipline of high character development allowing a person to attain wisdom to share, courage to avoid harm, temperance to attentively listen, and justice that balances and centers everything they do. This all comes in Islamic pastoral theology from our beloved Prophet Muhammad ﷺ whose life and legacy are a complete guide to the care of hearts and souls. The act of shepherding is an exercise of religious faith and a practice of belief that results in the realization of *al-iḥsân* (the doing of the beautiful) as the highest level of this religion.

I realize now how my childhood Jewish Community Center rabbi, my Evangelical pastor, Catholic nun, and Episcopal CPE supervisor all were integral to my internal development as a pastoral caregiver as a chaplain. Chaplaincy is a professional practice of compassionate caregiving that, most often, is carried out in secular institutions seeking accommodation for all without the establishment of a specific religion. This makes chaplains different from clergy in houses of worship. Though Muslim, professionally I am not a "Muslim chaplain" nor an "Islamic chaplain" but rather, a chaplain who identifies religiously as Muslim. A chaplain, by definition, is always a chaplain for all; this necessitates a working knowledge of other faiths and their religious foundations for pastoral care, in addition to one's own.

At Hartford Seminary, I have the honor of teaching in classrooms with students who are studying to become pastoral caregivers from all faith backgrounds. Muslims are able to delve into Islamic studies in classes taught by practicing Muslims alongside a diverse group of Muslim peers who collectively challenge the Sunday school style of Islam as a monolithic unchanging practice that most have grown up with. Muslims studying to become chaplains will enter classrooms within a multifaith context studying ministry for a multifaith context with scholar-practitioners who have served as shepherds themselves. This is how my mentors taught me to integrate theory into practice, form a professional identity, maintain excellent moral conduct, practice prophetic pastoral skills of care, and lead ethically.

Notes

1. See al-Maʿârij/70:32; al-Muʾminûn/23:8.

2. Ibrahim Long and Bilal Ansari. "Islamic Pastoral Care and the Development of Muslim Chaplaincy," *Journal of Muslim Mental Health* 12, no. 1 (2018).

3. al-Qasas/28:23–30.

4. Imam W. D. Muhammad was the seventh son of the Honorable Elijah Muhammad, founder of the Nation of Islam. After the death of his father, he was elected to succeed him. He then immediately led the majority of his followers, Malcolm X among them, to Sunni Islam.

5. For a good description of what I am calling Imam W. D. Muhammad's hermeneutic of engagement, see Timur Yuskaev, *Speaking Qur'an: An American Scripture* (University of South Carolina Press, 2017), 69–110.

6. Abraham's prayer found in al-Shuʿarâ'/26:89.

7. See again al-Maʿârij/70:32; al-Muʾminûn/23:8.

8. My thinking around this is informed by Don Browning's "Pastoral Theology in a Pluralistic Age," *Pastoral Psychology* 29 (1980): 24–35.

A Theology of Spiritual Care Inspired by Allah's Attributes

ALI R. CANDIR

MY JOURNEY INTO chaplaincy was not an easy one. "What am I doing here, really?" I asked myself while I was trying to get some rest during one of my first on-call shifts as a chaplain intern. I was alone and my shift had been quite busy. It was almost 3:00 in the morning. I was looking at the bookshelf from where I was lying down; there were copies of holy scriptures, prayer books, rosaries, crosses, and inspirational reading materials. The question that came to my mind was, in fact, an effort to grasp the reality I was in and to find my own answers about why I was participating in the Clinical Pastoral Education (CPE) program. In a broader sense, it was actually the beginning of my inner journey toward a well-founded spiritual care practice.

"The one who visits the sick is in an orchard of Paradise until he returns."[1] These words were uttered by Allah's beloved messenger, the Prophet Muhammad ﷺ as a different perspective on illness. Anyone who

---

Ali R. Candir is board certified with the Association of Professional Chaplains (APC) and serves at CHI Baylor St. Luke's Medical Center in Houston, Texas. He has an MA degree in Islamic Studies and Christian-Muslim Relations from Hartford Seminary. Originally from Turkey, Ali is the founder and president of Wellspring Chaplaincy Initiative, which aims to advance hospital chaplaincy among Muslims in the United States. Before becoming a hospital chaplain, he led several nonprofit organizations that promote interfaith and intercultural dialogue for fifteen years. He is the author of two publications, including *Give Glad Tidings to the Patient*, an inspirational reader for Muslim patients. Ali speaks Turkish, English, and Spanish, and is married with two children. As a family, they love traveling around the world and spending time with their friends.

---

works in or visits a hospital knows that patient rooms and hospital hallways are far from seeming like "orchards of Paradise" from their external appearance. Hospitals are often perceived as places where people experience vulnerability and suffering, and face some of the toughest decisions of their lives. As a chaplain, I feel inspired by the example of the Prophet because I understand his words as an invitation to see the contrast and connection between the two realities of patient rooms: suffering and God's *rahmah* (mercy and compassion),[2] illness and *shifâ'* (divine healing), and those who are sick and those who offer care—in this case, chaplains. Next to a patient, we find God's mercy and compassion, even though the patients may not feel or see it in that way. I aspire to offer a sacred space that might remind patients of that divine compassion by being an active listener who listens nonjudgmentally and without trying to "fix," a holding hand, a praying voice, and, hopefully, a softened heart that deeply feels their suffering.

On the first day of our CPE training, I was told that I was the first Muslim student in this hospital's CPE program. This surprised me given the fact that Houston has a large Muslim population and receives many Muslim patients from around the world. As the first Muslim chaplain intern, I experienced being "the other" right from the beginning. I later learned that administrators of the Spiritual Care department were also feeling nervous about admitting a Muslim student into a hospital where most patients and staff are Christian. They were, understandably, concerned about what kind of situations I might find myself in and how it would be for me: responding to Baptism requests, offering extemporaneous prayers, reading from the Bible to a patient, and so on.

I did not originally intend to become a hospital chaplain. I had other aspirations on my mind. I was considering college chaplaincy and working toward my MA/GC from Hartford Seminary, which required one unit of CPE. I was struggling to squeeze 400 hours of CPE along with my job as a full-time executive director of a local nonprofit organization. Three things kept me going when I felt stretched so thin I might split. First, my continuous prayers for Allah to guide me in this uncharted territory. Second, the everyday support of my supervisor, a very caring and skillful individual who had tremendous sensitivity and advocated for me. And third, the encounters I had with my patients, as well as some dreams that I consider *sadûqah* (authentic).

With those three reassurances, I did not quit CPE, and, moreover, I began planning to do another unit. Yet I kept hearing the question, "What am I doing here, really?" over and over again throughout the weeks, sometimes during a patient visit at the hospital, when writing a verbatim at home, or while traveling away from Houston. I sensed something was going on. What I was doing at the hospital had already transformed from being a mere requirement toward exploring a career option into something personal, deep inside me. I was determined to find the answer to my question.

As part of CPE requirements, my peers and I were required to write a personal theology of spiritual care paper as an end-of-unit assignment. As a Muslim spiritual caregiver, I felt I was starting from scratch since there is not much material that outlines a theology of spiritual care in a healthcare setting with an Islamic approach. I needed to find inspirations from my own faith that would guide me to become a chaplain who could attend to patients of all faith traditions as well as those who had none. The sections included below are my collection of important foundational aspects of Islam, my faith, that inform my spiritual care.

Ridâ: *God's Pleasure*

Faith plays a crucial role in my life in relating to God and His whole creation, especially human beings. My core values and principles draw from my faith as well. The concept of *ridâ* (contentment with God's decree) is one of my key motivations. God says in the Qur'an, "God has promised the believing men and the believing women Gardens with rivers running below, to abide therein, and goodly dwellings in the Gardens of Eden. But Contentment from God is greater; that is the great triumph!"[3] According to this verse and similar teachings, some Islamic scholars consider *ridâ* as the highest spiritual reward, even greater than Paradise itself.[4] Among them is the Turkish scholar Fethullah Gülen, from whom I learned about Islamic spirituality. His teachings, which are based on the Qur'an and Prophet Muhammad's ﷺ example, have profoundly impacted me since my college years. Gülen teaches that Muslims pursue obtaining God's pleasure in everything they do. *Ridâ* requires a sincere, selfless act that is done for nothing except the sake of God. I believe that "being" with patients in their difficult moments and offering deep listening and presence are devotional acts that put patients at the heart of the visit, beyond all my personal expectations and assumptions.

Common Humanity and Divine Rahmah

All humans are equal before God, as was clearly taught by Prophet Muhammad ﷺ in his final sermon: "All men are equal before God as are the teeth of a comb. All mankind is from Adam and Eve, an Arab has no superiority over a non-Arab nor a non-Arab has any superiority over an Arab; also, a white has no superiority over a black nor a black has any superiority over white except by piety and good action." God, as *al-Rahmân* (the Most Compassionate), encompasses everyone in His mercy and generosity, regardless of their color, gender, faith, culture, or race. Based on this divine attribute, Muslims should aim to treat everyone with mercy, generosity, love, and respect. Before we come into physical existence, our spirit has no shape, culture, color, or race yet; I admire our common humanity in this regard. I see my patients through these lenses of *rahmah* and diversity: I feel as if I am communicating with another human spirit, beyond all markers of identity. In this encounter, there are no barriers, nothing that impedes two humans from embracing each other wholly because we both are two mirrors of God, two mirrors looking at each other. In physics, when two literal mirrors face each other, an infinite number of images happen. I think it is similar in the spiritual realm as well; there is no end to two humans' journey into each other as long as their hearts are open.[5]

I feel inspired by God's giving from two of His Divine Names to the Prophet Muhammad ﷺ, which are *al-Ra'ûf* and *al-Rahîm*: "A Messenger has indeed come unto you from among your own. Troubled is he by what you suffer, solicitous of you, kind [*ra'ûf*] and merciful [*rahîm*] unto the believers."[6] This verse speaks to how we can emulate the Prophetic example. If Allah chose these two names, among many others, to give to His most beloved servant, it is not only because it is a reaffirmation of the Prophet's character, but also, in my opinion, an invitation for me to be the carrier and reminder of that kindness and mercy to all. I believe deeply that *al-Ra'ûf* and *al-Rahîm* are two names that connect me to God, the Prophet, and all human beings.

Diversity of Human Beings: A Divine Will

I have had countless experiences where I felt truly humbled by my patients' faith, good manners, and humanity. One such patient required a device to sustain his heart, and his nurse notified me that he had decided to turn off the heart pump and asked for a chaplain visit. When I entered the room, he was sitting next to the window where the sun was shining brightly. He told me with a big smile on his face, "Look, Ali, it is a beautiful day to die." As I was talking to this man, whom I knew would probably be dead within a few hours, I realized he was in total surrender. He said, "I am going to meet God today. I am going to meet Jesus in paradise." I was in awe of his acceptance of his current state as he was facing death and maintaining such a peaceful and almost joyous spirit. As we continued, I realized that no family would be present at the time of turning off the pump. I asked if he wanted any of us to be with him, to which he replied, "You." I held his hand as he was breathing his last. To this day, I remember him as an example of true faith in God and *islâm*—not as the name of a particular religion but as surrendering or submitting to God's will.[7]

I see beauty in all our differences. As somebody who lived in places other than his native country for two decades, I grew accustomed to diversity in race, culture, language, and religion. I learned to appreciate these differences through personal reflection and education. I saw how barriers that I had in my mind in earlier years kept disappearing or being replaced with the positive images, and I strove to adapt those positive changes to my life as much as I could. A verse in the Qur'an says, "O mankind! Truly We created you from a male and a female, and We made you peoples and tribes that you may come to know one another. Surely the most noble of you before God are the most reverent of you. Truly God is Knowing, Aware."[8] I believe that diversity is part of God's divine will, and it is this divine will that enjoins us to get to know each other, thereby fulfilling the concept of *ta'âruf*. Knowing one another is not a superficial interaction but rather is to possess a genuine curiosity, humility, and grace to look at another human being as a unique mirror of the Divine, deserving to be treated with tenderheartedness, dignity, and respect.

Many other experiences helped me deeply appreciate the meaning of diversity in the light of this verse: "And among His signs are the creation of the heavens and the earth and the variation in your tongues and colors. Truly in that are signs for those who know."[9] As a trilingual chaplain, I talk to my patients and offer prayers in their languages. As I live in Texas, there are many Spanish-speaking patients. As we pray together in Spanish, I feel the beauty of God through a different language. I feel astounded by how God listens to all, in thousands of different languages and ways of expression, and hears what is at the heart of what they want, and how He responds to them in thousands of ways. Speaking the language of a patient, even sometimes with only a few words, helps break the barriers and connect with patients and their loved ones. I have seen many times the relief and the surprise on the face of a patient or a loved one when they hear their own language in the vulnerable atmosphere of a hospital room.

Remembrance of One of the Two Greatest Blessings of God: Health

Almost no day goes by without seeing a patient who has been yearning to have one sip of water, eat something, or take two steps unassisted. Health is considered a blessing of God in Islam. Yet, the Prophet 🕌 teaches us that health is one of the two blessings which many people take for granted, the other being free time.[10] When I come into the hospital, I remember the things I forget or undervalue so quickly: a healthy family and myself. My on-call shifts at a local pediatric hospital were particularly challenging, bearing witness to children suffering and trying to fight back with their tiny bodies. Once, a Catholic priest asked me to visit a Spanish-speaking parent. Her child was not responding to treatments anymore and she was left having to decide whether to place a DNR (do not resuscitate) order. Her eyes were filled with tears, a language everyone can understand, and she said, "What am I supposed to say? If I say yes to DNR, I feel like I am not doing enough for my baby. If I say no, doctors tell me that his ribs may be broken and he would suffer a lot. . . . O Lord, what can I say?" I imagined if I had to decide such a thing—what would I do? After leaving the room, I felt deeply impacted by her grief. At the same time, I also gave thanks to God for having healthy children.

Remembrance of Death

In keeping oneself from succumbing to worldly life and forgetting our return to God, Prophetic teachings recommend the frequent remembrance of death.[11] By doing so, one does not sever his or her bond with God. From time to time, Prophet Muhammad ﷺ used to visit the cemetery where his Companions were buried. He would salute them, say prayers for them, and weep. The concept of death is visible where I grew up in Turkey, where cemeteries exist alongside businesses and mosques. They reminded me of death and of the transitory nature of my world that is destined to transform into an eternal afterlife. After I moved to the United States, I noticed many cemeteries are located outside of cities and require special effort to travel there for such reflections.

The situation in a hospital is different, though. It is not uncommon during our morning staff meetings to hear that several people died in the night. I also have seen some of my patients die in front of my eyes and have provided death ministry many times throughout my years in chaplaincy. It is a very powerful experience: people seeking forgiveness from each other, talking anxiously about unfinished matters, and fearing what comes after death. One patient of mine, a forty-five-year-old woman, was processing death and dying during her end-stage cancer: "I am scared of death. I don't know what's going to happen when it is time. When I think of myself not breathing, being in the coffin, I feel very scared. And I accept death whichever way it goes, may God's will be done. But I am still scared." Along with these feelings of fear, there is also a peaceful sense of closure and letting go, expressions of "ready to go," feeling accomplished with one's life, leaving a legacy and cherished memories to the world. Another patient, a sixty-eight-year-old man, told me as he was approaching death, "I believe everything comes from God. I have nothing to worry about." I was later told that he was not accepting morphine despite his excruciating pain. When we talked, he told me that he was concerned that his mind would be clouded, and he feared that he was going to lose his *imân* (faith). Those moments have been sacred and humbling for me. It helps me reflect on my life frequently and serves as a reminder of death as transition.

Du'â: *Invocation/Prayer*

God says, "When My servants ask thee about Me, truly I am near. I answer the call of the caller when he calls Me."[12] *Du'â* is pure worship.[13] To be able to call upon God is the most beautiful gift for me. No matter when and where, we can turn to God and know for sure that He is listening to us. This empowers our hearts and spirits and motivates us to keep moving forward, especially in those times when we feel broken or are broken. Hospitals are among those places where one can powerfully witness and experience that brokenness, helplessness, and sometimes anger and despair. When I am with a patient or his or her loved one who goes through such feelings, I offer a *du'â* (prayer) or am asked to do so. Through offering and reciting a *du'â*, we open ourselves to al-Samî' (the All-Hearing); when there is no one else around, we utter the words we would not utter otherwise and ask for comfort, serenity, and healing. With these feelings, I offer prayers to experience the nearness of God not only with the other human being I am praying with but also with myself. Sometimes these prayers are in the form of conversation, which demonstrates a deep link with God.

I offer prayers to my patients when they ask me to because, in my opinion, it is more powerful when it comes from them and not from me. I will sometimes take the initiative to offer a prayer if I assess that prayer might be comforting to patients. I hear when my patients add their own ways of finishing the prayer, or say words and amen as I am praying, or extend their hands for me to hold. Sometimes they burst into tears after the prayer or seem joyous at the conclusion of prayer. Some families ask for prayers for their patient almost daily. In addition, I pray for staff, nurses, PCAs, or the entire team as part of my support to them in their compassionate care. Nurses frequently request prayers because they are overworked, their patient is not doing well, they are grieving the loss of a patient in their unit, or they are having issues in their personal lives. Prayer brings a moment of solace amid all this, a moment to step away from the realities of the world and a move into a state of peace beyond everything.

So, I have found the answer to my question, "What am I doing here, really?" It seems that God brought me here to be with Him through being a healing presence for those in need. I conclude this article with a prayer that I remember to offer at the end of my week at the hospital:

God, I thank You for all the patients, families, and our staff that I visited during this week and for all the times that I was able to bring them a moment of joy, peace, and comfort. If I was able to do so, it is because of Your grace.

I also ask Your forgiveness for all the times I did not hear what they wanted to say, all the times I missed an opportunity to understand them, and all the times that I was not a healing presence. Overlook my shortcomings as I am a human being.

Âmîn

Notes

This article is an expanded version of "Experience and Application of the Faith of a Muslim CPE Student," *Plain Views* 12, no. 7 (2015), a publication of HealthCare Chaplaincy Network.

1. Muslim, *al-Sahîh* Vol. 6, Hadith 6551–6555.

2. M. Asad in his *The Message of the Qur'an* explains: "Both the divine epithets *Rahmân* and *Rahîm* are derived from the noun *rahmah*, which signifies 'mercy,' 'compassion,' 'loving tenderness,' and, more comprehensively, 'grace.'"

3. al-Tawbah/9:72.

4. Abu Sa'id al-Khudri reported that Allah's Apostle ﷺ said that Allah would say to the inmates of Paradise: "O, Dwellers of Paradise," and they would say in response: "At thy service and pleasure, our Lord, the good is in Thy Hand." He (the Lord) would say: "Are you well pleased now?" They would say: "Why should we not be pleased, O Lord, when Thou hast given us what Thou hast not given to any of Thy creatures?" He would, however, say: "May I not give you [something] even more excellent than that?" And they would say: "O Lord, what thing can be more excellent than this?" And He would say: "I shall cause My pleasure to alight upon you and I shall never be afterwards annoyed with you." Muslim, *al-Sahîh* Vol. 40, Hadith 6787.

5. Rumi tells of a competition between two groups of artists. He inspiringly makes the mirror a symbol for the heart:

"That purity of the mirror is, beyond doubt, the heart which receives images innumerable.
That Moses (the perfect saint) holds in his bosom the formless infinite form of the Unseen (reflected) from the mirror of his heart.
Although that form is not contained in Heaven, nor in the empyrean nor in the sphere of the stars, nor (in the earth which rests) on the Fish,

Because (all) those are bounded and numbered—(yet is it contained in the
heart): know that the mirror of the heart has no bound."

Read the full story (scroll down for English translation): http://rumiurdu.blogspot
.com/2012/03/masnavi-book-1-63-contention-between.html.

6. al-Tawbah/9:128.

7. "Who is better in religion than the one who submits his face to God, and is
virtuous, and follows the creed of Abraham, as a *hanîf*? And God did take Abraham
for a friend." al-Nisâ'/4:125.

8. al-Hujurât/49:13.

9. al-Rûm/30:22.

10. al-Bukhârî, *al-Jâmi' al-Sahîh*, Book 81, Hadith 1.

11. al-Tirmidhî, *Sunan* 2307.

12. al-Baqarah/2:186.

13. "Supplication is worship itself." al-Tirmidhî, *Sunan* 3247.

Su-Shi

Bridging the Intrafaith Divide

MUHAMMAD A. ALI

BEFORE I BEGAN MY CAREER as a Muslim chaplain, I called a nearby facility to offer volunteer services. The Muslim staff chaplain answered the phone, and the first question he asked was, "Are you Shi'a?" I responded hesitantly and inquisitively, "Yes?" The chaplain replied, "We do not need volunteers at this time," and hung up the phone. Several other community members were given the same response. I had recently been invited to join a group seeking to respond to the many letters from incarcerated Shi'a Muslims complaining of a lack of Shi'a representation regarding religious materials and volunteers. It did not seem as though they could imagine asking for a Shi'a chaplain. The letters also complained of discrimination on the part of Muslim staff chaplains toward the Shi'a school of thought. We were disheartened to find how real that challenge would be.

Muhammad A. Ali is a graduate of Bayan Islamic Graduate School with an MDiv in Islamic Chaplaincy and an MA in Islamic Education. He chaplains in university and prison settings. He has served in many leadership roles, leading youth programs, and as a lecturer in Islamic centers in North Carolina and California. He has an extensive Islamic education beginning with Qur'an and Arabic as a child at the American Institute of Quranic Studies. He is proud to have studied under the auspices of teachers of Sunni, Shi'a, and Sufi persuasions. He holds a BA in Psychology and completed four units of Clinical Pastoral Education (CPE). His major interest is in exploring the chronology of revelation and its application to individual and community development. His pondering the Qur'an keeps him sane, while his love of basketball and his children keep him fit. He lives in Pennsylvania with his superhero wife and their four children.

My first encounter with incarcerated Muslims had come six years earlier when Ch. Oliver Muhammad connected with me while looking for a volunteer from the Shiʻa community. I remembered so clearly when I first stepped foot into a North Carolina prison to lead a Jummah prayer. I was afraid! The air felt heavier than usual. The clanking of the outside gate was like a gunshot signaling my heart to start a race. I had entered a terrifying world. My primary reference points were scenes from various films. The walk to the chapel through the long hallways and multiple locked gates felt like a lifetime. My heart was racing as I repeated quietly, "*Astaghfirullâh! Astaghfirullâh! Astaghfirullâh!*"[1] The discomfort of that place drew me toward the remembrance of Allah, unlike anything I had experienced. I drew courage from recommitting my intention to be there only for the sake of Allah; I could therefore leave everything out of my control to my Creator. I tried to convince myself that if I got shanked walking in that intention, I would be content.

Ch. Oliver and I waited briefly in the chapel before inmates began to arrive. As I saw them enter, I thought about how they all look like me. I remembered my father, who was one of the pioneering Sunni Muslims in the Northeast, saying, "It is only by the mercy of Allah that I am not up under the jail." Thinking of my family history and that of many African Americans, I felt that only the changing of winds could have landed me in their shoes. I was grateful for the sacrifices my Shiʻa mother made to safeguard me from many of the influences that push young Black men toward lifestyles likely to result in prison. The men greeted me with the familiar Muslim greeting, "*Assalâmu ʻalaykum*," which made me feel more comfortable. They lined up in the straightest rows I had ever seen while one of them made a heartrending call to prayer. These familiar rituals settled me enough to lead the prayer as I had done in my local community. In conversation after, several men offered positive feedback and questions. They expressed their gratitude for my coming to visit and their hope that I would see them again. I was moved by what I experienced as their eagerness for knowledge and communal connection.

The seed of a prison chaplain was planted, though I had no idea that such a path existed for me until several years later. Today, I am thankful that Allah allowed me to mature beyond that point before being aware of the opportunities to pursue chaplaincy in California, where I moved in 2010. The group I had been invited to join in the Bay Area included Maulana Sayyid Qamar Hasani, who had dedicated many years to corresponding with incarcerated Muslims about Shiʻa Islam. After hearing me speak on several occasions, he told me, "You should be a chaplain. It would be perfect for you." No one in the group knew of my previous experience visiting a prison, but my being African

American and well educated in the Shiʻa school of thought made me an ideal prospect. Along with Sayyid Nabi Raza Abidi from Saba Islamic Center, he developed a certification program to help individuals meet qualifications to become chaplains in California state prisons. The program required a visit to a prison, but this was challenging as nearby chaplains would not accommodate Shiʻa Muslim volunteers.

My interest in prison chaplaincy is rooted much more deeply in my identity as an African American Muslim than as a representative of Shiʻa Islam. However, as I learned more about the obstacles faced by Shiʻa Muslims behind bars, my mindset was undoubtedly affected, leading me to wonder if, not fitting the Sunni norm, I would always be restricted to being seen as Shiʻa. Through my upbringing with parents who ascribed to the two primary schools of Islamic thought, I was forced to engage these differences early in life. Additionally, both practiced Sufism under the guidance of shaykhs representing several Sufi orders.[2] The theological underpinnings of these perspectives and their accompanying practices have been matters of continuous study and contemplation for me. My investigation has revealed the degree to which identity politics have so often eroded reason, respectful discourse, and cooperation. In prison, these identity politics, when embraced by the likes of former criminals and gang members, can lead to violence. People who were previously fighting over neighborhood turf find themselves in opposition over religious identity. It can be a matter of life and death for some. In an encounter with a Shiʻa Muslim who was transferred to my facility, he informed me he had been beaten nearly to death because of his Shiʻa background. This inmate was deeply spiritually oriented, yet he reported fearing for his life around other Muslims.

His experience evoked memories of my own encounter being forced into a room and questioned by Saudi guards at the Prophet's ﷺ mosque while I was on hajj. One of the *mutawwiʻîn* (religious police) saw me speaking to a Shiʻa scholar in the courtyard of the Prophet's mosque and immediately rushed over to ask why I was talking with him. He barked at the turbaned scholar, saying, "You are not allowed to speak with anyone outside your group!" I told him, "I was simply speaking with my Muslim brother." He replied, "He is not your brother!" He then asked me if I was Shiʻa. I said, "I am Muslim." Three more guards appeared. Two of them escorted him away while the other two took me to a room where a couple of young seminarians sat around me with several *mutawwiʻîn* standing guard. As they asked me questions about my background, I began to worry I might not make it out of that room if I answered in a way that alarmed them. (A prominent Shiʻa scholar from Canada was allegedly beaten and strangled as he was thrown into a Madinah City Prison

cell with twenty-eight other people for twenty-four to thirty-six hours.)[3] I eventually realized they saw me as a young Black American who needed to be
saved from Shi'a influence—that is, unless I had already been corrupted. The
seminarians proceeded to tell me about Shi'as, who, according to them, believe
in a different prophet, worship stones and the dead, among many other misconceptions. I listened and only asked a few questions, curious to see what
other absurd ideas they had. After nearly four hours, they let me go. Not knowing what happened to the man I met in the courtyard still weighs on me.

I do not wish to belabor the point that many Shi'a Muslims have been mis-
treated in U.S. prisons by fellow Muslims, but I believe it bears naming that
Sunni Islam, especially in the prisons, is colored by Saudi Wahhabism and
Salafism through Saudi-distributed literature. Mateen Charbonneau, who
embraced Shi'a Islam in a South Carolina prison, has documented the experiences of Shi'as in prison. His work offers helpful insight into how some
"Sunnis"[4] seek to marginalize Shi'a perspectives in the prison context. He
reports what I have also seen: books written by Ibn Taymiyya and his students
with titles such as *Demolishing the Shi'a Creed* have often been readily available in prison chapel libraries or in possession of inmate influencers.[5] He also
documents the violent inclinations of some of those who are motivated by and
gravitate toward such readings.

The majority versus minority dynamics among Sunni and Shi'a create a
Sunni privilege with little motivation to learn about Shi'ism. Following a law-
suit by inmates alleging discrimination against Shi'a imams in hiring, the *Wall
Street Journal* questioned the head of the organization that advised the State
of New York on hiring more than forty Sunni imams with no Shi'a representation. The leading member responded with, "The Prophet said we are all
Muslims, not Shi'ite, not Sunni, just Muslims."[6] While this sounds nice, the
mindset typically erases the beliefs, practices, and history of Shi'as, creating
the religious version of being a "colorblind society." Typically, Sunnis do not
need a qualifier for their Muslim-ness; indeed, many practice the Sunni version of Islam without even knowing it. Furthermore, few are aware of the great
diversity of thought within the history of Sunni Islam. Meanwhile, Shi'as are
often compelled to learn about Sunnism to defend themselves, as they are frequently asked to present evidence for why they do something that appears to
be different. To be included as "just Muslim" is often a privilege.

When I was young and quite zealous, I hoped that I could guide people to
my perspective of Islam. I am thankful that my journey through Clinical
Pastoral Education (CPE) helped me develop humility around my own understanding and appropriate curiosity about others. Engaging in that process

helped me embrace the Qur'anic injunction calling different segments of the human family to get to know each other.[7] Listening to understand others first rather than to refute expanded my understanding of humanity's vast spiritual and intellectual landscape. I see the Shi'a imams endorsing the diversity within the Muslim community while meeting each person where they are and developing each according to their capacity and frame of reference. They urge those close to them to "speak to the people according to their understanding."[8] I do not believe that truth is subjective, I only acknowledge that the lenses through which we see are relatively imperfect.

Sunni and Shi'a Muslims share the basic tenets of belief: *tawhîd* (divine unity), *nubuwwah* (prophethood of all prophets with Muhammad ﷺ being the final messenger), and *ma'âd* (belief in the hereafter, including Judgment Day, punishment, and reward). The main dispute is around political authority after the Prophet's death (and its bearing on the *ummah* religiously and spiritually). Historical evidence shows early disagreement from Ali (son-in-law of Prophet Muhammad) and a small number of supporters with the selection of Abû Bakr al-Siddîq (close friend and father-in-law of Prophet Muhammad) as the first political successor. Ali's concession resolved the political disagreement, and Muslims lived with their differing perspectives. Through time several more conflicts arose, and responses to those conflicts manifested in more pronounced political and religious factions and fissures. While the Qur'an is not explicit about succession, several verses can be interpreted and understood to support each position. The challenge is knowing how those interpretations have been influenced by subsequent historical developments. The development of hadith literature in the generations after adds layers to that challenge.

In general, those brought up or exposed to Islam in environments where one sect is dominant are familiar with the evidence and interpretations that support that position. Moreover, many do not require much evidence for themselves. I recall a conversation in which an inmate approached me argumentatively for my textual evidence for prostrating on a *turbah* (small piece of dried mud), a common Shi'a practice. I told him I would be happy to bring him all my evidence in writing to exchange for his evidence in writing for what he prostates on. He seemed halted by my request and admitted he did not know of the evidence. "Is it fair," I asked him, "that you require others to present evidence for their practices but do not require it of yourself?" I went on to explain to him the different ways that Sunni and Shi'a Muslims understand the statement attributed to the Prophet ﷺ, "The earth has been made a place of prostration for me."[9] One might interpret "earth" to mean anything on the planet Earth is appropriate for prostration, while another might understand "earth" to mean something from the earth that is not manmade, like dirt, leaves, or grass as opposed to carpet. I also pointed him to several narrations within the most prominent Sunni books reporting that the Prophet would pray on something from the earth like mud or palm fibers. Those narrations are also understood in different ways, and much context is missing from hadith narrations filled in during the process of interpretation.

Initial indoctrination from childhood or during one's conversion has an anchoring effect that is difficult to overcome even when confronted with competing evidence, weighty as it may be. I see the Qur'an pointing out this phenomenon when it speaks of each faction being unabashedly pleased with what they have.[10] Each group would like to believe themselves to be the orthodoxy of Islam as believed and practiced by the Prophet ﷺ himself despite the many intellectual, political, and cultural developments during the 1,400 years since his death.

A man who was nearing the end of his sentence came asking for addresses to masjids in the city where he would be living. He said, "I don't want to go to a masjid with the wrong beliefs." I asked him how he would know whether a group of people have the correct beliefs. He said, "Well, if we agree on all the same principles." I said, "I hear you saying you determine truth by its agreement with what you know, but what do you not know?" He stopped himself and said, "You know what? You are right. But brothers told me not to go to a Shi'a mosque or a Sufi mosque." This individual had been Muslim for a short time and had been told all the kinds of Muslims he should stay away from without ever encountering them, their beliefs, or practices. My advice to him was to maintain humility, visit all the masjids, and sustain his beliefs while learning about others. Perhaps he could learn something new, recognize a deficiency in himself, or help someone else do the same. I reminded him that we are instructed to repeatedly pray, asking God to "guide us upon the straight path."[11] I read this as a reminder not to assume we have arrived; instead, we are pursuing the mark together. The Qur'an does not require us to be perfect; it requires us to strive.

When I eventually began my first position in a California state prison, I quickly learned of the power the Muslim chaplain had to influence the climate of the prison community. The denial of Shi'a volunteers, my experiences during my hajj journey, and the many stories from Shi'a practicing prisoners made me want to educate people about Shi'ism. I also realized the importance of not abusing my own authority to suppress Sunni Muslims. As a chaplain, I could now decide what literature stayed in the chapel library or what volunteers could visit. One day one of the leading members of the community approached me. He said, "So you are throwing away all the Sunni literature now." I said, "What? Where did that come from?" He said, "Some of the brothers said you are throwing away the Sunni literature." I explained to him that the Sunni chapel clerk and I were in the process of cleaning up the library, which had become a mess. We threw away some random papers, but all the Sunni books remained in the library. I had no intention to throw them away. Those men were expecting me to treat them as they had seen some of the Sunni chaplains treat the Shi'as, and it was scary! I spent many evenings with inmate representatives in my office, answering questions and clarifying my intention to build a united community across sectarian lines. That would prove to be exhausting work.

The Sunni members of the community were used to being dominant. Some Shi'as were used to being on the outskirts, and I struggled to bring them back into the fold of the community. Some were initially disappointed that I was not trying to make Shi'ism dominant. The jadedness from past conflict was evident, and everyone needed time to heal. I am thankful for the support of several leading Muslim brothers among the Shi'a and Sunni who welcomed a united community and supported me. Most of the community did buy into a diverse yet inclusive community. We welcomed volunteers with varying perspectives. Some of the hardliners identified as Shi'a, and some identified as Sunni; I struggled with both equally. I expanded the library so Muslim inmates could have access to a broader understanding of Islam, and all were invited to humbly pursue the straight path together.

Developing solid relationships with people with different perspectives and consistently increasing my own knowledge moves me further from the need to identify myself by sect. As a student of Islam, I do not seek to be a Shi'a scholar or a Sunni scholar. I strive to take advantage of the vast landscape of the Muslim tradition while recognizing the beauty and fallibility within. I do not aim to be a Shi'a Muslim chaplain; I aim to be a Muslim chaplain who serves all Muslims and beyond. The contrast between the chaplain who sought to deny Shi'a volunteers and Ch. Oliver Muhammad, who sought to include Shi'a volunteers, shows the vital role that chaplains have in bridging the division in the Muslim community. This work can be seen in various chaplaincy settings being modeled by well-trained chaplains who are more invested in humbly pursuing the straight path together than in identity politics. This is truly a part of the legacy of Ch. Sohaib Sultan that our profession must preserve.

Notes

1. A prayer for forgiveness and protection.

2. Sufism, frequently mistaken for a third sect, is a flavor of spiritual practice present in both Sunni and Shi'a traditions.

3. "Canadian Imam Released from 'Horrid' Saudi Imprisonment," CTVNews, October 31, 2011, https://www.ctvnews.ca/canadian-imam-released-from-horrid -saudi-imprisonment-1.718845.

4. I use the term "Sunni" here because that is how so many identify, not to represent all of Sunnism, especially those forms not subject to heavy Wahhabi Salafi influence.

5. Sheikh Mateen Charbonneau, "Life as a Shia Muslim Inside the U.S. Penitentiary," December 24, 2014, https://mateenjc.com/2014/12/24/life-as-a-shia -muslim-inside-the-u-s-penitentiary/.

6. Terry Eastland, "Inmates and Imams," *Washington Examiner*, April 28, 2003, https://www.washingtonexaminer.com/weekly-standard/inmates-and-imams.

7. al-Hujurât/49:13.

8. al-Bukhârî, *Sahîh* 127.

9. an-Nasâ'î, *Sunan* 736.

10. al-Rûm/30:33.

11. al-Fâtihah/1:6 (this opening chapter of the Qur'an is recited multiple times in the Muslim daily prayers).

Centering Identities in the Divine

AMIRA QURAISHI AND AILYA VAJID

Sitting on a patterned Turkish rug, sipping from mugs of chai spiced with cardamom and clove, we chat and wait for everyone to arrive from their evening classes. We then begin to hand out the small white papers containing dhikr *and* salawât *(remembrances of Allah and His Messenger ﷺ). From our heart-center, we move to this week's topic: "Why are we here, and who is Allah?" And so begins our Spirituality Series.*

Amira Quraishi currently serves as a chaplain at Wellesley College, previously having served at Johns Hopkins. She holds an MA in Religious Studies from the University of Pennsylvania, an MA in Middle Eastern Studies from New York University, and a BA in Political Science from the University of California, Davis. Amira has previously served on the board of the Association of Campus Muslim Chaplains. She attributes her love for a deeply spiritual and intellectual expression of Islam to her experiences growing up at the Muslim Youth Camp of California, for which she served as a board member. She brings to her chaplaincy thirty years of counseling experience.

Ailya Vajid has served with the Hadi Initiative at the University of Virginia, as well as at Carleton, Macalester, Gustavus Adolphus, and Swarthmore Colleges. Ailya was raised in Southern California in a Pakistani American household. She holds a BA in Religion and Islamic Studies from Swarthmore College and an MA in Theological Studies with a focus in Islamic Studies from Harvard Divinity School, and previously served on the board of the Association of Muslim Chaplains. She enjoys spending time in nature, reading sacred and reflective texts, learning about traditional forms of healing, and listening to people's life stories.

THIS WEEKLY GATHERING is one of many different ways that college chaplains walk alongside students on their journey in infusing the presence, remembrance, and blessing of Allah in every moment of their lives. This includes their social justice endeavors—students' activism in combating systemic racism, inequity, and violence aligns with Islamic values of justice and truth. Chaplains can support them in maintaining God at the center of these efforts so that they are grounded in a deep striving to manifest God's Attributes as *al-Muqsit* (The Just) and *al-Haqq* (The Truth) in the world. They become a part of the broader journey of self-discovery of our *fitrah*, our true self within.[1]

During their college years, students are surrounded by a diverse array of cultures, philosophies, traditions, religions, and ways of being. Many, having left home and their families for the first time, are seeking self-knowledge. Their learning takes place both in the classroom and among their peers as they start to navigate who they are, what they believe, what their values are, how they live their faith, and how they seek to contribute to the world. Through this experience, they are testing formed identities and discovering new ones. Identity is multidimensional and fluid, encompassing biological and psychological factors (such as race, gender, sexuality, and mental, physical, and psychological wellness and disabilities) as well as sociocultural factors (beliefs, upbringing and cultural context, peers, education, social/economic/political status), and vocational factors (such as career goals, activism, or volunteering).[2] Often in this seeking, students begin to explore aspects of themselves that provide the strongest affinity. In the classroom and around campus, as minorities, students often feel unsafe or that they have to hide parts of themselves (if they are able) to be accepted, to belong, and to feel secure. Spaces with peers who share similar experiences and backgrounds provide a sense of safety, understanding, and deep connection where they can fully be themselves and express themselves freely. Sometimes, however, these outward identities become our center, especially when the outside world affronts us with stereotyping, discrimination, and danger. A chaplain can support students in celebrating their identities and grounding them in faith, which provides resilience and spiritual depth.

Sometimes in our search for self and a connection to others who provide safety and security, a shared bond can be expressed as an "us versus them" mentality. The fourteenth-century historian Ibn Khaldun observed how this affinity functions as a "group feeling [in] which a human being feels most closely connected to his relatives" or those who share a "common descent."[3] He referred to it as *'asabiyyah* (tribalism). Today, we experience this group consciousness and connection as social solidarity, nationalism, political parties, or as any other form of partisanship around a shared cause or identity. This social solidarity through identity can be a powerful, positive, uniting force in mobilizing us around a shared cause for justice and truth. For example, a pan-African or pan-Arab identity has been an important tool in uniting nations in fighting colonialism, and such identities are also a binding force in contemporary movements for justice across the globe. It is important, however, that they do not become the center of our self-understanding and our intentions in this work.[4] Moreover, we must be aware that such solidarity around identity can also cause strife, disconnection, antagonism, dehumanization, exclusion, and even genocide. Indeed, the Prophet Muhammad ﷺ, sent as "a mercy to humankind," is our greatest model of how to strive for justice. During the first thirteen years of his prophethood, he and his followers suffered the physical and emotional pain of persecution, injustice, and loss. This they endured while the Qur'anic verses being revealed emphasized worshipping God alone. Clearly spiritual practice rooted in faith transformed them, such that an act of 'ibâdah (worship) included standing up for God's Truth and Justice with humility, sincerity, mercy, courage, and compassion.

As a chaplain, I (Amira) have seen that when a struggle for social justice is founded on external identity markers, it can easily lead to pain and fracture. One night, an ordinary group meeting I had with students erupted in expressions of discontent and anger over lack of allyship within the Muslim community. Their energy had them all talking at once, and suddenly I had to shift gears to moderate the conversation, listening with care and concern to each individual. I assured them that I would try my best to understand how their experiences were shared and/or different. I turned toward each person, making eye contact, asking clarifying questions. I listened intently to how they interpreted the events that were so frustrating to them. I stayed with them until late into the night, making a plan to facilitate reconciliation with those who were absent. Black and brown Muslims expressed that they felt dismissed by "white-passing" Muslims. Arabs felt they bore the brunt of Islamophobic attacks. I heard students grapple with expectations they had of their Muslim peers, hoping they would come to each other's aid in the face of the government's new homeland security policies. The friendships they thought were strong were now fractured by the revelation that they assumed they shared the same reality. Caught up in their own pain, they missed seeing the other's pain. As a result, their efforts to combat Islamophobia were isolated and their relationships damaged. I validated their feelings as I tried to lay a path forward based on the Qur'anic model of reconciliation: enjoining one another toward truth and patience.[5]

Even though reconciliation was not achieved, I observed firsthand that when someone feels attacked, it is very hard for them to see another point of view, and when someone feels dismissed, they desperately want to be recognized. In addition, the strains of college life make it difficult for students to always find emotional reserves to see another's pain, let alone face the possibility that they may be the cause of it. The path forward, then, had to be bringing together those who were willing to rebuild relationships. Recognizing that one cause of the fallout was not sufficiently knowing one another, the new leaders of various cultural organizations agreed to reduce the amount of their own programming in order to attend the programs hosted by the other groups, thereby building friendships and mutual understanding of different identities. To broaden thinking about multiple identities, I also led interactive exercises to engage students in discussion about their life experiences and to illustrate how they are different and the same.

Several weeks later, I sat with the newly elected Muslim student leaders to reflect on their experience and how they wanted to rebuild the culture of the Muslim student group. Previously, they focused on producing programming, and individual success was based on a student's ability to accomplish a task for these programs. Now it would focus on creating a welcoming, supportive community built on the loving example of Prophet Muhammad ﷺ who smiled at people because he loved them, who laughed with them, listened to them, showed patience with them, and cared for them because they were unique creations of Allah, capable of channeling Divine love and Divine attributes. Together, we decided to focus on two tenets: (1) building deep friendships based on trust, understanding, support, and forgiveness, and (2) celebrating the diversity of the Muslim community, creating a space where everyone is welcome.

Years later, I still try to use this story to make the Qur'an and the Prophetic example relevant to students today. One of the main challenges the Prophet Muhammad ﷺ faced was convincing people to look past certain identity markers to see the heart and soul within an individual. In other words, his message of Islam invited them to seek what unified them across differences, like light that goes through a prism, bending its wavelengths to reveal separate colors as they exit the prism. This world operates like a prism, forcing us to see each other as different colors. These distinctions, while beautiful and intentional, that demonstrate the breadth of Allah's creation can sometimes make us forget that we were originally part of the singular light. Indeed, Allah offers "examples to humanity" to teach us about the exponential brilliance of Divine light that is as if emitted from oil that is "neither from East nor West."

Allah's singular light, "encased in glass, appear[ing] as a brilliant star," is "light upon light."[6] Allah tells us that our differences are signs of God's creation, which we should treat with humble curiosity and appreciation: "O humanity! Truly We created you from a male and a female, and We made you peoples and tribes that you may come to know one another. Surely the most noble of you before God are the most reverent of you. Truly God is Knowing, Aware."[7] Today, we understand individuals as embodying multiple identities. They are all Divinely intended and are a gift for us from God to connect to the richness and diversity of creation and to know one another. Self-understanding through them is a significant part of knowing ourselves and living into the various roles and responsibilities we embody. Moreover, knowledge of others and of creation through these identities is a beautiful way of connecting to Allah's Attributes as they manifest in the world. Thus, we come closer to appreciating the oneness of God (*tawhîd*) when we see Allah's singular light through the multiplicity of creation. However, *limiting* our self-understanding to these identity markers can veil us from our inner self that seeks the Divine.

Whether through Qur'anic-based reminders, spiritual practice, or conversation, chaplains tenderly support students in connecting to the soul within. On a university campus in Virginia, students gather on Wednesday nights for Spirituality Series, a gathering in which we (Ailya and students) journey together in seeking to move inward into our heart-center, reflecting on the purpose of our existence as humans, cultivating self-knowledge, witnessing Allah in all of creation and within ourselves, drawing near to Allah through remembrance, and striving to worship Allah with *ihsân*.[8]

In this gathering, we reflect on Islamic scriptures that provide understanding on our purpose and nature as human beings. In a Hadith Qudsi relayed through the Prophet ﷺ, Allah makes clear the purpose of human life: "I was a hidden treasure, and I loved to be known; hence I created creation so that I would be known."[9] In Surah al-Dhâriyât, Allah tells us, "I did not create jinn and mankind save to worship me."[10] In another well-known Hadith Qudsi, Allah tells us, "My heavens and My earth cannot contain Me, but the heart of My faithful servant does contain Me."[11] In the Islamic tradition, the heart is "the center of our being on all the different levels of our existence."[12] Dr. Seyyed Hossein Nasr writes that the heart is "the isthmus between this world and the next, between the visible and invisible worlds, between the human realm and the realm of the Spirit."[13] Through the heart we witness, worship, and connect to Allah. The Prophet Muhammad has said that "the faithful heart is the throne of the All-Merciful."[14] In Spirituality Series, we journey together to re-center ourselves in Islamic principles on the purpose of existence, and we seek to deepen our self-knowledge so that we begin to live more intentionally from our heart-center, connecting to our *fitrah*,[15] to the *rûh*[16] that Allah breathed into each of us. We lean into the teaching related by the Prophet: "He who knows himself knows His Lord."[17] Thus, we seek to return to the center of our being and remove the rust on the mirror of the heart which holds and reflects the very presence of Allah.

Seeking to deepen our knowledge of and connection to Allah, we also reflect on various topics and questions on knowing Allah through His Names and Attributes, as well as inner meanings and purpose of worship, suffering and hardship, the nature of human beings and the ephemeral world, and recalling Allah's Mercy and closeness to us. In this space, we learn to witness and cultivate knowledge of Allah through "His signs on the horizons and within ourselves."[18,19] This gnosis resides in the heart, as the heart has the capacity to understand in a way the mind cannot comprehend. Students have recounted how such conversations have opened their hearts to perceiving Allah's presence and Attributes in the world and within themselves:

> I didn't know how much I needed Spirituality Series until it pushed me to dive into the depths of my heart. Over the course of two years, I've come to see myself and the world around me through a God-conscious lens. It transformed my perspective for the better.[20]

As students enter into their heart-center, they start to experience themselves, their identities, their work, and their activism through this lens, such that God is at the center of who they are and all they do. They cultivate what psychologist Dr. Abdallah Rothman calls "heartfulness," or "coming into a full awareness from the center of ourselves."[21] We further engage this through the practice of *murâqabah* (self-observation) in which we more intentionally come into our hearts where Allah is present, and we ask for forgiveness, praise and give thanks, and seek help and guidance from Allah.[22] This practice has allowed students to slow down, to breathe, to become present to their very selves, to cleanse their souls, to cultivate gratitude, and to let go and leave their difficulties in the Hands of Allah. By engaging in these various practices of contemplation and remembrance, we begin to detach from our outward selves and our ego selves. We do so not to entirely transcend our outward self and the ways that it informs our life and being, but rather so that it is not the center of our identity and being. Mawlana Rumi guides us in this regard:

> What is to be done, O Muslims, for I know myself not,
> Neither a Christian am I, nor Jew, nor a Magean, nor Muslim.

Neither of the East am I nor West, nor of the land, nor sea;
Nor of nature's quarry, nor of heavens circling above.
. . . My place is the placeless, my mark the markless;
Not either body or soul for I Myself the Beloved am.
I cast aside duality seeing the two worlds as one,
I seek the One, I know the One, I see the One, I call the One,
He is the First, He is the Last, He is the Outward, He is the Inward.
I know no one other than He, none but He who is He.[23]

In this *ghazal*, Mawlana Rumi seeks to detach himself from all forms of out-ward identity, his soul a beautiful polished mirror to the Divine. Here, he is calling us to empty ourselves of our ego and our attachments so that we are not veiling our *fitrah*, the Divine within our heart. This is not to undermine the Divine intentionality and beauty[24] of our outward identities, our heritages, ancestors, traditions, languages, and cultures. Allah has created us different to know one another and to learn and transform through the richness of these differences by interacting with one another. Moreover, the journey of know-ing one's inner self is also through these outward identities that build self-knowledge and awareness and help us know Allah, as long as they themselves do not become the destination.

Social justice work is a part of a Muslim's life. Numerous verses of the Qur'an highlight Divine Justice and call upon Muslims to combat injustice and oppression.[25] The Prophet ﷺ called upon Muslims to take action against, speak up against, or at least inwardly acknowledge an injustice, which is the weakest form of faith.[26] Engaging in this activism from our heart-center for the sake of Allah infuses it with selflessness, intentionality, and blessing. It transforms both the work and our own self, as we rub the rust off the mirror of the heart that reflects the Divine. Chaplains can support students in culti-vating this through spiritual practices of self-accountability (*muhâsabah*), developing virtues, aligning with *fitrah*, and reflection on and remembrance of Allah's Names and Attributes. Chaplains themselves can follow the Prophet Muhammad's model, which compassionately provides perspective on the ten-sion between the self that is attached to this world and the self that is the breath of the Divine. The relationship between chaplain and student is also meant to develop resilience for life's challenges, to connect to Allah more deeply, and to grow into our better selves that are naturally inclined to radi-ate compassion. Dr. Omid Safi explains that when we enrich every relation-ship with love and compassion, which are Divine Attributes, justice is essentially radical love in the public sphere. We then begin to understand how injury to the dignity of God's creation is an affront to God, and honoring that dignity is an act of worshipping God. The role of a chaplain is, at the core, that of a shepherd who walks alongside human souls on this journey of self-knowledge, inner transformation, and drawing near to the Divine.

Notes

1. al-A'râf/7:172.

2. Muhammad U. Faruqe, *Sculpting the Self: Islam, Selfhood, and Human Flourishing* (University of Michigan Press, 2021).

3. Binti Ismail, Nurul Fadhilah, and Adibah Binti Abdul Rahim, "Ibn Khaldun's Theory of 'Asabiyyah and Its Impact on the Current Muslim Community," *Journalism and Mass Communication* 8, no. 6 (June 2018): 290–291, doi:10.17265/2160-6579/2018.06.002.

4. A special thanks and recognition of Dr. Naseemah Mohamed Ogunnaike for her insights that deeply informed these reflections.

5. al-'Asr/103:3.

6. al-Nûr/24:35.

7. al-Hujurât/49:13.

8. The Prophet ﷺ was asked, "'What is *ihsân*?' Allah's Messenger replied, 'It is to worship Allah as though you could see Him, and if you cannot see Him [achieve this state of devotion], [know that] He sees you.'" (Hadith Jibril). Al-Bukhârî, *Sahîh*, 50.

9. William Chittick, *The Self-Disclosure of God: Principles of Ibn Arabi's Cosmology* (SUNY Press, 1998), 21.

10. al-Dhâriyât/51:56.

11. Seyyed Hossein Nasr, "The Heart of the Faithful Is the Throne of the All-Merciful," in *Paths to the Heart: Sufism and the Christian East,* ed. James Cutsinger (World Wisdom, 2004), 32.

12. Nasr, "The Heart of the Faithful," 37.

13. Nasr, "The Heart of the Faithful."

14. Nasr, "The Heart of the Faithful," 32.

15. Our innate nature which encompasses knowledge of Allah.

16. al-A'râf/7:172.

17. Seyyed Hossein Nasr, *The Garden of Truth: The Vision and Promise of Sufism, Islam's Mystical Tradition* (HarperCollins, 2007), 5.

18. Fussilat/41:53.

19. The Qur'an is filled with vivid imagery of the natural world: of the changing of the night into the day and the day into the night, the meeting of the seawater and freshwater, the constellations in the sky. In them, the Qur'an tells us, are signs for

those who "intellect" (*ya'qilûn*), those who "contemplate" (*yatafakkarûn*), those who believe, and those who listen. Yûsuf/12:2, Yûnus/10:24, al-Baqarah/2:164, al-An'âm/6:99, Yûnus/10:67, al-Ra'd/13:17–19.

20. Undergraduate student participant.

21. Abdallah Rothman, "Heartfulness," Shifaa Integrative Counseling, June 28, 2019, http://www.shifaacounseling.com/blog/heartfulness.

22. In this practice, we turn our consciousness toward the presence of Allah, recite *adhkâr*, and then reflect upon the following: asking Allah for forgiveness for our missteps of the day, recounting and giving thanks to Allah for our blessings, and asking Allah for our various needs and desires. We then recount a place or moment in which we were deeply present with Allah and return our consciousness here. Then we close with *salawât* and return to one another.

23. R. A. Nicholson, *Selected Poems from Divan-e Shams-e Tabrizi* (Ibex, 2001).

24. al-Hujurât/49:13.

25. "Allah raised up the heavens and established the scales of balance." al-Rahmân/55:7. "*Fitnah* (oppression) is graver [even] than slaying." al-Baqarah/2:217. "Truly We created humankind in the most beautiful stature, then We cast him to the lowest of the low, save those who believe and perform righteous deeds; for theirs shall be a reward unceasing." al-Tîn/95:4–6.

26. "Whosoever of you sees an evil, let him change it with his hand; and if he is not able to do so, then [let him change it] with his tongue; and if he is not able to do so, then with his heart—and that is the weakest of faith." *Hadîth al-Nawawî*, 34. One of many Prophetic sayings about injustice, including the Prophet ﷺ relaying God's Words: "O My Servants, I have forbidden injustice upon Myself and have made it forbidden amongst you, so do not commit injustice." Muslim, *Sahîh*, 2577.

From Banana Leaves

SAMSIAH ABDUL-MAJID

TO ME, BANANA LEAVES signify the time of my childhood in Malaysia. The leaf was a multipurpose commodity: to wrap things with, to cook in, to be used as an umbrella when it rains. Things have changed; once a convenient go-to item, banana leaves have been replaced by ubiquitous plastic. The leaf, therefore, is also a reminder of the changes that have occurred over time in me personally. My life was swept by changes in my social, cultural, economic, and religious environment, at first in a country that had just become independent and was aggressively trying to create a place for itself in the world, and later through my own choices.

After a long career at the United Nations, I am now a chaplain, a surprising development even to me. The call happened seemingly by accident, which I now recognize is the design of The Best of Planners. On many occasions, I acted like a chaplain before I knew what a chaplain was. One experience stands out prominently in my memory. Two staff members of an international

---

Samsiah Abdul-Majid is a palliative care chaplain at a medical center in New York State and is board certified by the Association of Professional Chaplains. A former board member of the Association of Muslim Chaplains, she currently supports AMC through research, initiating its oral history project and the survey on mapping Muslim chaplaincy in the United States. Samsiah holds an MA from Hartford Seminary's Islamic Chaplaincy Program and a Certificate in Palliative Care Chaplaincy from California State University. Born and raised Muslim in Malaysia, Samsiah gravitates to good food and follows a strict physical exercise regime to compensate, a regime that also keeps her nimble for her granddaughter. Her husband of forty-five years is her unwavering cheerleader.

---

organization I was working for in London died within a week of each other. I can still hear the howl of the sister in the middle of the night in her living room when my colleague and I broke the news that her brother had died in a plane crash in Africa. The wife of the second staff member kept repeating that this was not true, as she trudged up and down the hospital hallway and circled his body in the viewing room. As the organization's interim head of human resources, it was on me to support and organize help for the families, the staff, and the leadership. I wanted to be a balm to them as the UN Secretary-General had been to his staff, myself included, several years earlier when the UN office in Iraq was bombed, killing 22 and injuring more than 150. With intentionality, I followed my intuition and my sense of common humanity, and supported the London families and staff through their emotions, fears, and hopes. I realize now that chaplaincy found me through that experience.

I am very much at home in a hospital environment. Its diverse staff and patient population remind me of the United Nations. However, initially, I did not take to visiting patients like the proverbial fish to water; I felt like an intruder, self-conscious, uncomfortable walking into others' very personal and private lives. For the first few weeks of my training, I requested that I be assigned only to female patients. I figured that it would be less stressful to be with my own gender while I sorted out my feelings and figured out the basic nuts and bolts of providing emotional and spiritual support.

As I grew more comfortable in my role, I expanded my visits to include male patients, which meant visiting Muslim male patients as well. I could tarry no longer; I had to confront my feelings about visiting them. Reluctance? Fear? Reticence? It was hard for me to locate it. While I had worked in a mixed gender context my entire career, my practice of faith had been in segregated spaces. I imagined my visits. I thought about my opening words, how to introduce myself. I wondered whether my gender would be an issue, about proper etiquette, whether to make *du'â* and recite the Qur'an, and if we did, whether I should lead. I read about caring for Muslim patients. Just as in reading a recipe or a tech manual, the test is in the doing. My agonizing was for naught. My gender was not and continues not to be an issue with male Muslim patients. From almost every Muslim, male and female, a question, posed in many different ways, calls for an explanation of what a chaplain is. That is followed by, "And you are Muslim?" Invariably, the response to my affirmative answer is *al-hamdu lillâh* (a statement thanking God). Rejection did happen occasionally. I generally rationalize it as a way for patients to express control and autonomy in a situation of limited choices.

Rejection for being female, though, came from an unexpected quarter.[1] I received a request to visit an actively dying patient, a non-Muslim. His wife was alone, pensive, sitting in a chair by his bed. When she learned that I was the chaplain responding to her request, she said, "My husband does not deal with women clergy." I explained that I was the only one that day, it being a weekend. She bolted out of her chair, literally physically made a 360-degree turn, faced me again and said, with a wave of her hand, "Okay, do whatever it is you do." I prayed for ease and for forgiveness; she declined my invitation to pray together.

Gender was also a consideration in another death situation. I was called for a Muslim man. I scanned the scene as I approached the unit. The patient's room and the area outside it were overflowing with visitors, all men. I suddenly became self-conscious that I was a woman. I claimed my space by consulting with the physician and the nurse to understand the situation. The nurse identified who the main persons were among the men and said that the wife was in the adjacent waiting room. I greeted the men, talked to the "leaders," and we agreed on the urgency of obtaining a death certificate and expressed mutual concerns for the family. Then I went to meet the wife. She was alone except for one other woman. After we talked for a bit, she mentioned she had not seen her husband, and when I inquired further, she affirmed that yes, she would like to view his body. I was aware that in some Muslim cultures this was discouraged, and I was concerned that we might be stopped. I spoke encouraging words softly to the wife to keep going as the men regarded us somewhat apprehensively. When we reached her husband's bed, I placed her in such a way that anyone who tried to take her out of the room would have to reach across and over me, something I knew culturally these clearly practicing Muslim men wouldn't do given my gender. After a while, the men began leaving the room. She was able to have a quiet, private time with her husband, maybe the only one before the funeral. It was one of many lessons that helped me learn I would need to claim my authority rather than waiting for it to be given to me.

As I've learned to navigate death with Muslim men, so too have I learned to navigate birth. Someone in the chaplaincy office said one morning, "Samsiah, a Muslim baby needs blessing before circumcision." This thought flashed through me: What? Me? I am a woman. Sunni schools of law hold differing views on whether circumcision is an obligatory or recommended act, but it is common practice for Muslim families to circumcise their sons.[2] Where I come from, circumcision is a rite of passage for boys, usually conducted during school holidays. I remember one such holiday some sixty years ago at the home of a grand-uncle. Some of my male cousins, about eleven or twelve years old, were there for a group circumcision. It was a somewhat celebratory time with prayers and a feast. After the circumcision, the cousins wore the traditional sarongs instead of pants, careful to hold them away from their groin areas. How the circumcision itself was conducted, I had no idea. Suffice it to say that it was an all-male affair held in the privacy of the front room. Having thus learned at that young age that circumcision was the domain of men, I parked it in the recesses of my mind. It's amazing how strongly childhood perceptions are embedded into one's psyche where they remain unexamined, powerful like an invisible fence that keeps one in check. I wonder what invisible fences I and other women hold within ourselves that circumscribe our reach.

I prayed for the baby; I placed my fingers lightly on his feet and told him that he was about to take part in a tradition that would link him to Prophet Ibrâhîm. As I raised my supplication, I teared up, humbled by the gravity of the situation and the opportunity to be a link in an ancient chain. I have since learned from a friend, who is a surgeon in Malaysia, that circumcision continues to be a group celebration for the six-to-twelve-year-olds; the difference from sixty years ago is that it is now held in hospitals and other specifically designated locations. She herself has performed the procedure, trained junior physicians for circumcision certification, and organized group circumcision programs.

Navigating the communal ritual of circumcision was only one of the many occasions in which I was called to navigate a ritual that would have traditionally been assigned to a male Muslim, such as public prayer. During my Clinical Pastoral Education (CPE) training, students were expected to conduct "chapel" services for the hospital that should be relevant for those from any faith and even no faith at all. As a chaplain, I am also called to pray for patients at the bedside or with families when requested. I am not unfamiliar with public speaking; I was once a spokeswoman for the president of the United Nations General Assembly. However, these two—spontaneous prayer and the service—terrified me. I spent hours into the night preparing for a fifteen-minute service. I harangued my colleagues for help; most were ordained Christians or Catholics who could conduct a service at the drop of a hat. Two of them were particularly helpful. One stood outside the room of the first patient I was ever to visit, a Muslim woman. He told me to signal to him if I needed support. What a morale booster—it was almost like a kid's first day at school. It was a brief visit, but a visit, nonetheless. I had dived in and survived, a celebratory moment for both of us. Another chaplain worked with me to develop my first prayer/reflection service. The theme I chose was light, thinking of the simile in the Qur'an about moving from darkness to light. I have no recollection of what I said, I mumbled and stumbled, I felt inadequate. Then the kind chaplain played his guitar; it never sounded sweeter. I felt sorry for the people who attended; luckily there were not many. They were most probably a forgiving lot, aware that I was a student. The struggle with "chapel" service continued into my chaplaincy residency at another hospital. I agonized over every service: to get a suitable topic, to write the service, and to deliver it.

A fellow resident once asked why I mumbled so quietly in prayer. I responded, "You know, prayer has always been very private for me. It has always been only two: God and me. It's very unnatural for me to pray out loud." Then it dawned on me that, other than a course in public speaking for Muslim religious leaders, I have not been trained for public performance of religious acts nor do I have the practice. Men are the ones who lead prayers and give sermons. Indeed, my Muslim male seminary classmates refined their public speaking by providing the *khutbah* (sermon) and lectures at mosques across the state. My situation is also exacerbated by coming from a culture that appreciates a soft voice as part of a much valued femininity in women.

I decided to seek help to learn to develop a firmer voice in religious settings and learn to project it as well. My bosses arranged for assistance from a voice trainer in the hospital. She spent her lunchtime with me a couple of times a week. I am ever grateful to her and to my bosses. With practice—of the voice and of conducting service—the agony has subsided. I would even venture to say that it has been replaced by greater ease and a lightness of being, enabling me to be more fully present in the moment, at the bedside or in front of an audience. I am now embarking on another self-improvement project: developing my Qur'an voice, a deep resonance for recitation. This desire was partly inspired by a call to tend to a Muslim woman laboring to bring forth her baby alone. I recited Surah Maryam to help ease her in her labor and her loneliness, and in providing it, I was taken by how powerful a gift it is to be able to offer Qur'anic recitation for those Muslim patients who desire it. I want to honor and dignify its verses and wisdom with beautiful recitation. God loves beauty.

"What about the belief that the female voice is part of her *'awrah* [concealment], like her body?" a friend asked, alluding to the rule held by some Muslims that a woman's voice cannot be heard just as her body cannot be seen. Would I recite the Qur'an to a male patient or in a mixed-gender group? I responded with a resounding yes; it is part of my chaplaincy practice when I discern it appropriate and is much appreciated. God's words moved many to reveal their vulnerabilities, delve into their souls and wounds, sobbing. I truly believe that the religious correctness of my action depends on context and intention, as modeled by a woman I admire from my family. She was the wife of my grand-uncle. She led *halaqah* (study circles) and gave public lectures in her local community. Before I learned of the many women authorities in Islamic history, hers was the image I held of a confident, dignified, articulate woman. When she spoke, adorning her hijab scarf otherwise worn around her shoulders, people listened, including the men.

Women from my cultural and familial narrative continue to inform the way I navigate female leadership roles, including the perennial topic of the hijab. I grew up without wearing religiosity on my sleeve or head. Among my early memories is going to the village mosque with my paternal grandmother, a long scarf loosely slung over her head and shoulder, her sparkling white shoes somehow untouched by the muddy lane. Early in the morning, after her *Fajr* prayer, in my hazy state, I would hear her softly reciting her *dhikr* (remembrance of Allah) as she stroked my head. Such tenderness from a woman who the previous evening had fiercely scrubbed me with coconut husks and bathed me with cold well water to get rid of the gunk from a day of playing outdoors.

My maternal great-grandmother, bent at the waist, was a picture of contrasts. She was among the few women in our community at that time who had performed the hajj (pilgrimage). On festive occasions she wore her hajj turban with a treasured cotton shawl from Mecca and crisp, freshly ironed clothes. At other times, she labored outside in her work clothes, head uncovered. She tapped the family's rubber trees; she went into the forest for pandan leaves which she processed and coaxed into mats for sleeping and sitting. She reared chickens and goats. Her house on stilts had chickens sleeping under it, which we could smell through the cracks of the wooden floor. She was always working, stationary only during her *salât* (prayer) when she would don her prayer clothes we call *telekung* (a fuller version of the hijab).

Ask any Muslim woman wearing a hijab in a Muslim minority area, she most likely will have a hijab story. I do, too, except that mine is a non-hijab story. I had just started my chaplaincy clinical training when a male Muslim volunteer I didn't know very well stopped me in the hallway and asked why I was without a hijab. My heart pumped furiously, blood rushed to my ears, my head, my face. I folded my arms to hold my body, willing it to be still and to stop the shivers. Is this how it feels to be violated? I wanted to shout, "What business is it of yours?" I wanted to run away. I regained my composure, and merely said, "Thank you, brother. It's a journey; please make *du'â* for me." We parted. In my CPE-grounded reflective mode (chaplains have a penchant for that), I wondered why I was so angry. It was not the first time that I was asked the question. Was it because he was a man, and he pushed my red paternalism button? And what about paternalism riled me? Or is it a reflection of my own sense of guilt? In my expansive moments, I tell myself that he was "calling people to good," an injunction of the Qur'an, in the way he knew, though Allah also emphasizes gentleness, "Then [it was] by a mercy from God that thou wert gentle with them. Hadst thou been severe [and] hard-hearted they would have scattered from about thee."[3]

Growing up in Malaysia when I did, hijab was not a societal focus point the way it has become there and elsewhere today. I was only made self-conscious about not wearing it in the United States. My friends and acquaintances from other faith traditions are fascinated by hijab, making it a frequent topic in early encounters, to which I respond with the concept of modesty and lowering the gaze. These questions afford me the opportunity to explain the wider meaning of modesty—in action, words, thoughts, and worship—and the significance of the hijab. More than a head covering, more than a part of attire, to me it signifies a commitment to a spiritual journey toward God. My bare head is a reminder that I am a beginner in that *jihâd* (struggle). Furthermore, some jurists do not consider it a problem if the hair of an older woman such as myself shows. Nonetheless, lately I find myself wearing the scarf over my head more frequently, instead of simply draping it over my shoulders, ready to draw it up to my head when I recite the Qur'an and offer supplications for Muslim patients as I've done in the past. I like to think that *al-Fattâh*, the Opener who makes all things possible, is beginning to remove the veil over my heart about hijab with one for my head. Also, I now think more kindly of the Muslim male volunteer, though I am still working on the feeling of being ruffled.

Apart from these rare bumpy encounters, I find that my work as a chaplain is communally appreciated and does not end when I leave the hospital door. Seemingly innocuous questions are brought to me frequently by members of my community knowing me as a chaplain. "What is a good Muslim wife?" wondered a new revert to Islam who also is a newlywed. "Will you marry us?" asked a young lady whose intended is a non-Muslim. "Can you say a prayer at my dad's birthday?" requested a friend with a multifaith extended family. An anxious mother sought help with the Qur'an for her teenager before she went away to college. A young professional wanted to talk about her mother's problematic marriage expectations of her: "I am lesbian," she said, and her mother did not know.

The approaches I received show the range of issues faced by Muslims as they navigate life in the twenty-first century. Some of the questions and requests involve considerations of *fiqh* (jurisprudence), which I consider in my interactions. But generally, individuals are not looking for a black-and-white answer;

often they already know the *fiqh* response. Rather, they seek space for reflection, without having "haram and halal" immediately pushed onto them. They want an opportunity to engage in a discussion with someone they perceive as having religious gravitas, not necessarily an imam—and, for some, I am that person. They wish to reveal the tension between their awareness of *fiqh* rulings and their personal take of them, to give voice to it. They want the dilemmas of their lived experience to be recognized and heard.

Apart from individuals, my mosque too has found it useful to have a chaplain in its community. Being a chaplain makes me a convenient representative to the wider interfaith communities: the title easily places me in their religious schema; my education and training allow me to make connections to their own faiths, provide context for mine, and speak to Islamic theology. I serve on committees, give talks, recite the Qur'an, and assist with interfaith activities. I remember a man who came up to me after my reciting the Qur'an in a church event celebrating the 100th anniversary of the end of World War I. He had lived in a Muslim majority country, and my recitation reminded him of what he missed. A lady remarked that she had not heard the Qur'an recited the way I did; she had only heard it read out. It's good to know that I play a small part in promoting the normalization of the recited Qur'an in the lives of people.

Importantly, my chaplaincy training allows me to serve my community, Muslims and non-Muslims, as we respond to communal tragedy, be it the COVID-19 pandemic or hate-driven attacks on houses of worship and congregants in the United States and elsewhere. While these are extremely rare in our immediate congregations, the ripple effect of faraway incidents has left many psychologically wounded. As a chaplain, I've been able to recognize when morale needs boosting, nerves need calming, and we need to be together to affirm our camaraderie and support for each other with what I call a communal fizz. Following a spate of such attacks, I co-organized an interfaith *iftâr* involving a dozen mosques and Muslim organizations in my county. This was an experiment on two counts: this was the first Muslim interorganizational collaborative event; and at the personal level, this was the first time I facilitated a group comprising primarily of imams and male leaders. I was somewhat nervous at first as to how the situation might play out, and specifically how they might react to my leadership. I was pleasantly surprised; everyone collaborated fully, and gender was not an issue in giving and taking direction. My opening speech that evening focused on good neighborliness drawn from Surah al-Ma'un of the Qur'an. My chaplaincy training leading services for non-Muslims and previous work experience had prepared me to take this role among my own people and our guests—numbering nearly 500—with calm confidence.

And so, I come back to my banana leaves. In their original state, banana leaves grow out of a rigid branch. The leaves themselves, about three to five feet long and twelve to twenty-four inches wide, are stiff and tear easily. To be useful, we would run them quickly over a flame to wilt them. Then we would cut the leaves off the rigid branches to desired lengths and trim the uneven edges. It is in this wilted state that the banana leaves can be molded into their most useful forms. When used to wrap food, the leaves impart a surprisingly fragrant scent into the food, bringing about a unique, subtle flavoring. Rather than detracting from the primary taste of the dish, the flavoring actually enhances it.

That may best describe my leadership as a chaplain, which researchers say is a new avenue for religious leadership for Muslims. Just as banana leaves are used for different purposes under different circumstances, my leadership is contextual. The experiences I had are the flames that "wilt" me; I have to mindfully "burn" the self slightly to help bring out the best of me, to become a container that not only holds up the contents placed in it but also complements and amplifies, ever so lightly, so that the self of the other remains intact and whole.

Notes

1. A study of Muslim patients in California indicated that 64 percent of Muslim patients did not consider the gender of their spiritual provider important. Kamal Abu-Shamsieh, "Barriers to Spiritual Care Among Muslim Patients" (master's thesis, Hartford Seminary, 2012), 64.

2. Brian J. Morris, Richard G. Wamai, Esther B. Henebeng, Aaron A. Tobian, Jeffrey D. Klausner, Joya Banerjee, and Catherine A. Hankins, "Estimation of Country-Specific and Global Prevalence of Male Circumcision," *Population Health Metrics* 14, no. 4 (2016).

3. Âl 'Imrân/3:159.

Mapping the Landscape of Muslim Chaplaincy in Higher Education

KHALIL ABDUR-RASHID

I BEGAN MY JOURNEY as a university Muslim chaplain accidentally. During my time as a graduate student at Columbia University in New York City, a major crisis unfolded in 2011. The Associated Press had broken a story about the NYPD spying on Muslims in the tri-state area in places that included mosques, businesses, and university campuses. Columbia was looking for someone who could support students through what they were experiencing; my background in social work and Islamic studies seemed a good fit. In this essay, I draw on this experience and my work on several campuses to map the landscape of Muslim chaplaincy in higher education. First, I address the foundations and institutional justifications for hiring Muslim chaplains. In the second

Dr. Khalil Abdur-Rashid serves at Harvard University where he is also chair of the Board of Religious, Spiritual, and Ethical Life and on the faculty at Harvard Divinity School. Born and raised in Atlanta, Georgia, he received his BA in Social Work from Georgia State University and subsequently worked as a state social worker before completing an MA and an MPhil in Islamic Law and Middle East Studies at Columbia University, and a PhD in Liberal Studies in American Islam at Southern Methodist University. Khalil pursued Islamic studies academically and traditionally in the Middle East and Turkey, where he obtained an MA in Comparative Islamic Law at Marmara University and completed two advanced Islamic seminary doctoral licenses (ijâzah) in Islamic Sciences. Cofounder of the Islamic Seminary of America, he has taught at a number of universities, served as chaplain at Columbia University and Barnard College, as an imam in New York City, and as a scholar-in-residence in North Dallas. He enjoys reading the Qur'an and spending time with family, and finds healing in reflecting on God's beauty alongside any body of water.

section, I classify the complex and diverse ways Muslim chaplains operate on campus into three distinct levels, adopted from the three levels of government in the United States: local, state, and federal.

Why Hire a Muslim Chaplain?

A Muslim chaplain is an integral part of the university's commitment not just to diversity but also to strategic diversity. Investing in faith communities is a fundamental way to situate religious, spiritual, and ethical life as part and parcel of diversity, inclusion, and belonging initiatives. The absence of a chaplain can undermine efforts at inclusion and may even create obstacles to belonging for students, adversely impacting diversity initiatives that seek to include Muslims who come from a wide variety of racial and ethnic backgrounds. There are specific religious needs for these students, as well as an administrative need for guidance pertaining to accommodations; both require expertise. A chaplain is a resource for students to support their spiritual cultivation, provide practical guidance, and be an institutional advocate when challenging circumstances arise. The chaplain becomes a conduit through whom students express their grievances, and a mentor who empowers them to articulate their requests to administrators. Universities equipped with chaplains are better positioned to provide interventions and support students when Islamophobia manifests on campuses and in the larger public sphere. Chaplains not only speak out against all forms of hate but also inspire and instill hope in students affected by bigotry.

Additionally, when faced with a challenging situation regarding faith communities on campus, senior leadership often find themselves searching for answers on how best to respond. Part of strategic leadership is diversifying the sources of ideas available to draw upon, and having a Muslim chaplain as part of the team helps ensure that the solutions crafted to meet Muslim students' needs are not ad hoc or temporary but pervasive and transformational as well as appropriate. Navigating Muslim students' needs requires university collaboration and consultation with someone who understands, firsthand, students' challenges practicing a regular set of obligational religious observances. Investing in a Muslim chaplain amounts to creating an infrastructure that will reliably serve as a stable agent of institutional transformation and progress.

The Landscape of Practice

A chaplain's practice ranges from simple work to quite complex duties requiring more than one institutional role and several layers of responsibilities, depending on the size of the student population and whether the chaplain is a volunteer or a part-time or full-time employee. In attempting to outline the range of these duties, I have delineated below three levels along with outlining the duties and tasks at each level. The degree to which each level will be applicable may vary from one type of campus to another, but in general, the three levels of practice articulated below in my view are representative of the work of any university Muslim chaplain. Institutions of higher education are best served when they employ a Muslim chaplain who can effectively serve the needs of Muslim students who identify as Sunni and those who identify as Shi'a in such a way as to unite the Muslim community while also celebrating its diversity. It is critical that Muslim women be hired in equal measure as their male counterparts and that this becomes a normative part of campus religious life. While some colleges have benefited from hiring two chaplains— male and female and/or Sunni and Shi'a—few have such resources and as such require a versatile chaplain capable of serving all of the campus's constituents.

MICRO LEVEL: PRACTICE AT THE "LOCAL LEVEL"

The term "micro" here refers to the grassroots, one-to-one engagement that is the core of the chaplain's work with students. The practice at the micro level involves the work of meeting with individuals and small groups of students on a regular basis through three basic chaplaincy offerings: religious education, community-building events, and mentoring/spiritual counseling.

Regarding religious education, the chaplain may meet with students for a regular *halaqah* (learning circle) and/or conduct or manage the weekly Friday prayer on campus. In my experience, students often request opportunities for religious learning, such as workshops, reading groups, Qur'an study circles, and the like. College is when students begin to encounter life outside the shelter of their home and reexamine the values they have grown up with. On numerous occasions, I have found that although American Muslim students may have been raised in a Muslim household as a Muslim, college life challenges them to understand their Muslim identity on their own terms, spurring a burst of curiosity and inquisition about Islamic teachings pertaining to a myriad of things ranging from social justice issues and identity issues to topics raised in their classes. Religious education is significant for students at this time in their lives because it can help them understand, challenge, and formulate their own understanding of the Qur'an and the practice of Islam.

The chaplain facilitates social gatherings such as mixers, dinners, and other programs that bring the students together as a community throughout the year. At a minimum, Ramadan *iftâr* dinners, for which universities typically provide funding through the chaplains' budget or directly to students' dining accounts, offer community for students away from their homes. In a robust and mature chaplaincy, programming may take on the form of monthly community dinners and gatherings and special events commemorating religious occasions, such as the *Mawlid*, the night of *Isrâʾ and Miʿrâj*, *ʿAshûrâʾ*, and Eid.

In terms of mentoring and spiritual counseling, chaplains are an invaluable primary university resource for spiritual development and healing for Muslim students on campus. It is not uncommon for students to reach out to the chaplain during exam periods, times of life-altering events such as grieving from a loss, and general moments of anxiety during the academic year. In light of the stigma that exists around mental health care in many Muslim cultures, students will often first seek out a chaplain. A properly trained chaplain can provide pastoral counseling and, when a student's needs warrant it, help facilitate connection with the appropriate mental health services.

All three frames of local engagement (education, community building, and spiritual counseling) constitute local-level interaction. These activities alone can easily fill the calendar year with events. Similar to the workings of a local government that manages municipal services for its residents, at this level the chaplain primarily develops and manages an array of services for students in order to facilitate individual and communal spiritual well-being. Work at this level directly impacts the enhancement of diversity at the university (though not necessarily inclusion or belonging). From work at the local level, the size and nature of the Muslim student community on campus become identifiable as a distinct population cohort. Therefore, from the perspective of the university, the fruits derived from this level of engagement are data-oriented, quantitative, and measurable, which enables the institution to enhance the quality of its services to this community and consequently to all students.

MEZZO LEVEL: PRACTICE AT THE "STATE LEVEL"

The second level is the mezzo level, which I define as activities a chaplain must participate in to develop partnerships and strong collegial alliances with non-Muslim communities in the university as well as the various departments or graduate schools, for larger strategic purposes related to inclusion. At the "state level," the chaplain is a builder of coalitions and developer of strategic partnerships throughout the university. These activities serve to better facilitate interfaith work and to achieve more efficient advocacy and understanding among university staff engaging with Muslim students. Practice at this level involves marshaling a larger set of resources to ensure students are included, enabling a fuller sense of belonging within campus life. Examples include, but are not limited to, ensuring campus dining offers a variety of halal options; developing and expanding prayer spaces and washrooms (i.e., footbaths); addressing issues of anti-Muslim statements or teaching materials used in classroom settings that contribute to a climate of bigotry; developing strong relationships with the other chaplains in order to work collectively to strengthen religious life; discussing issues related to Islam and Muslim life with university staff members to aid understanding of campus diversity; participating in convocation and baccalaureate services and recommending students capable of sharing Muslim sacred texts during such programs; helping advise members of the dean of students office and other university personnel about crucial factors necessary to provide the best accommodations possible for Muslims, and so forth. The "state level" practice of the chaplain centers around the larger issues regarding the best way to apply existing university resources to the Muslim student population at large.

The data from the work at the "local level" becomes a requisite for work at the "state level," for when the size and nature of the Muslim student population become known, this allows for better allocation of resources to meet students' unique needs. Furthermore, because the Muslim student population also intersects with other minority groups such as immigrant, DACA, first-generation, African American, Latinx, as well as students with disabilities, serving the needs of Muslims often entails establishing strategic partnerships with other university offices devoted to serving various affiliated groups. Similar to a task force or committee established at the state governmental level whose mandate is to solve a state problem, the chaplain must also at times be a member of, or even initiate, a task force of diverse members of the university to address an issue pertaining to the Muslim community on campus. It is not uncommon, for instance, for a university chaplain to convene a committee that meets several times a year, composed of senior members of campus dining services, a senior member from the dean of students office, a representative of campus security, and other senior administrators, to address students' needs in Ramadan. At this level, a chaplain helps the university by guiding undergraduate and graduate administrators toward achieving a climate of excellence as it relates to the Muslim students' sense of inclusion.

MACRO LEVEL: PRACTICE AT THE "FEDERAL LEVEL"

At the macro level or "federal level," the task of the chaplain is that of liaison, ambassador, senior administrator, and at times senior educator. At this level, the chaplain may serve on committees; meet with the university president or provost regarding decisions that impact communities of faith; assist in developing or amending policy regarding diversity, inclusion, and belonging; advise deans regarding developing schoolwide communiqués on religious accommodations for exams and during Ramadan; educate various aspects of the university leadership through workshops and forums on critical issues not widely known but necessary to adequately train Muslim students; conduct workshops to raise awareness on campus of Islamic biomedical issues for the medical school, Muslim funeral procedures for the divinity school, and issues related to American Islamophobia in graduate schools of public policy; and keep current with relevant policies, procedures, and resources related to the Title IX Office, Office of Counseling and Behavioral Health, and numerous other university resources.

Furthermore, leading and speaking at campus vigils, addressing a grieving campus community during a university-experienced crisis, and even on occasion representing students' best interests off campus when necessary may be required. Examples of this may be meeting with local or state elected or appointed officials to discuss matters relating to student well-being. Such matters can be quite delicate, and it is always necessary to consult with university leaders and decision-makers first before engaging in speaking engagements or off-campus initiatives. Nonetheless, for certain issues, at certain times, a letter from a university chaplain addressing student needs, speaking to media outlets, or serving on a municipal or state board may be appropriate to address a particular issue related to student well-being. Such an ambassadorial role must only be undertaken with the best interest of students and institution in mind, and never without approval from the university. An example of this is when I was asked in 2012 to serve on a special task force to advise the NYPD police commissioner on policing in cases where Muslim students were targeted and surveilled on and off campus. I took the request to my supervisor, who received approval from the university president. I also secured permission from the university Muslim Student Association to serve on their behalf in that capacity.

The three areas of university chaplaincy—micro/local, mezzo/state, and macro/federal level practices—all complement each other and are all uniquely part of cultivating an atmosphere of diversity, inclusion, and belonging for Muslim students on campus. It is a role that is best accomplished by someone with a commitment to service, an appreciation of scholarship, and a love for the climate and culture of higher education in America. Paradoxically, it is a vocation that requires serious training, yet one that you can never entirely be trained for. In that sense, it is an art more than a science.

Open Door, Open Heart

OMER BAJWA

CAMPUS CHAPLAINCY FOLLOWS A ROUTINE, but it can be unpredictable. "Would it be possible to reschedule the dates for Ramadan? Or at least the times?" an administrator once asked me. Apparently, the *iftâr* (fast-breaking) times—determined by sunset—interfered with mandatory new student orientation meetings, and the dean's office did not fully understand how to accommodate this. I discussed this with my fellow chaplains in the Yale chaplain's office, whose experience and support have been invaluable to me, and sought the advice of my supervisor, university chaplain Sharon Kugler, to help me craft a response.

I love that my work includes this element of unpredictability. No two days are really ever the same. But my vision of campus chaplaincy is constant: to

---

Omer Bajwa serves as director of Muslim life in the chaplain's office at Yale University and has been engaged in religious service, interreligious engagement, and educational outreach since 2000. He earned his graduate certificate in Islamic Chaplaincy from Hartford Seminary, has an MA in Near Eastern Studies and an MS in Communication from Cornell University, and a BA from Binghamton University. Omer has also studied several classical Islamic sciences with traditional scholars from Pakistan, Turkey, and the United States. His interests include Islam in the United States and the intersections of culture, media, politics, and spirituality. He regularly lectures about these and other topics around the country. Omer was a founding member of the Association of Muslim Chaplains and is one of the longest serving campus Muslim chaplains in the United States. He loves taking long hikes with his family and friends, and when not working, he can often be found sampling local desserts.

---

nurture the mind, body, and soul, through spiritual care, mentorship, and empowerment. My pastoral counseling—and care for the souls of my community—are inspired and driven by two pieces of timeless advice of the Prophet Muhammad ﷺ: "All of you are shepherds and each of you is responsible for his flock,"[1] and "Make things easy, do not make things difficult. Give glad tidings and do not frighten them away."[2]

There are many differences between colleges, the nature of campuses, institutional structures, even chaplaincy styles, but I believe that in all cases the work of the Muslim chaplain encompasses five fundamental roles: spiritual counselor, advocate, interfaith interlocutor, teacher, and minister.

Spiritual Counselor

One Tuesday afternoon, a student walked into my office in tears but was reluctant to speak. Noting his anxiety, I invited him into my space as I would a guest into my home. I offered him cookies and made small talk as I made some coffee. As I engaged him as warmly as I could, he visibly relaxed. I sat across from him and faced him with my full body and attention, in the manner of the Prophet ﷺ. He cautiously started telling me his story: he came from a mixed family, one parent was a religious Muslim, the other nonreligious and unaffiliated. Growing up, a feeling of alienation meant he was in constant search of community: "I don't know where I belong. I want to find Muslim friends, but I always feel like I don't know enough or know the right things to do or say, or I'm not good enough to be friends with other Muslims."

As we spoke, he described his difficult experiences with religion and authority, from his parents to religious figures. I listened and asked reflective questions when appropriate, but I sensed conflicting emotions which may have been part of his transference toward me as another parental or religious figure. In different students' imaginations, I range from accessible older brother to understanding uncle to judgmental religious authority. I always try to be aware of this transference, just as I am also mindful of my own possible countertransference. He eventually opened up about his concerns: "My father used to push me to be a better Muslim, but I pushed back because he just expected me to do things like him without really explaining anything. After years of fighting in high school, he eventually gave up trying and I gave up caring. I feel pretty insecure around other Muslims, and I feel guilty for not knowing more about Islam. Now I'm starting to want to learn more, to be accepted, but I don't know how to start learning what I'm supposed to know."

Leaning into my training to refrain from solving or fixing immediately, I thanked the student for coming to me with his concerns, and we discussed setting up regular conversations and slowly taking it from there. I offered that we could attend some campus Muslim events together and then discuss what he was learning, processing, and experiencing; he left satisfied and reassured. This is just one example of countless permutations of counseling conversations I have had with students and community members, either single encounters, or in regular sessions over the course of several semesters, and even after graduation.

Over the years, students have shared an amazing array of stories about spiritual curiosity, spiritual crises, difficult family relationships, complex romantic relationships, career doubts, social anxieties, traumatizing race relations, Islamophobia, justice advocacy, friendship woes, and much else besides. Stories are vital to how we see ourselves and our roles in the world, and I believe that amid the various differences, chaplains are story-catchers helping careseekers process and make meaning of their experiences.

Advocate

One morning, I was called into the university president's office for a private meeting. Having no idea why I was summoned, I imagined different scenarios. "Maybe he's going to fire me?" I said to my wife, to which she retorted, "You're not important enough to get fired by the university president." It turned out that a famous Yale professor had invited the infamous Danish cartoonist Kurt Westergaard to campus for a provocative event on free speech, and the administration was nervous about protests and negative publicity. Muslim students were distressed by this campus invitation, so I initiated several conversations between Muslim students, Muslim faculty, and administrators to discuss different strategies to address the situation so that everyone's voice was heard and duly considered. Eventually, we agreed that students who wanted to protest would be allowed to do so peacefully outside the venue, while others would prepare cogent questions to engage with the speaker. In this way, both groups of students were empowered.

As an advisor and liaison, I am constantly called on to consult and collaborate on everything from halal dining to holiday observance, housing issues to designated prayer spaces, social gatherings to toilet use. In effect, I serve as a go-to Muslim voice, based on my expertise, experience, and the reputation I have cultivated as someone of integrity. One of the challenges of this role in particular is having potentially difficult conversations with both your community and the administration about conflicting perceptions of needs and wants. For example, an ongoing concern is mixed-gender campus housing, which typically requires students to share bathrooms. This creates tension between administrators, who maintain that it is part of the contemporary campus housing philosophy of teaching students to navigate difference, and Muslim students, who maintain that they are not comfortable sharing bathrooms with other genders out of modesty.

Being in the middle can be inspiring as well as exhausting. It is inspiring to be involved in the meaning-making dialectic just as it is also exhausting trying to navigate intransigence. Arriving at reasonable compromises is often quite challenging and dispiriting because someone will likely be disappointed, but it is nevertheless also rewarding, because it is a critical component of community building. I am heartened by the following words attributed to Abû Bakr al-Siddîq, close companion of the Prophet ﷺ: "Taking pains to remove the pains of others is the true essence of generosity."

Interfaith Interlocutor

It's Thursday evening. As part of an interfaith series, a local church has invited me to preach and briefly reflect on the five pillars of Islam. In my allotted ten minutes, I recount the "Gabriel hadith" and use it to discuss the wisdom and meaning behind the five pillars, tying this to comparable Christian practices. Afterward, a visibly stunned parishioner, a nurse, approaches me to say that she's never heard Islam explained like that before. She confesses that she's always been quite afraid of Muslims and hearing about Islam. I am left to wonder how this has impacted the care she has provided to Muslim patients.

The church subsequently invited me for regular multifaith conversations on contemporary topics to continue the work of building bridges of understanding. As a result of these visits, relationships deepened, which allowed for more meaningful conversations, especially about such challenging issues as racism, bigotry, and violence.

The chaplain inevitably serves as a Muslim interlocutor in a variety of conversations. This includes being dialogue facilitator, coalition convener, and informed authority. At one level, this is based on the Qur'an's view about the purpose of diversity, "so that you get to know one another,"[3] something that is accomplished by promoting religious literacy and interreligious engagement. This educates students and communities, as global citizens, to be more aware of religion's role in people's lives in a globalized world.

Interfaith work often requires sensitivity and an ability to navigate the intersections of religious life, cultural traditions, social mores, and scriptural understandings. I am inspired by the prophetic advice to select appropriately qualified people for specialized tasks: as a chaplain, I have the training and capacity to make connections and to translate between religious traditions, particularly by contextualizing events. On campus, too, I encourage the collaboration between various religious groups and associations as a way to model effective interfaith experiences for students. People often undervalue the role of multifaith conversations and experiences, but when done well it is empowering because it includes probing questions about meaning, purpose, values, and convictions.

Teacher

When I teach, I invite students to approach their *dîn* (religion) as a journey to love Allah and His Prophet ﷺ. This can sometimes be quite different from the ways they encountered Islam with their parents and in Sunday school. Since 2012, I have been co-leading an annual *'umrah* (minor pilgrimage) trip for students and young professionals. We first visit Medina, the Prophet Muhammad's city, where I give daily spiritual lessons and walking tours around the Prophet's mosque and the city's famous religious landmarks. I was fortunate to perform both hajj (annual pilgrimage) and *'umrah* (occasional pilgrimage) during my formative years with my spiritual teachers. Their insights, love, and reverence for Medina left an indelible mark on my heart. Since then, I have aspired to bring the *sîrah* (Prophet's biography) to life when I teach, just as they did for me, as both enriching and edifying. The scholars say, "To know the Prophet Muhammad is to love him: you learn to know him by studying his life."

After several days in Medina, we bid farewell to the tranquility of the Prophet's ﷺ city and prepare to journey to Mecca. Departing Medina is always sad, and I gently advise our group to take some personal time to say goodbye, especially as we walk around the mosque on our last night. One time, a distressed student approached me in tears to say that she was heartbroken at leaving Medina because she had fallen in love with the city. "No one has ever spoken to us about the Prophet the way you have, and I cannot imagine leaving after having really learned about him. I never thought that I would be here or that the Prophet would mean so much to me."

In Mecca we visit the Kaaba, which has its own powerful attraction. Scholars often contrast the *jamâl* (beauty) of Medina with the *jalâl* (majesty) of Mecca. Seeing the Kaaba for the first time is also often a very powerful spiritual and emotional experience, and I take special care to lead my group into the Grand Mosque with their gazes respectfully lowered. Once I've found a suitable vantage point, I invite them to look up, set eyes upon the Kaaba, and make their heartfelt supplications. Seeing for the first time something they had until that point only seen in pictures and images nearly always brings everyone to tears.

I believe it is a privilege and responsibility to help facilitate these meaning-making moments for our community.

Teaching groups of Muslims of diverse backgrounds, practice, and religiosity helps us all think beyond our different cognitive-frames for understanding Islam. Effective teaching should nurture emotional connections by inspiring the requisite heart-work to cultivate a personal commitment to being Muslim and growing in your Islam so that it is spiritually and intellectually transformative.

Minister

After attending a few campus Friday services, a first-year female Muslim student approached me and asked, "How can I get involved and really help with Jummah?" I asked her what she had in mind, and she said, "Before I came to college, I wanted to attend Jummah but didn't feel like I really could. But here, I love the way Jummah is set up; I feel like I want to come to listen and learn every week. It's pretty inspiring and it's something I could even bring my non-Muslim friends to. I'm always learning something new, and I love the lunch afterwards! How can I get involved?" I smiled, affirming her enthusiasm, and encouraged her to share some *khutbah* (sermon) topics she might be interested in. I also asked her if she would be willing to give me feedback on my *khutbah* the following week.

I serve as the official spiritual leader and director of religious programming for the campus Muslim community. My most visible role is *khatîb* (sermon-giver) on Friday. It is an influential yet serious responsibility because the *khatîb* stands on the pulpit, just as the Prophet ﷺ did. My campus community includes male and female undergraduates, graduate and professional students, staff, faculty, often their families, and both Shiʻa and Sunni worshipers. Given the diversity of my constituents, it is vitally important to not just offer relevant and engaging preaching but also to thoughtfully create welcoming and inclusive space. In terms of preaching, I intentionally and equally reference the Prophet's family and companions to foster affection and reverence for them. I ensure that we have proper audio so that both men and women can comfortably hear and I make equal eye contact to acknowledge listeners. We serve free lunch after Jummah to promote fellowship and I circulate among the attendees to check in and chat. The goal is to offer quality, access, engagement, and encouragement. *Al-hamdu lillâh*, our Jummah attendance has more than quadrupled as we continue to attract increasing numbers of community members and students from other campuses.

Closing Thoughts

While guidance and advocacy remain important functions, in my thirteen years of service I have found that the most important function of the campus chaplain is sustaining presence. This presence means being an identifiable pastoral figure and being the most visible Muslim persona at the university. The campus community, both Muslim and non-Muslim, must literally see me around campus, which means that I must participate in and organize events, attend public lectures, have meals in the dining facilities, and even just regularly traverse campus. In addition to being seen, I strive to be easily approachable and accessible, which means not only phone and email access but also direct physical access—being in my office, in prayer spaces, and in communal spaces. Ch. Sharon Kugler calls this "creative loitering": observing, listening, chatting, reflecting, engaging. She has taught me and shown me that the chaplain needs to be approachable so that students, staff, faculty, and community members feel comfortable striking up a conversation, asking a question, and gauging interpersonal warmth before discussing a pastoral need. Although I never know who is going to walk through my door or in what role I am needed, my door is always open, literally and figuratively.

Notes

1. al-Bukhârî, Al-Adab al-Mufrad 212.
2. al-Bukhârî, *Sahîh* 69; Muslim, *Sahîh* 1734.
3. al-Hujurât/49:13.

Islam at "Alcatraz of the Rockies"

FIAZUDDIN SHUAYB

MUSLIM INMATES CONSTITUTE the second largest religious group after Christians[1] in the U.S. federal prison system, where Islam is the fastest growing religion.[2] They are ethnically diverse (Black, Latino, Arab, Asian, and white), predominantly Sunni, and the largest congregation at prison chapels. They are perhaps the most litigious inmates—"paper jihadists"[3]—appropriating *jihâd* (spiritual struggle) to guarantee their religious rights under the U.S. Constitution. With Muslim chaplains constituting just 4.7 percent of Federal Bureau of Prison (BOP) chaplains, Muslim inmates are significantly underserved.[4] This narrative explores my experience with the dynamics, challenges, and role of Islamic ministry at the federal super-maximum (supermax) prison in Colorado—nicknamed the "Alcatraz of the Rockies."[5]

How does a minority chaplain (brown and Muslim) fit into the federal correctional setting dominated by white Christian chaplains? There is no

Born in Trinidad and Tobago, **Dr. Fiazuddin Shuayb** immigrated with his wife and two children in 2000, after studying Arabic and Islam at the University of Medina. He holds a BA in Political Science/Cultural Anthropology from Queens College, New York; an MA in Islamic and Social Sciences from Cordoba University, Virginia (formerly Graduate School of Islamic Social Sciences); and CPhil and PhD in Islamic Studies from UCLA under the mentorship of Dr. Khaled Abou El-Fadl. Having previously served with the Federal Bureau of Prisons at the Federal Correctional Complex in Florence, Colorado, he now serves at FCI Ft. Dix and is a member of the Association of Muslim Chaplains. His self-care includes quality family time, healthy diet and exercise, worship, visiting the sick and elderly, and reading.

handbook for Muslim chaplains, and I did not know anyone to ask for advice when I started. BOP chaplains are familiar with the technical manual on federal chaplaincy, policies, duties, and responsibilities in general, but how does one conduct Islamic chaplaincy? A colleague gifted me a book entitled *Correctional Chaplains: Keepers of the Cloak*,[6] which was informative on the history of correctional chaplaincy, issues, concepts, dimensions, and an individualized ministry plan. But it lacked an Islamic ethos. I decided to examine Muslim history in search of ministerial connections between imams and prisons. I came across the story of Yûsuf (Joseph) in the Qur'an. Its *tafsîr* (exegesis) highlighted the tradition of a prophet of God who, dreading the strife of seduction in society, sought refuge in prison, where he was divinely bestowed with knowledge, especially dream interpretation. Yûsuf submitted to the Divine Will, adhering to the monotheistic religion of his forebears Jacob, Isaac, and Abraham. He conducted religious ministry in prison, preaching *tawhîd* (monotheism) to inmates, counseling them on patience when they despaired, comforting them when they were sad, and visiting them when they were sick. His wisdom and good character endeared him to prisoners and prison officers alike. The latter wished to shelter him in the best quarter of the jail, but Yûsuf refused, preferring to stay in the lowly quarter among the riffraff to serve them. I understood Yûsuf to be the first Muslim prison chaplain and model Muslim prisoner, abiding his prison time constructively.[7] Thus, the "Yûsuf Model of Muslim Chaplaincy" became my guide in implementing an individualized ministry plan that reflected my Islamic ethos, having three layers of the proverbial pastoral cloak—(1) deep knowledge of Islam (*'ilm*), (2) good character (*husn al-khuluq*), and (3) doing good to others (*al-ihsân*)—tailored to suit the needs of inmates in general and Muslim inmates in particular.

"Alcatraz of the Rockies" (AOR), at the Federal Correctional Complex in Florence, Colorado, is a prison complex comprising a collection of institutions: a supermax security facility, an administrative maximum security facility, a high-security U.S. penitentiary, a medium-security federal correctional institute, and a federal prison camp. In terms of group structure, Muslim inmates in my facility are of two types. The minority form themselves into a tightly disciplined group known as the Community (similar to the use of *jamâ'ah*[8] used by some groups outside of prison) complete with *imam* (leadership), *wazîrs* (officers), constitution, *shûrâ* (council), and membership. But the majority are not affiliated with the Community for diverse reasons, including perceiving it as a prison gang operating under the facade of Islam, staying away because of power dynamics of its Muslim leadership (rivals from Washington, D.C., Florida, Chicago, New York, Philadelphia), having little or no confidence in its leader (who is not considered a bona fide imam because he is a prisoner), preferring to be unaffiliated because of no compelling need to join it, aversion to scrutiny of their activities by its members, or other mundane reasons. I tried to nudge the Community toward calling their leader *amîr* and not *imam*, thereby reducing ambiguity over the term *imam* among inmates in light of my own presence at the facility serving as a chaplain and an imam with regard to prayer.

Muslim inmates at AOR have come to Islam through various paths: some were born and raised Muslims in America or abroad, some converted/ reverted in prison—self-proclaimed "prison Muslims"—and others before their incarceration. I find three primary motivations to embrace Islam among prison Muslims: First, *da'wah* (proselytizing) efforts of fellow prisoners; second, positive interactions with a Muslim chaplain, volunteer, or contract imam;[9] third, the inmate's own volition having been fostered through keen observation of fellow Muslim inmates' practice and/or critical study of Islamic literature.

There are many faith-based practices that are also powerful religious symbols of a new sense of belonging, fresh identity, and spiritual benefit in a dense incarcerated environment, which attract some non-Muslim inmates. The giving and receiving greetings of *as-salâmu 'alaykum* (peace be with you) and *akhî* (my brother), sharing the frequent verbal remembrances of Allah, joining for *salât* (ritual prayer), wearing *kûfis* (male Muslim head cover) and growing beards, the wearing of pants hemmed above the ankles, and refraining from pork provide pride and confidence in their Islamic identity. The Qur'an says: "Surely thou dost not guide whomsoever thou lovest, but God guides whomsoever He will."[10] Hardly a month goes by without an inmate, or two, or more declaring to me his *shahâdah*—the first pillar of Islam stated as means of conversion—the testimony that "none is worthy of worship but Allah, and Muhammad is Allah's final servant and messenger." It is always a deeply humbling experience to receive.

Additionally, there are those the other inmates call "hypocrite Muslims," a label they use to refer to the actions of some inmates who identify—often only briefly—as Muslims for different reasons, including participation in the annual Eid ceremonial meal, gaining access to halal meals, joining the Muslim Community for protection against gangs or threats, or simply to explore the Islamic faith out of idle curiosity. Additionally, AOR has a small population of transgender Muslims—or transsexual Muslims, as they call themselves. Some are struggling to integrate their gender identity with their

Islamic faith and practice. Some keep their relationship to gender private and their Islam public. Others do the opposite. The posture of the rest of the Muslim inmates is that, while they do not condone transgender Muslims, they will not allow them membership, hurt them, or come to their defense in the yard. This socioreligious arrangement works to give transgender Muslim inmates a safe space in the general population without necessarily endorsing their transition. In conversation, I informed them that a person's transition does not negate his Islam, just as a person's murder, robbery, rape, or other crime does not; furthermore, all types of Muslims are welcome to attend Jummah at the chapel. The Prophet ﷺ did encounter *mukhannathûn* in his community, who some see as akin to certain transgender identities, yet he did not persecute them, harm them, or force them to change their effeminate ways.[11]

Jummah for Muslim Inmates

The Prophet ﷺ said, "The best day on which the sun arises is Friday [Jummah]."[12] Jummah is the best day of the week for conscientious Muslim inmates. It is the largest weekly religious congregational service held in the chapel, which is sacralized on Friday, becoming a virtual mosque, as inmates roll out prayer rugs, stack chairs to create an open prayer space (*musallâ*), vacuum the carpet, and sit in neat, quiet rows. Before coming to the chapel, inmates take their *ghûsl* (ritual bath) in the units, perfume themselves, and dress neatly. They sit quietly in rows. If the *khutbah* (sermon) resonates with them, it becomes a talking point among them until the next Jummah. I have never led Jummah congregational prayer with straighter lines of worshipers than I have in the federal prison. Leading Jummah prayer with Muslim inmates—felons of sundry crimes, including drug trafficking, murder, aggravated robbery, rape, and terrorism—and hearing them praise, glorify, and declare Allah's greatness is a surreal cultural experience, which I have not fully processed or will ever forget. Yet, I have never felt fearful or nervous doing it. Jummah is also a day on which Muslim inmates get to meet their "homies," former "cellies," or friends from other units, exchange news, meet new Muslim brothers, and have a strong sense of faith identity, community, and empowerment. Whenever Jummah service is canceled for whatever reason at the institution, there is big disappointment.

I prepare the themes of my *khutbah*s to meet the expectations of the inmate audience, keeping them inspirational, informative, or pertinent to challenges that they face in prison or might encounter in the free society, bearing in mind that, for most of them, their understanding of Islam is basic and of Arabic rudimentary. At times, a few inmates suggest topics for me to address on the *minbar* (pulpit). Some of them request copies of my *khutbahs* to keep for future reference, share them with others who did not attend Jummah, or use upon transfer in the event of no BOP chaplain, contractor imam, or volunteer.

During the 2020–2021 COVID-19 pandemic, chapel programming was halted, as inmates were locked down indefinitely in their units due to protocols. I wrote a series of *bayâns* (expositions) providing updates on the coronavirus with Islamic perspectives on plagues drawn from commentaries of the Qur'an, hadith, and Muslim history. I delivered them to every Muslim inmate on Jummah day, providing them an Islamic frame of reference to discuss the pandemic and resist conspiracy theories. They were appreciative, sharing it with others and with their families via phone calls, emails, and letters. One inmate caught me off guard when he asked me how I was coping with the coronavirus situation. When I responded that I was fearful about my family and myself contracting it, he replied, "Nothing can befall us except what Allah wills. Allah is the Greatest, and He controls everything." We talked about what the Prophet ﷺ said: "No servant experiences a plague and remains in his town, being patient, hoping for Allah's reward, and knowing nothing can befall him except what Allah has decreed for him—except his reward will be like that of a martyr."[13] It was a humble reminder that Islam is the religion of good advice, sharing, and learning from one another.

Challenge of Radicalization

For decades, a strategic effort has been made in the government, media, and public to instill fears about radicalization of American Muslims, particularly with regard to corrections facilities. Academic critics and researchers like SpearIt,[14] Faiza Patel,[15] and others, however, have identified political agendas as the driving force for inquiry into radicalization rather than documentable evidence of such a problem in the United States.

In my observation, a tiny minority of Muslim prisoners are radicalized, believing Islam is at war with the non-Muslim world that seeks to destroy it and viewing themselves as jihadists. Notably, they seemed to have arrived at this position in advance of their incarceration. They comprise three groups. The first group, through various media, were brainwashed into heeding the call of militant *jihâd* to fight against belligerent enemies of Muslims but have had no in-depth knowledge of Islam. They engaged in terrorist activities or attempted to do so physically, financially, or rhetorically. The second group are not scholars but are well read in Islam and arrived at their own conclusions to engage in a particular form of *jihâd* rejected by most Muslims. The third group are wannabe militant jihadists. They have no in-depth knowledge of Islam and did not engage in militant *jihâd*, but have embraced Islam in prison and are exploiting it as a channel of protest, resistance, and ideology against authorities perceived as unjust. Clearly, the three types of radical Muslim inmates did not have a background of formal study in Islam but have the potential to become deradicalized in thought and deed. In sum, I had some success, albeit on a minuscule scale, mediating the radical views of some through exposing them to a structured study of Islam with different scholarly opinions in contradistinction to monolithic narratives of ideologues and demagogues that they knew. They realized how much of Islam they did not know and reprioritized their goals in life, stating that when they were released, they wanted to become more knowledgeable about their faith and practice, contribute to Muslim community building, or raise a Muslim family. Others willingly participate in Islamic studies and enjoy intellectual exchanges but remain hardcore radicals. At the USP and FCI, jihadists are isolationists and not members of the dominant Black Sunni Muslim Community, excommunicated, or "run off the yard" Muslims because of aversion to their "foreign" brand of radical Islam with ISIS or al-Qaeda symbols and rhetoric, endangering the Community.

Yûsuf Model of Muslim Chaplaincy

My entry into the federal chaplaincy services with three graduate degrees in Islamic studies inadvertently made the impression on Muslim inmates that they were getting a shaykh to serve them. Their expectations are high. Some want me to visit them often (at least weekly), be readily available to counsel them, fulfill their requests for religious diets, literature, welfare checks, compassionate telephone calls to their families if one of their relatives died, and speedily answer their questions about Islam. They expect me to be humble, respectful, caring, patient, humanize them, and not be judgmental. Those are the seemingly big shoes that I am to fill as a BOP chaplain. Others desire more from me—beyond the mandate of the Religious Services department—as if I have a magic lamp that I can gently rub to conjure up a genie to grant their every legal, health, nutritional, and other wishes!

By Allah's Grace, I have managed to painstakingly develop a solid rapport with the Muslim inmates at AOR regardless of their ethnic, educational, social, and cultural backgrounds and Islamic orientation, something I credit to the Yûsuf model of Muslim chaplaincy mentioned earlier. To follow the example of Yûsuf, one must be sincere, benevolent, and view his work as a call from God Almighty to serve others. Coming from an academic background,

I go the extra mile to teach inmates Arabic and Islam, which was well received throughout the prison complex, connecting them linguistically and culturally with their religion. They measure their educational progress by my grading and rewarding them with certificates of achievement. They are as studious, disciplined, and passionate as my college students were, even more so given that many of them are at the GED level or lower and have been berated in the free society as nonachievers. Apart from teaching, I offer Islamic guidance on purchasing of food items sold at the commissaries—on what is *halal* (lawful), *haram* (unlawful), and *mushtabihât* (doubtful). I also worked with the Bury Me Muslim (BMM) organization, the Islamic Circle of North America, masjids in Denver, and U.S. attorneys at AOR to put in place *janâzah* (funeral) arrangements with jurisdiction in Colorado for indigent local Muslim inmates and foreign nationals facing difficulty in having their deceased bodies repatriated to their respective countries were they to die in federal custody.

Serving as a chaplain in a correctional setting has been self-actualizing, rewarding, and given me a higher meaning in life. The job environment has its unique stressors, too, as BOP employees say, "It is the least public federal job in one of the most dangerous work environments!" One never knows what a normal day is like because things can go wrong easily, quickly, and unexpectedly with suicides, fights, stabbings, even murder. One day I think I am doing much, making an affirmative difference in the lives of inmates; next day I think I've done nothing or not enough and maybe it is not the right job for me for myriad reasons, least of which is working in such an unnatural environment. Administering chaplaincy services to inmates in general, and the forgotten or neglected part of the American Muslim community (*ummah*) in particular, keeps me humble and prompts me to nurture my own spiritual development, continue my research on Islam, and practice what I preach, in order to be a respected servant of Allah. When Prophet Yûsuf finally left prison on the king's order, he wrote on its walls: "This is a place of calamity, abode of sorrow, grave of the living, test of those who are sincere, and malicious joy of the enemy."[16]

Conclusion

There is a dearth of Muslim chaplains in the BOP, which recruits via outreach to the Muslim community, advertising Islamic chaplain vacancies, and asking existing chaplains to recommend candidates. This need is likely to grow as the Muslim inmate population grows. Muslim chaplains are sought to serve Muslim inmates, expand religious diversity of the federal chaplaincy, and promote a holistic approach to Islam. As we foster the recruitment process and enhance Islamic chaplaincy, the next step may look like involving the wider Muslim community in post-prison rehabilitation efforts of ex-prisoners, retraining them in job skills, finding them jobs, temporary shelter, access to legal, mental, and physical clinical services, family reunification, continuing Islamic education, marriage counseling, and so forth. While many predominantly African American Muslim communities have been striving to do this work for decades, immigrant-dominated masjid have been slower to partake and are often isolated from the communities to which Muslim parolees return.[17] These communities are often impoverished food deserts with few jobs, high rates of unemployment, crime, and the accumulated impact of systemic racism, but, like Prophet Yûsuf, I remain hopeful in Allah's generosity.

Notes

1. According to BOP records on inmate religion stats (posted February 27, 2017), "Muslim" was the religious preference of 10,373 inmates, including males (10,059) and females (314), in federal custody, not including Residential Re-entry Centers or secure privatized facilities. See https://www.bop.gov/foia/docs/inmatereligion statsjune2016.pdf.

2. This is gleaned from a comparison of BOP stats on inmate religion over the years. In 2004, 9,000 inmates identified as Muslim out of a total inmate population of 150,000. In 2016, the number of Muslim inmates, as mentioned above, was 10,373 out of 159,315 inmates. The actual figure is probably much higher because many inmates convert to Islam but do not request their religious preference to be changed as Muslim in SENTRY, as I have personally encountered on many occasions. The BOP considers Nation of Islam and Moorish Science Temple of America as Islamic groups. See also Rami Nsour, "Islam and Muslims in the U.S. Prison System," at https://www.taybafoundation.org/articles/2020/islam-and-muslims-in-the-us -prison-system.

3. An epithet loosely used by some BOP staff to refer to the frequent, multiple, and intense litigation efforts of Muslim inmates within the federal prison system.

4. Dalia Faheid, "There Are 11,073 Muslims in Federal Prisons but Just 13 Chaplains to Minister to Them," National Public Radio, July 2, 2021.

5. Federal Correctional Complex, Florence, Colorado.

6. W. Thomas Becker, *Correctional Chaplains: Keepers of the Cloak* (Cappella Press, 2012).

7. Yûsuf/12:32–42; and *Tafsîr al-Baghawi* (Dar al-Hazm, 2002), 645–648.

8. Arabic, "community." A *jamâ'ah* typically refers to a Muslim community or congregation.

9. BOP chaplains, like most professional chaplains, are contractually prohibited from proselytizing, which is also a breach of the code of conduct for the Association of Muslim Chaplains and the Association of Professional Chaplains code of ethics.

10. al-Qasas/28:56.

11. An effeminate man (*mukhannath*), who had dyed his hands and feet with henna, was brought to the Prophet ﷺ. He asked, "What is the matter with this man?" He was told, "(O) Messenger of Allah! He imitates the likes of women." So he [the Prophet] issued an order, banishing him to an-Naqi'. The people said, "(O) Messenger of Allah! Should we not kill him?" He said, "I have been prohibited from killing people who pray." Abu Dawud, 4928.

12. Muslim, *al-Sahîh*, 1374.

13. al-Bukhârî, *al-Jâmi' al-Sahîh*, 5734.

14. SpearIt, "Muslim Radicalization in Prison: Responding with Sound Penal Policy or the Sound of Alarm?" *Gonzaga Law Review* 49, no. 1 (2014), available at SSRN: https://ssrn.com/abstract=2387928.

15. Faiza Patel, *Rethinking Radicalization* (Brennan Center for Justice, New York University School of Law, March 2011).

16. *Tafsîr al-Baghawi* (Dar al-Hazm, 2002), 650.

17. Dream of Detroit, Inner City Muslim Action Network, Believers Bailout, and Link Outside are doing important re-entry work.

Out of Necessity and of Love

EL-FAROUK KHAKI

"Justice is what love looks like in public."
—*Dr. Cornel West*

MUSLIM CHAPLAINS MAY be drawn to chaplaincy for a wide variety of reasons, but one thing they have in common is that, at some point, they will find themselves working with queer[1] and transgender Muslims or their families. Unfortunately, few have the appropriate training to do this work. On a recent interfaith panel of queer/trans clergy I took part in, one of the panelists noted that a "welcoming space" meant you were in someone else's home, while an "affirming space" *is* home. While many may not be able to directly offer LGBTIQ Muslims the theological affirmation that I feel is inherent to Islam, and which is integral to my own ministry and the care I provide, all should be able to affirm that queer Muslims *are* Muslims *and are a part of the ummah.*

El-Farouk Khaki is an activist, public speaker, writer, and media commentator. He identifies as a "sunni-normative" nondenominational Muslim with Shi'a and Sunni histories, and is initiated in the Rifai Sufi Muslim tradition. El-Farouk is the founder of Salaam: Queer Muslim Community, and serves as imam of el-Tawhid Juma Circle: The Unity Mosque, an inclusive healing space he cofounded with his (now) husband Troy Jackson and Dr. Laury Silvers. Previously a student at Emmanuel College's master's program in pastoral counseling, he officiates marriage for all orientations, genders, and faiths.

EDITOR'S NOTE: Having not received a submission from a chaplain on this topic, we are profoundly grateful to Imam Khaki for graciously collaborating with us on this piece and to Tynan Power for his editing assistance.

Chaplains can do this by providing nonjudgmental presence and spiritual companionship as queer Muslims journey with identity formation and by providing means for them to connect with others who have been on similar journeys so that they can begin to see a future that feels possible and hopeful. With the increased attention the profession of chaplaincy is receiving among mosque-going Muslims, chaplains are also well positioned to shift the discourse toward one of a prophetic model of spiritual care rooted in passion and compassion for all of humanity.

As a teenager living in Canada, the child of Tanzanian political and religious activists, I came into my activism around the intersectional issues of racial justice, Muslim matters, and interfaith bridgebuilding. As my awareness of my own identity grew, I became an advocate for gender justice, and justice/equality for LGBTIQ people. Much of my work has risen from my personal journey for integration and wholeness and through my advocacy for LGBTIQ refugees, and understanding how gender, sexual orientation, and gender identity can be weaponized against individuals and groups. Not having found many such spaces where the fullness of my humanity—my Muslim faith, my queerness, my race, my immigration experience, and now my identities as husband and father—can be affirmed and held in dignity,[2] I have been called to create them.

Certainly, that was the context in 1991 when I started Salaam: A Social/Support Group for Lesbian and Gay Muslims. However, issues of inclusion and marginalization for LGBTIQ people, including Muslims, are never only about social support. For LGBTIQ people of faith, spiritual scars can run deep. In 2009, Dr. Laury Silvers, Troy Jackson, and I started 'el-Tawhid[3] Juma Circle: The Unity Mosque, in response to the spiritual violence we observed and had ourselves endured, as a safe space for ourselves, for those de-Muslimed (Muslims not seen as Muslim enough) and those un-mosqued (Muslims lacking a mosque that reflected their values and/or beliefs). Mosque president Troy Jackson, upon receiving the 2017 Harmony Award on behalf of The Unity Mosque, shared poignantly, "We started . . . out of necessity and of love. We believed, then and still, that all people are equal in and before Allah. . . . It is a place to heal, and reclaim their Islam. Many are so incredulous that such a mosque exists, that we regularly witness tears." Eventually, my increasing engagement in pastoral care at the masjid (mosque) led me to embark on a master of pastoral counseling at Emmanuel College, focused on Muslim spiritual care.

My calling to pastoral care has earlier roots in my refugee-law practice of nearly three decades in which, having represented refugees from over 110 different countries, I've seen patterns in the way different kinds of violence, including spiritual violence, manifest and are interwoven into people's lives. The majority of my clients have sought protection due to their sexual orientation, gender or gender identity/expression, or HIV status. My work requires not only listening to client experiences but working with them to extract the different traumas and violence they have endured, much of which is often normalized and internalized. Many of my clients have experienced religious doctrines and teachings being imposed as tools to dehumanize and demonize them due to their actual or perceived sexual orientation or gender identity/expression.

In one case, "Mina," a young, Black African Muslim lesbian, broke down in tears in my office, believing she had disobeyed God by fleeing the sexually, physically, and emotionally abusive marriage her father had forced her into after he discovered she was a lesbian and brutally assaulted her himself. Together, Mina and I explored the Qur'anic story wherein God tells Ibrâhîm to respect and care for his parents but not to follow their misguided ways. Mina came to recognize that her father's actions were abusive and contrary to the *amânah* (responsibility or trust) God places on parents. This understanding freed her from the burden of believing—and the ensuing guilt—that her only way to be a good Muslim and child was to stay in a violent and abusive marriage.

Christian writer Jean Stairs laments the neglect of the soul in Protestant pastoral care trends and calls for the reclamation of "soul care" and "listening for the soul" for the pastoral care ministry. She defines "soul listening" as listening for the holy in the ordinary.

> To listen for the soul means helping people connect with God, live in the image of God, and learn to participate in God's ongoing creative and redemptive work through a multi-tiered strategy at the individual, family and community level.[4]

In my experience, the call to deep listening is as relevant in the Muslim context, if not more so, especially in the contemporary urban and Western landscapes where extended family and community elders, who traditionally played such roles, may no longer exist. Too often, religious guidance is premised on the belief that "enjoining good and forbidding evil"[5] means enforcing ritual observance, rather than the creation of a just and equitable society or fostering a healing, loving relationship with the Divine.

Often, questions by Muslims are framed by religious leaders as questions of *fiqh* (jurisprudence);[6] unfortunately, the meaning of *fiqh* as "deep understanding" or "full comprehension" seems to have been lost in contemporary society. Responding with soul listening rather than jurisprudence can help to discern what is needed to care for the soul. An unfortunate example was once related to me: A young woman went to the chaplain on her campus and articulated feelings that hijab made her "look fatter and more ugly." The chaplain disregarded her feelings, which revealed an underlying struggle with body image rooted in the history of emotional abuse in the home, and simply told her hijab was obligatory. Had he listened to her soul and her pain, or simply acknowledged the diversity of opinions about the hijab,[7] he could have avoided inflicting more harm.[8]

Many queer Muslims relate similarly alienating stories. Unity Mosque congregant Samra Habib writes: "Many of us [have] been made to feel rejected by Allah, at times when we needed Him most."[9] Spiritual care providers thus become obstacles, impeding Muslims from stepping toward God.[10] Chaplains have the opportunity—and I would argue the responsibility—to remove obstacles to enable seekers to step toward God. Removing obstacles isn't always hard, as another member shared: "I wish somebody would have told me all the Qur'anic verses about God's compassion and love for all Creation, and about loving God, rather than obeying rules out of fear."

A story from Ch. Abdul-Malik Merchant demonstrates what soul care can look like for queer or trans Muslims.[11] When a student disclosed to Ch. Abdul-Malik that he was gay and asked what he thought, Abdul-Malik affirmed his love for him as a fellow believer and turned the question around to ask the student his own thoughts, thereby creating a compassionate space for the student to share his struggles. The student, believing he couldn't be gay and Muslim, had stopped praying. However, in speaking with Ch. Abdul-Malik, he came to recognize that he remained Muslim because of his *tawhîdic* (Divine unity) framework and belief in the Prophet Muhammad ﷺ. Subsequently, he resumed his prayers and, on his own volition, even began doubling up to make up for those missed.

This return to prayer is notable because of the traumatic relationship so many queer and trans Muslims have with prayer. For trans Muslims, the gendered aspects of prayer—from attire to line locations—can exacerbate gender dysphoria and make participation in congregational prayer stressful and even unsafe. Additionally, when many queer and trans people first begin to recognize our differences and the subsequent grief as we grapple with the implications, we've turned to God and begged and bartered to be changed, misled by imams who have preached that such is possible.

Ch. Abdul-Malik's example stands in contrast to what most of us experience with Muslim authority and leadership figures. Often queer and trans

Muslims seeking support and guidance from religious leaders are simply told, "You can't be gay/trans and Muslim." This immediately creates a dichotomy forcing an individual to choose between integral parts of one's being. Sadly, this statement is often decreed without any knowledge or insight into how we live our lives or how we honor our faith—and, in the case of trans Muslims, without awareness of Sunni and Shi'a rulings that support gender transition.[12] Beyond soul listening, when chaplains speaking publicly are asked what Islam says about *any* topic, they can begin by acknowledging the truth first: Islam says nothing. Muslims, however, say a lot. Multiplicity has been a foundational feature since the time of the Prophet ﷺ, and indeed queer and trans Muslims have a variety of ways that we reconcile our existence.[13]

Without theological and pastoral options for integration, queer and trans Muslims are often left fragmented: internalized homophobia and/or transphobia and deep shame add further complexity. Suicide risk is at its greatest when a person is struggling to envision a hopeful or happy future for themselves.[14,15] Chaplains, who can understand a person's "Muslimness" without needing it explained, can provide critical space for someone to begin envisioning a future by simply listening, acknowledging the struggles as normal and common, affirming that there is space for them within the *ummah*, and upholding God's love and compassion.[16] Additionally, referring careseekers to groups for queer and trans Muslims[17] can be especially helpful as these are "horizontal identities" in that they are typically not learned "vertically" from one's family, but from others of similar experience.[18]

While everyone's journey to self-awareness and integration is unique, Vivienne Cass offers a framework for understanding the process of gay and lesbian identity formation.[19] It is important to note that Cass's model isn't designed to address trans development, and is predicated on a Western cultural model that may not always work with some, including many Muslims. For example, a person who has overcome shame (both imposed and internalized) may still have to be selective about coming out, yet identity integration can still occur.[20] Despite its shortcomings, Cass's framework, summarized below with a composite example, is a helpful starting point.

Identity Confusion: Initial development of awareness of one's sexual orientation and incongruence with their personal—as well as peers' and family's—expectations.

I realized that I was different from the other boys as a very young child, even though I couldn't put my finger on why. When puberty hit, I began to realize I was attracted to men.

Identity Comparison: Often a time of isolation, acceptance of the possibility of being queer, start of a closer examination of the implications that would have on the above-mentioned expectations, and experience of grief.

Even though dating wasn't allowed in my family, I thought maybe a girlfriend could help. It didn't. I joined Tablighi-Jamat convinced that if I put all my focus on being a good Muslim, Allah would cure me. It enriched my soul, but didn't cure me. I was devastated and alone. My parents, my teachers, the imam—they'd all said gays choose to be gay and go to hell for it . . . but what if we don't choose it?

Identity Tolerance: Acknowledgment of likely being LGBTQ+, increased commitment to this as a lifelong reality, starting to connect with other LGBTQ+ people and stories.

There was a lot of pressure to marry; the idea of lying to a wife felt like an injustice. This was when I started to better understand what it was going to mean for me to be gay, and that it wasn't going away. I checked out a queer Muslim group website secretly on a school computer, but I didn't reach out.

Identity Acceptance: Coming to terms with sexual orientation and starting to develop new visions for the future; may begin coming out to individuals and feeling more comfortable attending queer events or groups.

As I was avoiding my parents' choices of marriage prospects, I circled back to that group and was surprised to see that they had all kinds of things—including a halaqah. It is sad now to realize just how much it surprised me that there were Muslims who were gay and pious. The friendships I made there were critical. When I decided I needed to be honest with my parents, one gave me a key to her home so I'd have a safe place to go if Abu threw me out. Alhamdulillah, he didn't, but I'd packed a bag in case.

Identity Pride:[21] Immersing in queer spaces and absorbing queer culture, while sometimes rejecting/distancing from heterosexual-dominated spaces and events.

My parents wanted me to pretend I was straight with their siblings. It was exhausting. I was done pretending to be something I wasn't. It became really important for me to let everyone know I was gay to free myself from their suffocating expectations. In the queer Muslim group, I found a chosen family where I could be me—all of me. I love that we can enjoy dinner together and then some of us go to the masjid for a talk while others go dancing.

Identity Synthesis: Sexual identity becomes fully integrated and is no longer the only/primary identity; sense of division between queer people and heterosexuals diminishes.

In college, it felt really important to be recognized as a gay brown Muslim; now I'm just Abdullah. I am all of those things still, but I'm also an uncle, a board member of a local social service agency, I'm a lot of things—my sexual orientation just isn't what defines all of me. I'm Abdullah, a servant of Allah trying to do the best I can in this lifetime.

Part of identity integration often includes determining how to be in a relationship with family. For those from Muslim families in North America, the family often serves as an important ethnoculturally relevant support system and a buffer from racism and Islamophobia. Coming out to family may put a person at risk of losing those relationships and the support they provide. Yet, to live closeted among family can be profoundly difficult requiring careful—and traumatizing—compartmentalization.

Those who do come out need space to process their families' reactions. I've come to see common themes: pressure for nondisclosure to other family members ("Don't tell your father, it will kill him"); placing a tremendous guilt-inducing burden on a child; self-blame and remorse on the part of the parent ("What did I do wrong?" and "Why is God punishing me?"); blaming Western influence ("We should never have come to this country!")—as if there are no queer or trans people in cultures outside of North America. I often say, "When we queer Muslims come out of the closet, our families often go into the closet" due to fear of shame, ostracism, and the punishment of hellfire. Families often need to grieve the future they'd planned, before they can catch up and join in dreaming of a new future with their queer/trans family members. Sadly, many suffer silently in isolation, never reaching out, because they do not believe it is possible to receive help from other Muslims. Additionally, I am aware of many LGBT converts who, fearing rejection in the Muslim community, have gone back into the closet after embracing Islam. Frequently this has been unsustainable, leading to great anguish and discordance for the individual and their relationships, including eventually their relationship with Islam.

As family life can be challenging, Muslim spaces are often places of stress and fear for queer and trans Muslims. Some must evade questions from "the aunties" about getting married and producing grandchildren. Some fear that having their sexual orientation or gender identity discovered would result in judgment, harm to their family's reputations, ostracism from the community/masjid, or even violence against them, including honor killings.[22] As one man reflected on the freedom of simply being able to walk into a masjid as himself: "I don't ever have that: in Muslim spaces I always hide my queer-self, you have to, just to be safe. It is exhausting . . . just to be me, all of me." Chaplains can counter this experience of fear and trauma—or even prevent it—by setting a tone of inclusion and affirmation. Speaking of what it was like to be invited to participate in a listening circle at a masjid, the same man reflected, "Simply being present in that space fully as ourselves and being heard . . . wow, it was amazing."[23]

Mevlana Rumi's invitation "Come, come, whoever you are" puts words to the spirit of creating space as a form of spiritual care. Mevlana names and invites those who were marginalized and stigmatized in his day and society—the "wanderer, worshiper of fire, idolater"—and goes further: calling his âdhân even to those who have "broken your vows but a thousand times." A contemporary case study of the impacts of inviting in versus pushing away can be seen in the aftermath of the 2016 Pulse nightclub massacre. As the media depicted the tragedy as a struggle between Islam (represented by the Muslim shooter) and LGBTIQ people (represented by the victims), queer and trans Muslims found themselves at a painful intersection. Ch. Kaiser Aslam immediately issued a statement recognizing the grief of queer and trans Muslims:

> Our deepest condolences to the families and loved ones of those affected by the horrific attack in Orlando. To anyone from the LGBTQI community, you have a safe space with us at the Center for Islamic Life at Rutgers University.[24]

Though Ch. Kaiser later lamented that the statement fell short of a truly empathetic response, as a result of his "inviting in" queer and trans Muslims, a number of students—straight and queer alike—contacted him to let him know how important that statement was for them.[25]

By contrast, "A Joint Muslim Statement on the Carnage in Orlando"[26] issued by over 400 imams and other Muslim community leaders pushed queer and trans Muslims away.[27] Neglecting the Islamic principle of shûrâ (consultation), no one consulted queer Muslims in its formulation. When this not-so-joint statement declared "most Muslims adhere to a strict Abrahamic morality," it failed to define what such morality means, and inaccurately presented the Abrahamic traditions as monolithic and exclusionary of LGBTIQ people. If chaplains and queer and trans Muslims had been fully included in drafting the statement and rooting it in a spiritual care framework, it could have provided a simple acknowledgment and offered healing:

To our queer and trans Muslim siblings, we see you. We acknowledge the ways this event has been more difficult for you than we can imagine. **Allah loves you, and we love you.** *We pray you will find the solace and support you need within the ummah.*

Notes

1. The acronym LGBTI for lesbian, gay, bisexual, transgender, and intersex can box people into defined categories that don't always transcend the diversity of experiences. I reclaim "queer" in acknowledgment of this diversity. See Khaled El-Rouayheb's *Before Homosexuality in the Arab-Islamic World, 1500–1800* (University of Chicago Press, 2015). Some, particularly those opting for abstinence, prefer the term "same sex attracted" (SSA).

2. Canadian Race Relations Foundation, "Accidental Activist: El-Farouk Khaki," May 14, 2020, https://www.youtube.com/watch?v=drjBVKhiOfs&t=1152s.

3. *Tawhîd*, often translated as Divine unity, is more fully understood through the exegesis provided by Amina Wadud: "Experienced as a reality in everyday Islamic terms, humanity would be a single global community without distinction for reasons of race, class, gender, religious tradition, national origin, sexual orientation or other arbitrary, voluntary, and involuntary aspects of human distinction. Their only distinction would be on the basis of their *taqwâ* [God-consciousness]." Amina Wadud, *Inside the Gender Jihad* (Oneworld Publications, 2005), xi–xii.

4. Jean Stairs, *Listening for the Soul* (Augsburg Fortress, 2000).

5. Âl ʿImrân/3:104.

6. Mohammad Taqi al-Modarresi, *The Laws of Islam* (Enlight Press, 2016).

7. For more on this, including a list of scholars who held that it was desirable but not mandated for women, see Khaled Abou El Fadl's *Speaking in God's Name* (Oneworld Press, 2005), 143–144.

8. Important in light of the Islamic legal maxim *al-darar yuzâl*, harm must be eliminated.

9. Samra Habib, *We Have Always Been Here: A Queer Muslim Memoir* (Viking Press, 2019).

10. Allah says: "Take one step toward me, I will take ten steps toward you. Walk toward me, I will run toward you" (Hadith Qudsi). Abu Barzah reported: "I said, 'O Prophet of Allah, teach me something that will benefit me.' The Prophet, peace and blessings be upon him, said, 'Remove harmful things from the roads of the Muslims.'" Source: Muslim, *al-Sahîh* 2618.

11. Email correspondence between Abdul-Malik Merchant and Jaye Starr, spring 2021.

12. For more, see Tynan Power, "Muslim People," in *The SAGE Encyclopedia of Trans Studies*, vol. 2, ed. Abbie Goldberg and Genny Beemyn (SAGE, 2021), 553–555.

13. Queer Muslims share their own diversity of opinions that include reading the story of Lût (Lot) as God's response to institutionalized rape, inhospitality, and domination; *tafsîr* (exegesis) related to *tawhîd* (oneness of Allah) paired with the *âyât* (signs and verses) demonstrating diversity; hadith criticism; and finding representation of queer Muslims in classical Muslim poetry and story. Many form loving relationships, some marry and have children, while others practice abstinence.

14. Naseeha (https://naseeha.org/) provides Muslim suicide prevention support.

15. Jaye Starr interview with Amelia Noor-Oshiro, April 2021.

16. Recognize and name the trap of what Martin Seligman identified as "The Three P's" in careseekers' narratives: the personalization that one is to blame, the pervasiveness that this is destroying everything in life (or will do so), and the permanence that one will always feel this bad or things will always be as bad as they are now. Also, recognize the limits of your training and capacity (i.e., if you can't offer a truly nonjudgmental presence) and the role of transference. Are the intersections of your identities (or perceived ones) helpful or a hindrance? Have a list of trusted Muslim-friendly LGBTIQ+ competent providers to refer to.

17. Gigi Ali and Summeiya Khamissa have developed a global resource list for queer Muslims (including resources for parents): https://linktr.ee/gigistherapy world (accessed July 2021).

18. Andrew Solomon, *Far from the Tree* (Scribner, 2012).

19. Vivienne Cass, "Homosexual Identity Formation: A Theoretical Model," *Journal of Homosexuality* 4, no. 3 (1979): 219–235. See UNC's Safe Zone for several models (including trans specific), https://safezone.uncc.edu/allies/theories (accessed July 2021).

20. Thank you to Rahim Thawer for providing this critique (email correspondence with the author, May 2021).

21. For many trans people, a healthy and integrated identity does not require pride in the experience of being transgender. Integration rests rather in acceptance and confidence in a person's gender identification. For more, see Walter Bockting and Eli Coleman, "Developmental Stages of the Transgender Coming-Out Process: Toward an Integrated Identity," in *Principles of Transgender Medicine and Surgery*, ed. Randi Ettner, Stan Monstrey, and Eli Coleman (Routledge, 2016); and the identity development model from Jack Simons, Leeann Grant, and Jose Miguel Rodas, "Transgender People of Color: Experiences and Coping During the School-Age Years," *Journal of LGBT Issues in Counseling* 15, no. 1 (2020): 16–37.

22. Roxanne Khan and Michelle Lowe, "Homophobic 'Honour' Abuse Experienced by South Asian Gay Men in England," in *Men, Masculinities and Honour-Based Abuse*, ed. Mohammad Mazer Idriss (Routledge, 2019), 95–113.

23. Anonymous subject interview with Jaye Starr, March 2021, speaking about a listening circle held after the Pulse nightclub massacre.

24. Islamic Center of Rutgers University Facebook page, June 12, 2016.

25. Jaye Starr interview and correspondence with Kaiser Aslam, spring 2021.

26. "A Joint Muslim Statement: On the Carnage in Orlando," June 13, 2016, http://www.orlandostatement.com. A smaller group of Muslim leaders and organizations joined with others in issuing a Unity Statement that did acknowledge LGBTQ Muslims: https://muslimadvocates.org/files/Unity-Statement-on-Orlando-2.pdf.

27. For further exploration of the role of Muslim chaplains in American Muslim leadership as it pertains to the joint statement, see Timur Yuskaev and Harvey Stark, "The American *'Ulama* and the Public Sphere," in *Routledge Handbook of Islam in the West*, ed. Roberto Tottoli (Routledge, 2021).

14

A Chaplain's Call for Pastoral Care in the Masjid

JOSHUA SALAAM

BEFORE BECOMING A CHAPLAIN, I spent almost a decade as a youth director for one of the largest Muslim communities in America. It was considered
a "mega mosque," and every Friday over 7,000 worshippers gathered for congregational prayers across multiple locations. I worked with over 1,000 youth
each week. From the moment I started working there, I was developing religious, social, and recreational programming. I was so busy that I never had
time to look up. Perhaps it was the overwhelming amount of work that delayed
my realization that I was operating to fulfill the needs of youth without proper
data on what those needs were. On a basic level, I was not even sure how many
youth members I was responsible for. Was I supposed to serve any youth who
registered for my programs? Beyond that, I wondered, what was the best way
to get youth to the masjid? Why do they come, or why not? Is the masjid a safe
and supportive place for them? And ultimately, how do I create a model where

---

Dr. Joshua Salaam has previously served as a lay leader and police officer in the U.S. Air
Force. He managed the Civil Rights Department for the Council on American-Islamic
Relations and helped oversee a Baltimore Muslim community and neighborhood development project. Before starting as a Muslim chaplain at Duke University in July 2018,
Joshua worked with youth and families for eleven years at one of the largest Muslim
communities in America. He holds an MA in Religious Studies and Christian-Muslim
Relations and a DMin from Hartford Seminary. Joshua is the vice president for education
chaplains on the board of the Association of Muslim Chaplains. For self-care, he enjoys
sports, chess, and quiet reflections.

I can listen to every youth in my charge to learn what they need, love, hate, fear, enjoy?

I experienced a similar challenge around the lack of data—specifically about the community's emotional, social, and spiritual needs—when I later became a chaplain at the same masjid. The masjid leadership shared my questions. Who is attending Jummah, and why? Are worshippers attending because the masjid is close or is it because they consider themselves members of the community? And what does it mean to be a member of the community? Are there any members of the community who are not attending, and why not? Are they okay? Many masjids do not have the answers to these important questions, leaving decisions to be made based on anecdotal evidence or concerns brought forward by the most vocal, but not necessarily the most representative, community members.[1] Focus is often placed on physical needs—a new carpet for the prayer area or a parking lot expansion.

Being in tune with the emotional, social, and spiritual needs of one's community takes a pastoral care mindset, a realization I came to through my chaplaincy training. Chaplains train to cultivate this mindset. The COVID-19 pandemic brought this gap to the forefront. As emails were circulating announcing masjid closures, many were forced to ask difficult questions. What is the purpose of the masjid? What is the role of the imam when the masjid is closed? Who are the community members and what do those members expect of the masjid during a pandemic? Is there a map identifying where members are, including information about those with increased risks and needs? Before these questions could be answered, the masjids were in desperate need of financial help. Instead of emails checking on the community, community members received masjid emails requesting additional funds for operations.

A pastoral care mindset calls us to look and listen a little deeper. Pastoral care is a term derived from the tradition of shepherding in a pasture and refers to the caretaking at the heart of chaplaincy. The skills needed to become a successful shepherd—patience, vigilance, and gentleness—have strong connections with prophethood in the Islamic tradition.[2] With a pastoral care mindset, we ask: Is there anyone in the community who is experiencing domestic violence? Who is struggling with drug addiction or dealing with food insecurity? Are youth having sex out of wedlock without any knowledge of STD transmission? Who no longer identifies as Muslim because of trauma they experienced or not having had religious questions answered? Asking these types of questions is the first step to providing the services and programs that best support the community's spiritual and emotional growth and resilience. Responding accordingly in a timely fashion is a difficult second step, especially when the answers to the questions or the data that is gathered is embarrassing and painful. However, as they say, "No pain, no gain."

Muslim chaplains have varying levels of Islamic knowledge, and some would even be considered scholars; however, the primary skill of a chaplain is pastoral care. My chaplaincy training at Hartford Seminary focused on this and included classes on the experiences of other American religious groups, which helped me tap into important data, research methods, and resources that are extremely helpful. I also learned to understand each person as a complicated human being with diverse needs. This is where the core of chaplaincy and pastoral care comes into play. In addition to addressing one's spiritual needs, the pastoral care framework and training that a chaplain brings also look at the emotional and social needs within a congregation. A chaplain is less eager to jump into questions of halal and haram. Instead, we focus more on questions like, "What's on your mind today?" and "What burdens are you struggling with?" Pastoral care helps an imam become aware of a family's financial troubles before they visit the zakat office; a youth director knows that a family is stressed before their child attempts suicide; a board connects with young professionals before they disappear into the American landscape. Trained chaplains providing proper pastoral care can help communities transition from a reactive model to one that proactively engages with its members.

Early in my career as a youth director, I was only focused on publicizing which programs were happening each week. I made sure everyone knew if a guest speaker was coming and if food was provided. My colleagues had similar responsibilities for the broader community—we were largely consumed with logistics and proper communication through our website and social media platforms. Later in my youth director career, after I'd begun my chaplaincy training, I learned to listen, reflect, and act through a pastoral care lens. As a result, my subsequent transition from youth director to a two-year position as community chaplain at the same masjid was full of lessons. One lesson as a chaplain was that the masjid leadership and I had very different understandings of what community chaplaincy meant. Since I was a trained chaplain and an employee of the masjid, the leadership envisioned me as a liaison with Muslims at the local jails, hospitals, and universities, as their understanding of chaplaincy was limited to those contexts. No one really knew what a chaplain was supposed to do within the masjid. "Why do we need a chaplain? We already have an imam and a social worker," was a common refrain. In their minds, a chaplain sounded like a duplication of efforts. While there is some healthy overlap, these are distinct but complementary roles. An imam is there to preach, teach, lead prayers, and if trained, to provide religious legal guidance. The social worker is best equipped to connect people with a variety of resources, including financial, housing, medical, and mental health. The chaplain can compassionately accompany people as they journey and explore their spiritual struggles. A chaplain provides a listening presence while congregants process times of joy or moments of stress and anxiety.

Contrary to the imam, who is typically selected by a community to uphold a specific set of interpretations of the faith, the chaplain is there to help people struggling to find their path. A chaplain should be able to serve Muslims not interested in ritual practices of the Islamic faith as well as people of other faiths or no faith who would like a nonjudgmental listening presence on their spiritual or emotional journey. In addition, it is important to separate the traditional image of a male imam from the role of chaplaincy. Many female chaplains are particularly well placed to provide a complementary role to or take some of the duties of the traditional imam position. They are experienced, well-educated, and often have natural listening gifts that give them an advantage.

Neither I nor the masjid quite got what we expected out of my community chaplaincy experience. My proposal to touch base with every community member with a pastoral mindset never got off the ground, and the masjid's vision of me being a liaison to local institutions never manifested either. Instead, I was tasked to implement a Jummah project that was designed when the masjid was still just a few families. The size of the community at the time of design could be why the projects touched on pastoral care. The project coordinated a series of *khutbahs* (sermons) around a topic chosen in coordination with parents, counselors, scholars, and other stakeholders. The *khatībs* (sermon-givers) across all the locations received training from mental health providers, family specialists, and religious leaders. A fun quiz was emailed out for children to play and win money by testing their knowledge of the *khutbah*. We were reimaging Jummah and the impact this fifteen to thirty minute window had on a captive audience. The focused project allowed me to feel the power of having a pastoral care mindset with a large community. And then . . . I left. Ultimately, the competing visions of the role of a community chaplain were too much.

I see similar challenges in higher education now that I have served as a university chaplain. A supervisor may have one idea of what a chaplain should be. The job description may have a different description. Students, however, may have other expectations. Without knowing exactly what a chaplain is, students may desire someone with the traditional Islamic education of an imam over someone with pastoral care training, which they may not even know exists. The definition of a chaplain is being pulled in different directions and thereby slowing the effects chaplains could have in the Muslim community. There is an urgent need to clearly define, understand, and strategically implement chaplaincy within the American Muslim community.

Many parents and communities seem ill prepared to have conversations with young people who see no issue with drinking, who are exploring their sexual orientation, or who no longer see Islam as a viable solution to their problems. Imams and community leaders often approach these conversations from a defensive position, trying to convert the person to the "correct" understanding. Chaplains, and pastoral care more broadly, aim to approach these conversations from a different mindset. A core part of chaplaincy training is around developing a nonjudgmental presence such that when one comes seeking pastoral care, it matters not whether one is pro-Trump or pro-Biden, Shi'a or Sunni, South Asian or Arab, conservative or liberal, gay or straight, indigenous or immigrant, Black or white. I aspire to reach this level of chaplaincy. I struggle to control my speech, my writings, and my actions so as not to appear unapproachable by members of my community. I've become more acutely aware of this struggle since becoming a university chaplain. In the masjid, I'd felt the community's expectation to uphold and promote the specific values the masjid was founded upon just as an imam would.

The more chaplaincy training and lived experience I've acquired, the less stressed I've become journeying with people. I am no longer the youth director expected to "fix" youth. I am not the imam expected to speak on masjid etiquette if too many people are violating tradition. I am not the social worker expected to solve social and financial emergencies through a network of local resources. I am the chaplain. My role is to step back, see all those pieces, then step in real close and listen very intently. Chaplaincy is sometimes called a *ministry of presence*. The art of truly being present with an individual without judgment is at the core of chaplaincy.

If there was a time I could go back to as masjid chaplain, where I wished I had listened a little closer and more intently, it would be during the time of a tragic murder of a young female Muslim congregant. The murder happened just blocks from the masjid during Ramadan and shook the entire community to its core. Too much was happening at the same time. An investigation needed to be done, parents and friends needed grief support, counselors were needed, lawyers had to be called, the media was calling, fingers were being pointed . . . but who was listening? Still a student, I was not fully prepared as a chaplain when this incident occurred. I don't know if anybody can really prepare for something like that. Along with others, I turned myself to the easier response of *doing* instead of simply *being.* I lament that we didn't have a better pastoral care framework already in place to help carry the community through that profoundly difficult time: chaplaincy is not an event, it is an ongoing process. Relationships are nurtured over time and the reputation of being a non-judgmental listener takes time to cultivate. When tragedy hits, chaplains and others will see the benefits of their pastoral mindset.

In conclusion, I maintain that there is a pastoral care void within many American Muslim communities. With many masjids struggling to pay an imam and basic utilities, I am not necessarily advocating for masjids to hire chaplains. Those that can should, but those that cannot would benefit from becoming more familiar with the concept of pastoral care. Communities should consider sending their imam to take a unit of Clinical Pastoral Education training at the local hospital. Additionally, connecting with local churches or temples is another option if they have a training program for pastoral care volunteers[3] so that masjids could start their own pastoral care committee. We should also ensure that anyone representing the masjid as a chaplain at the local university or corrections facility is trained appropriately. Together, we can create a cultural shift such that pastoral care becomes fundamental to the American masjid experience.

Notes

1. While organizations such as the Institute for Social Policy and Understanding (ISPU) and the Family Youth Institute (FYI) are working to fill the data gap pertaining to the national Muslim community, institution-specific needs assessments like those done by Center DC, a third space, are critical to guiding masjid leadership.

2. See Bilal Ansari and Ibrahim Long, "Islamic Pastoral Care and the Development of Muslim Chaplaincy," *Journal of Muslim Mental Health* 12, no. 1 (2018).

3. Such committees, common to many Christian congregations, can provide programs such as meal trains, home-based wellness and companionship visits, and transportation assistance to support the emotional, spiritual, and social needs of vulnerable congregants.

15

"Hurt People Hurt People"

LAUREN SCHREIBER

WHEN I CONVERTED TO ISLAM, I felt the need to connect with folks who shared the challenges and outlook on Islam that I did. That search led me to a video of Usama Canon inviting viewers "home" to Ta'leef with the tagline "Come as you are to Islam as it is."[1] As someone who had spent my first three years being Muslim peeling back and discarding layers of myself, this invitation was exactly what I needed to hear. I joined a ten-day residency program at Ta'leef where we got to talk about our inner workings and what drew us to Islam and community in the first place. When Usama spoke, I took notes. I spent some time picking his brain about how Ta'leef started, looking to glean best practices for the third space I was envisioning for Washington, D.C., but I unexpectedly found myself in his pastoral care. Through tears, I explained how I felt like an impostor attempting to do this as a young female convert. He looked me in the eyes and said, "Girl, you trippin'—Lauren, you are a quarterback! Run the plays. You know what is needed. And you know what to do.

Lauren Schreiber is the executive director and cofounder of Center DC, a growing third-space community in Washington, D.C., serving over 4,000 Muslims, that focuses on building authentic relationships between those practicing and exploring Islam and the Divine. Currently a student in Hartford Seminary's Islamic Chaplaincy Program, she also studies under Suhaib Webb and Ieasha Prime, and serves as vice president of community chaplains for the Association of Muslim Chaplains. Her most important jobs are being a wife and mama. In her spare time, you can find her making pupusas, writing music, and convening monthly gatherings of Muslim Practitioners of Restorative and Transformative Justice, a peer learning group she cofounded in 2020.

These people will follow you if they know what's good for them. And if you ever get boxed out of any circle you need access to—any group of brothers—you just grab me by my necktie and I'll be there to help get you in." In the years that followed, I would fly out to Cali to sit and learn with him, eat at his home, and play with his children. He was on speed dial if I ever had a new idea or needed feedback. He was one of the first people we texted when I went into labor, and he insisted on sleeping on our couch whenever he would visit D.C.

Almost a year after his 2019 ALS diagnosis became public, Ta'leef Collective severed all ties with Usama Canon in a board email to members that went viral, citing that he had "deeply betrayed the sanctity of the position of spiritual teacher." Allegations were vague but included "verbal abuse and abuse of authority" and accusations of a "more serious nature," which he was said to have admitted to. My earlier memories are now filed away, spoken in a whisper now that he's been labeled an abuser. I walk on eggshells whenever I'm praised for a strategy or approach I learned from him. I edit myself, fearful of mentioning the good parts of Usama in public spaces knowing that doing so risks rehashing the harm he caused. The ripples of the disclosure were felt nationwide. Muslims, and particularly women, were left grieving the loss of trust and violation of safety at the hands of a male scholar, yet again. Collectively, we were left questioning every conversation had with him, every gift he'd given, any compliment that had been offered. Sisters lamented to me, "If I'm not even safe with Usama Canon, *then who am I safe with?*" To be a woman leading a third space at that time, especially one who was mentored by Usama himself, was suffocating. I felt responsible to lean into the community—to revisit our agreements, to talk about safety, to design so as to meet the need of broken trust. Though I've not been in contact with him since the disclosure, Usama Canon continues to influence Center DC in ways I could never have foreseen.

On the surface, Center DC is like many Muslim third spaces across America: belonging and connectedness are at the center of our approach to building community. Muslim third spaces have generally endeavored to create inclusive spaces that challenge many of the negative stereotypes about mosques.[2] The term "third place" first appeared in Ray Oldenburg's community building masterpiece *The Great Good Place*.[3] Early Muslim third spaces such as Ta'leef, the first Muslim community to use the term, were not intended to replace the role of the masjid, but rather to complement and help bind people to the faith who were otherwise slipping away. Following Oldenburg's theory, at third spaces, conversation is the main activity. Jummah was intentionally not held; people were directed to the masjid for that. In Oldenburg's description, third spaces are open, accessible, and meet the needs of the people who gather there. There are "regulars" who help hold the culture of the space, and the environment is characteristically wholesome, playful, and comfortable like a home away from home.[4] This is all true for Center DC—in our surveys, the word most often used to describe Center DC is overwhelmingly "welcoming." But what happens when that isn't the case? What happens, instead, when people are harmed in community?

One day, three years after our founding, I received a WhatsApp message from a woman I hadn't seen at Center DC in a year. In a panicked message, she skipped the formalities and jumped right to the point: she was reaching out because a brother in the area had been going to Center DC in search of his next "victim." She had proof of his track record, had spotted him in our recent event photos, and felt it her duty to inform someone who could protect other women from him. She told me he was a narcissist, a compulsive liar, and had lured her and another woman she included in the message into separate simultaneous relationships with him where he exploited them financially and took advantage of them sexually, all under the guise of marriage. There were other women too, she told me, once we moved the conversation to a phone call. I was speechless. In a shaky voice, I fumbled out how sorry I was that this was happening to her, and asked a simple question: *What did she want me to do?* Thinking to myself as I did, *What could I possibly do?* Her answer gave me clarity as we continued to speak: this man was a threat to others and needed to be banned from Center DC. The women were extremely hesitant to allow us to reach out to the brother directly, for fear of retaliation, slander, and possibly compromising their own personal safety. A court case was also alluded to, but no restraining order was in place. Though they wanted him to be banned, I was unable to engage him in conversation without inadvertently revealing the identity of his accusers; as such it was impossible to hear his side of the story. Still, something needed to be done, and as they put it, it was now on me as the leader of this community to act.

When we started Center DC back in the summer of 2015, I hadn't yet heard of the term "restorative justice" and had no idea that that framework would become so pivotal in my understanding of how a healthy community should operate. I would have never imagined that my executive director role would turn into a pastoral role either. My guess is that many people enter the field of community chaplaincy as I did and take up the mantle with the belief that community is naturally for everyone. That human beings are imperfect, but that mercy and forgiveness are from the Divine. That our job, as chaplains, is to hold space for those on the margins and to walk with them until they are ready to be welcomed back into the fold of the faith and reintegrate into community. My assumption has always been that this readiness was implied and that ultimately, if my work as a chaplain is successful, they'll eventually be ready to jump back in. Allah, after all, designed us as communal creatures. I first came to know Islam through the Muslim Student Association as an undergraduate and then more intimately during a semester studying abroad in Gambia in my college years, where I was immersed in community life with Muslims. Community has been the mechanism by which I have come to know the Prophet ﷺ, through whom I have come to know God. The act of communal living puts us in direct relationship with God's creation and provides us invaluable insight into our own moral constitution and shortcomings that we might progress toward God. To me, this means that we need each other at our core if we are to travel on the path toward God. As the saying goes, "When one part of the body is aching, the whole body aches."

For the next few months after that WhatsApp exchange, I spent many sleepless nights in conversations with the women who became frustrated with our approach as time went on: with our team, with our board, with scholars, with the teams at HEART[5] and FACE,[6] with anyone I could think of reaching out to for counsel without providing too many details. What do organizations do when someone in their community is accused of being a predator? How does a faith-based community keep people, especially women, safe? How do we hold people who cause harm accountable? Can we evaluate with only one side of the story? What was the most just, most Islamic way to engage this dilemma? There were no clear answers.

Although Ta'leef had a general policy of aggression as grounds to ban someone, they didn't investigate personal matters or incidents that took place between community members outside of their physical space. My friends at Seattle's Wasat and Ohio's Salaam Community empathized and expressed interest to learn more about where we landed. I remember late nights of Title IX research and digging for hadiths and *fiqh* (jurisprudence) rulings in English that might shed light on Islamic perspectives about what to do in the absence of witnesses or access to evidence.

With the help of Sameera Qureshi, who worked for HEART at the time, along with some emergency conversations with Alia Salem from FACE, we waded through the facts and did our best to develop both a punitive policy outlining the breaches that would require intervention, including what might constitute someone being asked to disengage completely from Center DC. We assembled a small group from our core team and board to form a decision-making body, which we called the Safe(r) Space Committee.

Ultimately, after getting the go-ahead from the women, the Safe(r) Space Committee sent the brother in question an email two months after the initial complaint, asking him to meet with us to discuss some concerns that were brought to our attention and instructing him to refrain from attending Center DC events until we had met. Despite text messages and follow-up emails, we never received a response. Everything came to a head at Eid al-Fitr when the brother casually showed up at our outdoor picnic with his sister. My whole body tensed up. I could feel my hands shaking. "Here we go," I thought to myself. This is the unseen emotional labor that I carry.

I intercepted him at the entrance. "Eid Mubarak," I squeaked out. We exchanged brief forgettable small talk. "Did you get my emails and texts? Can we go over here and chat?" What happened next was one of the hardest moments I've experienced. Here we were with friends and familiar faces at a community celebration. Laughter. Children playing. Burgers on the grill. Prayer mats laid on the grass. I was the one to tell him he wasn't welcome. "If you would have just responded to the email, we could have had this conversation months ago and sorted this out." But by then, it was too late. He felt judged and slandered without due process or justice. He left, with his sister in tears, assuring me that they would never come back to Center DC and informing me that it was *my* fault they were being pushed out of the community. That I was responsible for this particular injustice against their family. There was pain all around. The women never reengaged with Center DC, nor did he. I was left with a feeling that I had failed everyone. I find myself searching for all of their faces, hoping that somewhere, they have found belonging again and that they've each been able to find holistic healing and community.

Not long after, we scrapped the punitive policy completely and leaned into the complexity. Conflict and harm are incredibly nuanced and the actual needs that arise often go unaddressed. We found no one-size-fits-all approach, and we tried to be "victim-centered," but it sometimes felt like an element was missing. After our second case emerged, Sameera introduced us to Tarek Maassarani, a D.C.-based restorative practitioner who has been focused on cases of sexual harm. As articulated by Howard Zehr, a champion of the modern restorative justice movement in the United States, it is best defined as "an approach to achieving justice that involves, to the extent possible, those who have a stake in a specific offense or harm to collectively identify and address harms, needs, and obligations in order to heal and put things as right as possible."[7] It is a method of engaging harm that is rooted in indigenous practices, found in similar fashion worldwide.

The key principles of this practice center on the impact of the harm and looking at the needs it creates. When someone harms another person, needs emerge from all parties involved: the person harmed, the person who caused harm, and the community itself. Some of these needs may include the need for answers, shared understanding, forgiveness, healing, and for the wrong to be made right or repaired as best as possible. In restorative justice, a resolution is sought that can meet as many needs as possible, without causing additional harm. The essence is rooted in the human desire to be in "right relationship" with others, and it was my hunch that early Muslim conflict resolution was based on its own unique form of restorative practices, rooted in theology. After that meeting, Tarek dropped off a copy of a book chapter from *The Spiritual Roots of Restorative Justice*. Lo and behold, Nawal H. Ammar had authored a piece documenting just that.

From there, I dove into the tradition looking to understand *maqâsid al-sharî'ah* (objectives of the law), *usûl al-fiqh* (principles of Islamic jurisprudence), and *fard kifâyah* (communal obligations), as well as other central concepts such as *'adl* (justice), *maghfirah* (forgiveness), *tawbah* (repentance), *taklîf* (moral accountability), *hurmah* (sacredness), *khulq* (spiritual composition), and *adab* (etiquette) to inform our developing policies. It consumed my graduate studies at Hartford Seminary. Several core team members opted into Circle Keeping training and other local restorative justice training to garner more skills. We also assembled a team of invested core team members to serve as an internal body to deal with issues as they arise, to ensure the weight of conflict and requisite emotional labor won't fall on one person's shoulders.

With Tarek's help, we took on our second case and facilitated our first restorative circle. After seeing how dramatically different this outcome was from the first case, I was left searching for more. We invited Tarek back for a private team meeting, where our team sat in a circle on the floor of our new community space, with pizza and mint tea, to learn more about the possible applications of restorative justice as a communal process. It was the first time I heard the term "transformative justice." One by one, we drilled scenarios, and Tarek walked us through hypothetical outcomes that could happen using a restorative justice framework. By the end of the session, our team was excited and overwhelmed. I remember hearing someone say, "This just feels so . . . Islamic." We decided we would develop language and a process grounded in our tradition that called people in rather than kicking them out whenever possible. It would take a tremendous amount of work and we had no road map, but *bismillâh*, we jumped in.

We've now engaged with ten official complaints, and two additional matters that were brought to our attention, though not pursued by the reporting person. Cases have ranged from accusations of sexual harassment, stalking, and assault to anti-Shi'a remarks and arguments about anti-Blackness, to brothers in the community who simply aren't understanding that sisters aren't interested in their marriage proposals. Notably, three of those ten cases involved speakers. We've held two restorative circles, facilitated the writing and sharing of apology letters, arbitrated space usage, made requests of those who caused harm from those that they harmed, and held countless one-to-one calls. The restorative justice values of participation, respect, interconnectedness, and hope guide this work. Our Safe(r) Space Committee has grown to include social workers, therapists, HR professionals, lawyers, victim advocates, and a Title IX expert.

I wish I could say that Center DC has the blueprint. Community accountability is not a written policy or template process that fits every situation. Every case is different. No two people perceive harm in the same way. This process asks a lot of the person harmed. Not everyone is interested in going down that road, and we don't force it. We've had circles that landed in some real meaningful growth and accountability being taken, and we've had ones that resulted in participants walking out in full-blown disagreement, opting out of community entirely to avoid seeing the other party again. Our goal isn't to reproduce a shari'ah-based court system and conduct investigations when claims are brought forward. The issue of pastoral concern for Center DC is the emotional and spiritual states of both parties—in this life and the next—and of the community itself. Repairing relationships, or at least preventing them from harming one another, is part of our duty toward our brothers and sisters in Islam. Allah tells us in the Qur'an, "Surely the believers are but brothers. So set things right between your two brothers, and be aware of God—perhaps you will obtain mercy."[8] Sometimes restorative practices support this.

The primary goal of our Safe(r) Space Committee is to help both parties arrive at a shared understanding with an agreed-upon path to move forward—a reality that can only take place if the facilitators are trusted and have the training and skills needed to hold space for difficult conversations and to recognize when they cannot. This is especially true when the conflict is between invested members of our community. To approach "setting things right" in situations like these, there are two main prerequisites: all parties involved must share an Islamic ethic, and a capable facilitator must be present.

Usama Canon was the first person I heard say the phrase "Hurt people hurt people." More than anything, I wish I could have called him when the allegations about him came out. But I didn't. His voice had already left him—and with it, the opportunity for closure. I have no doubt that he hurt people in irreparable, perhaps unforgivable ways. And I also know that God worked through him in my life in ways that have manifested tremendous good in the shape of Center DC. The duality is real. I hate that I can't call him for advice *and* I hate that I can't help but hold him accountable for the pain he caused the American Muslim community. I hope it would have been something he would have leaned into. And so Usama has influenced me once again, to build the type of system that's missing from the American Muslim community: one that is both brave and vulnerable. A space where it's safe to talk about the harm we experience and the harm we cause. At the end of the day, I cannot ensure that harm won't be experienced at Center DC or at the hands of our leaders. I am merely a witness of God, seeking to make right between believers as best I can by developing a systematic approach designed to meet the needs of those of us who are harmed *and* those of us who cause it. It is my hope that our spaces can be both prophetic and pastoral, once again facilitating healing and a route back to God.

Notes

1. I've heard this phrase attributed to Imam Zaid Shakir.

2. For more information on the "third space" phenomenon and how it is perceived, watch the documentary film *UnMosqued*, http://www.unmosquedfilm.com/.

3. Ray Oldenburg, *The Great Good Place: Cafes, Coffee Shops, Bookstores, Bars, Hair Salons and Other Hangouts at the Heart of a Community* (De Capo, 1997).

4. Oldenburg, *Great Good Place*, 42.

5. HEART is a U.S.-based nonprofit organization that works to ensure that Muslims have the language, resources, and choice to nurture sexual health and confront sexual violence.

6. FACE is a U.S.-based nonprofit organization that addresses the Muslim leadership accountability gap within the United States and Canada.

7. Howard Zehr, *The Little Book of Restorative Justice* (Good Books, 2015), 48.

8. al-Hujurât/49:10.

16

An Immigrant's Journey to Chaplaincy

MUSTAFA BOZ

I WAS BORN IN A traditional Kurdish Sunni Muslim family in a small mountain village in the eastern part of Turkey. Life in our village was simple, free of modern conveniences like electricity, indoor plumbing, and other luxuries. In many ways, we were living a medieval nomadic life. As a child, I experienced long, cold, and snowy winters in the village, and when summer came, I accompanied my grandfather and older brother to the mountains to tend to our sheep. My grandfather was a very wise, religious man. His guidance, advice, and stories have had a great impact on the way I have lived Islam. With my father often away working construction in the city, my mother, a devout and traditional woman, despite being illiterate, oversaw much of my religious formation, including sending us children to the village mosque where the imam taught *'aqîdah* (beliefs), *sîrah* (Prophetic biography*)*, and Qur'anic recitation.

With my grandfather's hard-earned life savings, I went to *madrasah* for three years in Istanbul after completing elementary school. It was at a boarding school; living away from my family in one of the most historical and diverse

---

Mustafa Boz is a graduate of Hartford Seminary's Islamic Chaplaincy Program and holds endorsement from the Muslim Endorsement Council. He is a graduate of the Turkish Imam Hatip system, and holds a BA in Islamic Studies from Ankara Divinity School where he nearly completed an MA in Tafsir before immigrating to the United States. He has previously served as vice president of corrections chaplains with the Association of Muslim Chaplains and currently lives with his wife and two young children in Michigan. He is an avid exerciser and enjoys unwinding over a cup of coffee in a café.

---

cities helped me to develop a wider perspective about life, religion, community, and the world. There, I studied basic Islam and became a *hâfiz*, memorizing the Qur'an, even though Arabic was not my native language and I did not understand what I was reciting. Subsequently, I enrolled in the Imam Hatip system, a high school program designed to teach future religious teachers and scholars. Residing in a dormitory with other *hâfizs*, I had access to additional Arabic classes after school and on weekends, with a summer intensive taught by visiting native speakers.

I was actively involved with social gatherings and *halaqahs*, and come senior year, my main quest was to find a satisfactory way to be "a true Muslim," according to the Qur'an and the Sunnah, leading me for a time on a path of great rigidity in my personal practice. At the invitation of an attentive teacher, I attended one of his private circles where I was fortunate to learn more of the depth of the faith. His teaching guided me to develop a more compassionate understanding of Islam, and his mentorship eventually led me to pursue Islamic studies academically, completing my bachelor's and pursuing a master's of divinity at Ankara Divinity School, focused on *tafsîr* (exegesis).

I began my studies after a yearlong Arabic language program developing a proper foundation to engage with theological texts (which I'd later expand upon, spending two summers studying in Damascus). Divinity school provided a rich academic background in modern Turkish theological studies. As an undergraduate in Ankara, I was able to take a multitude of courses on Qur'an, *Tafsîr*, *Hadîth*, *Kalâm* (theology), *Fiqh* (jurisprudence), Islamic history, Islamic philosophy and *Tasawwuf* (spirituality), along with social sciences, history, and general philosophy courses. Divinity school helped me to develop a deeper understanding based on compassion and mercy, how to apply those teachings into my life, and how to teach other Muslims. Reading scholars from the East and from the West helped me understand the impact of religion on societies and vice versa. I benefited tremendously from the writings of Kurdish scholar Said Nursi, whose writing about the meaning of human life, faith in God, and living with Islamic values both at a social and individual level held great influence on me. Pakistani scholar Fazlur Rahman offered me a deep methodological understanding of the Qur'an and ways to practice its moral values in modern life. Alongside my studies, I served as an assistant imam to a local mosque. This was a great opportunity for me to practice my education and theology in a real-life setting and experience some level of ministry.

Nearing the end of my program, I applied for the U.S. green card lottery on a whim one day with a friend who had been trying unsuccessfully for several years. Quite to my surprise, my number was selected. I spoke barely any

English and everything that I thought I knew about America was acquired from watching movies. A former professor-turned-mentor connected me with the Turkish diaspora in Connecticut where he'd spent time as a visiting scholar at Hartford Seminary, and I set off. I worked in pizza delivery until I'd saved up enough to enroll in a community college ESL program and subsequently worked as a hospital security guard to put myself through Hartford Seminary's Islamic Chaplaincy Program. As in Turkey, while studying, I served as a volunteer in different mosques around Connecticut, leading prayers and teaching Qur'an. It was there that I heard about the work of chaplaincy for the first time from Dr. Ingrid Mattson and, eventually, I decided to extend my studies to include chaplaincy training.

I cannot emphasize enough how important my Hartford Seminary studies have been to my work—despite years of training as an imam. Classes like Pastoral Care and Counseling, Muslim Mental Health, and Addiction and Ministry in an Incarceration Setting were critical for me to understand what chaplaincy is and prepared me to serve in a role very different from that of an imam. Especially important was the interfaith and multicultural environment—until I arrived at Hartford Seminary, I'd never had Christian or Jewish friends. Engaging with professors and students outside my tradition forced me out of my comfort zone and required me to evaluate my stereotypes about other religions. I had to learn fundamentals that are important for my institutional chaplaincy work, which requires me to provide for people of all faiths as well as those who do not identify with one. The pastoral care and ministry courses helped me to learn the importance of deep listening, nonjudgmental presence, care, love, and empathy—especially those that required role-playing. A central part of my job now is providing death notifications to inmates when a loved one dies. As a staff chaplain, I provide these to inmates of all faiths. Additionally, I liaison with visiting clergy and volunteers from a multitude of faiths—I'm better prepared for having had those friendships and those classes.

The Clinical Pastoral Education (CPE) portion of training was also critical for me. In CPE, I encountered people asking the questions that people are often afraid to ask: Who am I? What is my purpose in this life? Why did this happen to me? Where is God in all this? As an imam, I'd been trained to give prepackaged answers to these questions. As a chaplain, I had to learn to sit with them in a place of empathy, often while those asking were facing trauma, isolation, despair, and suffering. The experiences I had were life-changing lessons that could not have come through books. While it was a process of learning about my own weaknesses, limitations, and triggers, CPE was also a process of growth and transformation in a spiritual sense. What could be a better way to serve my Creator and Lord than being present in the lives of His servants in distress?

While still a student, I began working as a chaplain with the Connecticut Department of Corrections, initially as a contract chaplain just serving Muslims before eventually advancing to a staff chaplaincy position where I was responsible to care for all inmates. After five years there, I transitioned to working as a staff chaplain with the Federal Bureau of Prisons in 2012. I have come to believe that working as a spiritual leader in prison, serving, educating, and providing pastoral support for the less fortunate segments of our society is an important task for me as a believer in my journey to serve God through serving humanity.

I faced significant challenges when I first became a chaplain, such as learning about prison culture, African American experiences, and how to navigate the prejudice of some prison staff. I have been learning about race and racism since my childhood. Born Kurdish in Turkey in the late 1970s, I grew up in an era when Kurdish culture was obscured and the language was prohibited from the public sphere. Since the emergence of the New Turkish Republic and throughout my childhood, Kurds were oppressed, discriminated against, arrested for speaking against the government, and treated as second-class citizens. While things were starting to open up when I immigrated, I was excited to go to the United States—a place I believed to be a land of hope, promise, and fair opportunity for all.

Working as a corrections chaplain, facing and confronting the cold reality of racism and systematic discrimination against people of color—especially African Americans—has been a critical part of my growth. My early years in the United States, I was isolated, living and working with other Turks. They, and American pop culture, were my cultural educators, and from them I learned racism—not what it was or how it operated, but the worst of the bias became ingrained in me. Without realizing it, I made generalizations that Black people were lazy, potential criminals and drug dealers, who might rob and kill for a few dollars, and that it wasn't safe to drive in their neighborhoods. Quite frankly, I was terrified by the idea of working behind bars due to my biased views. At the same time, I had wonderful interactions with African American classmates during graduate studies at Hartford Seminary that led me to examine my biases. Unlike my stereotypes, these individuals were extremely hardworking, intelligent, and kind. I am ashamed now looking back on how much this surprised me and how, initially, I saw my friends only as exceptions, but I am also grateful that God provided me this opportunity to begin questioning myself.

The majority of inmates who come to my services are African American and most converted to Islam while incarcerated. I knew that would be as such when I took the job, but I was arrogant in thinking that I was a better person and a better Muslim and that I, as a Turkish trained imam, was most capable of serving them because of all my training in the Islamic sciences. I was quite ignorant of the circumstances that brought them to prison—not their crimes, but the crimes of the society and the systematic racism it is imbued with. I could not reconcile the contrast I witnessed between my stereotypes and those I was now serving, who were kind and respectful toward me. Furthermore, I was disturbed to enter prisons in entirely white rural communities to find staff that were almost entirely white while inmates were overwhelmingly people of color. I was struggling with this dissonance until I read Michelle Alexander's *The New Jim Crow*.

This book provided me with important insights into how systematic racism has created deep disparity, especially with regard to drug laws in the 1980s and 1990s that disproportionately filled prisons with thousands of African Americans and created a booming prison industry. I slowly committed myself to learning about African American history and racism, and, importantly, examining my own biases. The Muslim Endorsement Council's support and mentorship in this regard has been tremendously helpful, widening my horizons to understand the complexity surrounding the realities of African Americans' experiences. The book lists, course suggestions, and conversations they've provided me have been invaluable. I believe it is critical for a chaplain, especially those of us who are immigrants or who did our studies overseas, to obtain endorsement from a professional endorsing body capable of evaluating candidates based on their education, experience, training, *and* cultural competency. An endorsement agency's ability to provide important feedback, recommendation, and guidance is critical.

I have come a long way, but I recognize that I have a long way to go and that the work of striving to be antiracist will be a lifelong journey. I consider this intentional and mindful seeking out and purging of racism an act of *tazkiyah* (purification of the heart), and the development of antiracism frameworks as one of striving toward *ihsân* (perfection of faith) for I believe that racism is a spiritual disease that separates me like a veil from knowing my Creator. Learning about the important roles that Black Muslims have played has been invaluable and enriched my love for the Prophet ﷺ, but learning the racism in American history has been equally important.

I continue to make mistakes that I strive to learn from. When the movie *Lincoln* came out, I watched it and thought it would be a great resource for the chapel library. I saw it as a great historical portrayal of the struggle African Americans had on the path to freedom and Lincoln's contributions. I was excitedly talking about the movie to one of the African American inmates a few days later, but I could tell from his expression that he did not share my enthusiasm. "Chaplain, you really don't know the history," he told me. "What he did was political rather than for the real freedom of my people. It did not change anything for Black people, they continued to be discriminated against, lynched, and treated as second-class citizens. We've never been seen as equals to white people in terms of freedom, equal opportunities, and pursuit of happiness." I was taken aback and really didn't fully understand what he was saying until I read Ibram Kendi's *Stamped from the Beginning*, which gave me a much more holistic understanding of Lincoln.

The institution at which I currently serve has a sizable immigrant Muslim inmate population. However, the majority of Muslim inmates are African Americans who mainly converted to Islam in prison. Sometimes, I encounter tensions between African American and immigrant brothers due to their stereotypes and prejudice toward one another. Some African American brothers, especially those who converted to Islam later in their lives, express judgment that immigrant Muslims are not true Muslims as their practices have been corrupted by their cultures of origin. Conversely, some of the immigrant Muslims judge the African American converts as ignorant and narrow-minded in their practice of Islam, dismissing their Muslim identity as one of a gang mentality rather than sincere faith. As the chaplain serving all of them, I've tried to use my own learning as a tool for helping them to see their humanity in each other.

In one occasion, during my last portion of *khutbah* (sermon), I asked Allah for help, guidance, and protection for the Muslim community around the globe, naming several situations that were particularly dire at the time. However, I failed to mention the suffering of African American communities, most notably with regard to police brutality. After completing the Jummah prayer, an elderly African American brother approached me and said, "What about the injustice here, Chaplain? You did not mention the suffering and pain of African American people here." It was late summer 2014, and national attention was focused on Ferguson, Missouri, where Michael Brown, an African American, had been killed by police.

I was caught off guard to have simply missed the real injustice in front of my eyes. Recognizing my failure, I responded, "You are right, brother, thank you for bringing this to my attention." In my next *khutbah* to the community, I shared this learning encounter and spoke about the importance of brotherhood and the danger of racism and injustice in our community, paying special attention to the implicit biases of immigrant Muslims toward African American communities. I held up the verse: "O you who believe! Be steadfast maintainers of justice, witnesses for God, though it be against yourselves, or your parents and kinsfolk, and whether it be someone rich or poor, for God is nearer unto both. So follow not your caprice, that you may act justly. If you distort or turn away, truly God is Aware of whatsoever you do."[1]

Even after a lifetime of education in Islamic sciences and studies, I continue to be surprised to learn how much was absent from my education when it comes to the presence and contributions of the dark-skinned companions of the Prophet ﷺ and the rich traditions of scholarship in sub-Saharan Africa. It seems that we, as an American Muslim community with all of our diversity, are finally tapping into this critical knowledge. I pray that my children will grow up with this fully integrated into their Islamic education—not just in our home but in our masjid and Sunday school, at the conferences and retreats we attend together, and the Islamic history books they read—and not just during Black History Month. This history is our collective Muslim history, and it needs to be woven back into the narratives that all of us learn. I feel there is still much for me to learn to truly be open-minded and nonjudgmental in my service as a chaplain. I pray that Allah will lift the obstacles to my self-education and place gracious people in my path who will enlighten me. *Âmîn.*

Note

1. al-Nisâ'/4:135.

Chaplains

A Voice for the Alienated

RYAN CARTER

I REMEMBER MY first experience with racism as if it were yesterday. I was five years old. I and a Sikh child were the only children of color in the class-room. I recall going to a group of kids who were playing with blocks and asked them if I could join. One kid responded, "No! White skin only." Bewildered, I looked to my palms and replied, "Look, I'm white like you." This event put a lot of things into perspective. Well into my adulthood, my mother told me that from a very young age I kept asking her, "Mommy, when am I going to be white?" She gave an almost nervous giggle when she shared that with me, and it made me realize how early I was socialized to see my skin as a deterrent for any sense of belonging.

Within the Qur'anic paradigm of societal relations is an unwavering empha-sis on justice and a commitment to equality:

> O you who believe! Be steadfast maintainers of justice, witnesses for God, though it be against yourselves, or your parents and kinsfolk, and whether it be someone rich or poor, for God is nearer unto both.[1]

Captain Ryan Carter is a chaplain in the Canadian Armed Forces, presently posted to the Canadian Forces Chaplain School and Centre where he trains incoming military chap-lains. He holds a BA in Criminology and Social Policy from the University of Ontario Institute of Technology, Canada, an MA in Middle Eastern Studies from Durham University, U.K., an MA in Islamic Studies and Christian-Muslim Relations from Hartford Seminary, and is a doctoral candidate in the history department of Queens University, Canada, where he studies race and ethnicity in medieval Muslim communities.

As chaplains we have traditionally operated within the public sphere as that neutral space between the human experience and structures of power. In the military context, where I myself operate, chaplains are both trusted advisors and advocates with the privilege to navigate between every level of the organization which is, in itself, our locus of power and influence. Acknowledging this power, it is my assertion that chaplains are the "prophetic voice" within the institution capable of being leaders in cultural change.

In order to achieve this, there must be an awareness regarding the power structures we function within, as well as an understanding of how systems of meaning permeate these structures. Racism and racial supremacy are among those systems of meaning that exist almost organically in the Western workplace. This, of course, is not new.

The cultural landscape changed significantly over 2020 following the traumatic killing of George Floyd, which proved a climactic event setting the world in motion discussing the very real reality of anti-Black racism. In the past, well-known Muslim figures have made pronouncements, with some level of immunity, which seemingly denied the reality of anti-Black racism in society. Muslim discourse absent of any real substantive societal engagement is laden with references to Bilal and other Black companions of the Prophet ﷺ as simplistic means of encouraging some sort of color blindness. Culturally homogeneous mosques were notorious for marginalizing Black Muslims in their community and, in many cases, espousing an unwritten code of racial supremacy. Exclusion, hurt, and trauma inflicted on Black Muslims are no longer a reality possible to ignore but something that the community must contend with. As a vocation that deals with the human condition, chaplains have a key role to play in combating this pernicious form of discrimination in institutions where we serve, the masjids where we worship, and the *ummah* that we are a part of.

Identifying the Problem

In a powerful pronouncement, the Qur'an declares in the context of the rising hostilities and oppression by the Quraysh and their confederates on the nascent Muslim community that "*Fitnah* is worse than killing."[2] *Fitnah* is a term that could be defined broadly as strife and tribulation resulting from any number of human ills, such as oppression. Oppression in this context was far more than just physical threat; with this revolutionary system of belief and practice came the eradication of a deeply entrenched social stratification.

It has long been identified that health and well-being are not determined solely by individual choices and genetics but also by social determinants. In the Canadian context, racism has been identified as an important driver for inequitable health outcomes, especially for Black and indigenous Canadians. This was well demonstrated in a recent government report which noted that:[3]

> Black Canadians experience health and social inequities linked to processes of discrimination at multiple levels of society, including individual, interpersonal, institutional, and societal discrimination. Experiences of interpersonal racism can be overt (e.g., harassment, violent attacks), or subtle and pervasive in the form of daily indignities.

We often fail to take into account the magnitude of racism's impact, in part a by-product of the individualization of our culture which leads us to see "things" (including people's behavior) in isolation of larger social phenomena. The concept of social determinants highlights the importance of addressing the larger system rather than the focus on the individual, which is remedied by working on internal responses to undesirable circumstances. With this in mind, we should consider limiting the questioning of "What is wrong *with* you?" to the more broad question of "What has *happened to* you?"

Policies may be rooted in equity; however, workplace culture could be permissive of discriminatory or exclusionary behaviors and practices that do not directly contravene those policies. This may seem counterintuitive, but racism in the modern workplace is seldom overt and requires us as chaplains to refocus our observations on the less obvious. The more subtle forms of racism have been labeled modern racism,[4] symbolic racism,[5] aversive racism,[6] and democratic racism.[7] The similarity in all these studies is that racism is most often disguised, often occurring in the form of microaggressions, and in this sense, presents a challenge to recognize.[8]

Research studies, well documented in a 2009 meta-analysis conducted by Pascoe and Smart Richman,[9] provide a comprehensive account of the negative impact of perceived discrimination on both mental and physical health outcomes, including consequences such as depression and anxiety.[10] Because microaggressions are typically stated by a well-intentioned person in a covert fashion, the subject lives with these repeat occurrences and is frequently at odds with how to react and cope with a social environment veiled in hostility.[11]

Research by Richman and Jonassaint has highlighted that these racial stressors result in alterations in physiological processes and adrenocortical responses.[12] When we start to worry about something, our bodies initiate a biological stress response, which is in most circumstances a valuable biological phenomenon that dissipates after the threat is gone. The harm, however, is when this process is initiated too frequently. As the study clearly indicates, repeat cortisol hyperactivity is subsequently related to several long-term stress conditions, noted above. Part of the problem is that it is far easier to respond to an incident of overt discrimination, but when it is covert, even when sustained over a long period, many chaplains and therapists alike resist labeling this as trauma or traumatic.

Unless we see something clearly overt, there is a tendency to not see the broader picture and focus more on providing the individual with coping skills, spiritual practices, or referrals to mental health, where they are placed along the spectrum of depression, anxiety, or some other psychological disorders. In some sense, what this does is place the reasons for someone's illness or decreased well-being in internal reasons—in other words, "something is wrong *with* you" not "something has *happened to* you." Keven Nadal coined the term "microaggressive trauma" to address this issue.[13] To better understand this phenomenon, I provide four examples with the intention of helping chaplains recognize how racism and discrimination function in the workplace.

a) 2nd Lt. Taylor, a Muslim of African Canadian descent, is new to the unit. To meet other officers and feel part of the brigade, she attends a weekly officers' coffee hour where a variety of hot foods are served. She observes that all the food offerings regularly include meat and requests a vegetarian alternative be provided for herself and her colleagues who do not eat meat. She is told that there aren't enough vegetarians to justify a vegetarian option and, furthermore, specialized kitchen facilities are required to provide such an option. She is directed to eat the cut vegetables and fruit. After repeated failed requests, she stops attending the coffee hour.

Possible intent of mess manager: Due to the absence of specialized facilities, certain diets cannot be facilitated with certainty. At least some vegetarian options exist; the member will have to consider these as this request is potentially an undue burden on the institution.

Message as perceived by 2nd Lt. Taylor: When I have needs that differ from the majority, I am treated like a second-class citizen who must accept whatever is offered. My nourishment is not as important as that of my colleagues.

b) Cpl. Nelson, a Black Canadian, attends a brigade dinner. At the dinner, a chief warrant officer approaches Cpl. Nelson in a crowd of his colleagues and asks him where he is from. Cpl. Nelson politely responds that he is from Toronto. The CWO proceeds to relate how he had a "really good Black friend" at the unit way back, reminiscing, "Jonny was awesome, the fastest runner in the unit, fit right in!"

Possible intent of the CWO: I want to connect with him through sharing a story which he may resonate with. I want him to know I have good experiences with other Black people.

Message as perceived by Cpl. Nelson: Everyone asking where I'm from makes me feel like I'm perpetually an outsider, like they assume I'm foreign first and Canadian second. When I provide an image that is different from what they think I am, I feel like I have let them down. Moreover, when I am told of other "good" Black people, I am being told that as long as I mimic white respectability, I can fit into society.

c) Pvt. Warsame arrives at his new posting and asks the unit chaplain where he can perform his prayers. He is directed to a base multifaith space but finds it has become a storage area for various religious icons and old kitchen supplies. Sharing this with the chaplain, he receives an apology and assurance it will not happen again, explaining that nobody used the space before so people began storing their supplies in there. After a week of finding the supplies each time he attempts to pray, he gives up.

Possible intent of the unit chaplain: My apology should suffice to demonstrate that I did not intend to offend him by having his sacred space defiled. Because I'm not Muslim, I did not know the exact needs of the member.

Message as perceived by Pvt. Warsame: My faith is not respected. I am being told that the reason why the space is used as storage is not the fault of the management but the fault of the other non-Christians who don't use the space enough to justify keeping it in a dignified state. Maybe they don't use it because it's a storage room.

d) Capt. Muhammad is a highly educated intelligence officer from Toronto. Although she never noted her ethnic origin in any conversation, a colonel remarks how much of an asset she will be should there be a deployment to Mali since she must have a good understanding of the language and culture. She is not from Mali and has no familial connection there.

Possible intent of the colonel: Linguistic ability is an important asset to the military. I'm giving words of encouragement that opportunities are on the horizon for her.

Message as perceived by Capt. Muhammad: The assumption is that all people with black skin must be the same. I am not being complimented on my acquired skills but on my visible difference. This doesn't happen to white intelligence officers. He is not invested in his unit's Black members enough to know us as individuals; we are interchangeable and therefore disposable.

The commonality in all these scenarios is that they appear as small random events, not indicative of any "real" problem. However, in all these scenarios, people are alienated by their experience. Questions arise about the authenticity of the event: if it should be addressed or if it was just a well-meaning misunderstanding. More distressing are the doubts that arise when Black members express their discomfort about situations. Rank plays an important part, compromising the subject's ability to address the microaggression on the spot. Rarely is it the first time such a slight has occurred, but if something is addressed—even casually—invalidation often occurs with the charge that they are "too sensitive" or "playing the race card." Passive-aggressive comments such as "we have become so politically correct these days," or victim-blaming statements such as "you are coming across as too confrontational" operate to invalidate a person's legitimate right to address aggressions. The feeling of alienation occurs when these types of scenarios become commonplace to the extent that events no longer become random but deliberate (perceived or not) covert discrimination attempts.

Creating Critical Safe Spaces

The locus of power for chaplains lies in the trust we are accorded by those we serve. Trust is not simply a matter of confidentiality but an experience of safety where a person can trust that they can reveal their suffering and receive validation, thus creating a critical safe space. Not a physical space per se, but a moment where suffering can dissipate through an acknowledgment and acceptance of another's experience. The truth of the matter is that for this to happen, you must start with *you*. It requires all the might of our will to critically look at our own identity: the uniqueness, the intersections, and moreover how this identity may impact our interactions with others. Tests for implicit bias (sometimes called unconscious bias), widely available on the Internet, have frequently shown that we all carry unconscious preferences on the basis of such things as gender and race. These often operate unconsciously, yet significantly impact our engagement with the world. Taking these tests can help chaplains develop their awareness about their own bias.

One of the greatest insights I have gleaned from my own experiences is that therapists, chaplains, and social workers have an issue *listening* when it comes to racism. There is a cognitive response to hearing suffering—we are good at providing coping strategies, being unconditional listeners, and so on, yet when the suffering implicates a whole system or a dominant demographic there is a dissonance which I suspect is generated from fear.

For minorities themselves, it may evoke their unprocessed experiences; some may take the disclosure as an indictment of their own race, making them defensive. For most, however, I suspect they know something requiring a far greater intervention is occurring—which creates fear for both parties.

A Way Forward

There is a common adage in the military: if you are going to suggest something, be prepared to have a plan ready to make it happen. Chaplains need to be critical about what the institution is doing to support its members. This is not a stance of protest but rather bringing to the forefront an issue that requires attention in which you are prepared to help find a solution. To cite an example, in 2020, I co-initiated with the local diversity advisory group an event called "Talking About Race" where people of diverse backgrounds got together to discuss their experiences of race in the workplace. It was intended to be real talk where people with similar experiences were able to engage in a facilitated discussion. The initiative has since garnered considerable support and recognition. Supportive conversations are a powerful way to build solidarity and a sense of community, and enabling this gathering provided an opportunity for a critical safe space. Moreover, it was a source of training for senior leadership and policy makers to hear the experience of Black, indigenous, and people of color.

Rage as Self-Care

Antiracism is a difficult project, especially for Black chaplains, because at the root you are appealing to others to listen to *your* experience, which is a tiring endeavor. My personal source of self-care has been to locate informal networks for support and moreover find a mentor who could help situate my feelings of injustice and rage, which can become paralyzing emotions. I'm inspired by the fact that the Prophet ﷺ himself during his final pilgrimage pronounced a revolutionary concept: "There is no superiority for an Arab over a non-Arab, nor for a non-Arab over an Arab. Neither is the white superior over the black nor the black superior over the white—except by piety." The Prophet *named* a social ill in society and, by doing so, he made it real for us. He expressed, in my mind, rage toward this perpetual societal injustice. We tend to see rage as harmful, and indeed it can be. However, in my experience, guided rage is the essential component for building resiliency in the face of voicelessness and repeat trauma.[14] To have rage means you have been hurt. Instead of pacifying the feeling of rage, we need to channel that rage in positive and constructive ways. Regardless of our positionality, as chaplains, *we need rage*: we need to feel rage about injustice and channel that toward real individual and systemic healing. That is our prophetic call.

Notes

1. al-Nisâ'/4:135.

2. al-Baqarah/2:191.

3. "Social Determinants and Inequities in Health for Black Canadians: A Snapshot," 2020, https://www.canada.ca/en/public-health/services/health-promotion/population-health/what-determines-health/social-determinants-inequities-black-canadians-snapshot.html.

4. J. B. McConahay, "Modern Racism, Ambivalence, and the Modern Racism Scale," in *Prejudice, Discrimination, and Racism*, ed. J. F. Dovidio and S. L. Gaertner (Academic Press, 1986), 91–125.

5. D. O. Sears, "Symbolic Racism," in *Eliminating Racism: Perspectives in Social Psychology*, ed. P. A. Katz and D. A. Taylor (Springer, 1988).

6. S. L. Gaertner and J. F. Dovidio, "The Aversive Form of Racism," in *Prejudice, Discrimination, and Racism*, ed. J. F. Dovidio and S. L. Gaertner (Academic Press, 1986), 61–89.

7. F. Henry and C. Tator, "The Ideology of Racism: 'Democratic Racism,'" *Canadian Ethnic Studies* 26, no. 2 (1994): 1–14.

8. Derald Wing Sue defines microaggression as "The everyday verbal, nonverbal, and environmental slights, snubs, or insults, whether intentional or unintentional, which communicate hostile, derogatory, or negative messages to target persons based solely upon their marginalized group membership. In many cases, these hidden messages may invalidate the group identity or experiential reality of target persons, demean them on a personal or group level, communicate they are lesser human beings, suggest they do not belong with the majority group, threaten and intimidate, or relegate them to inferior status and treatment." Sue, *Race Talk and the Conspiracy of Silence: Understanding and Facilitating Difficult Dialogues on Race* (Wiley, 2015).

9. E. A. Pascoe and L. Smart Richman, "Perceived Discrimination and Health: A Meta-analytic Review," *Psychological Bulletin* 135, no. 4 (2009): 531–554.

10. D. R. Williams, H. W. Neighbors, and J. S. Jackson, "Racial/Ethnic Discrimination and Health: Findings from Community Studies," *American Journal of Public Health* 93, no. 2 (2003): 200–208.

11. Derald Wing Sue, "Microaggressions: More Than Just Race," *Psychology Today*, November 17, 2010, https://www.psychologytoday.com/us/blog/micro aggressions-in-everyday-life/201011/microaggressions-more-just-race.

12. Laura Smart Richman and Charles Jonassaint, "The Effects of Race-Related Stress on Cortisol Reactivity in the Laboratory: Implications of the Duke Lacrosse Scandal," *Annals of Behavioral Medicine* 35, no. 1 (February 2008): 105–110.

13. "The excessive and continuous exposure to subtle discrimination (both interpersonal and systemic) and the subsequent symptoms that develop or persist as a result. Although not all microaggressions are life threatening, they can certainly be pervasive and compromise one's sense of psychological and emotional safety, resulting in typical symptoms associated with trauma." K. L. Nadal, *Microaggressions and Traumatic Stress: Theory, Research, and Clinical Treatment* (American Psychological Association, 2018), 13.

14. Kenneth V. Hardy, "Healing the Hidden Wounds of Racial Trauma," *Reclaiming Children and Youth* 22, no. 1 (Spring 2013): 24–28.

Islamic Chaplaincy and Black Muslim College Students

NISA MUHAMMAD

THE MUSLIM STUDENTS Association executive board at a large, East Coast, predominantly white institution (PWI) received this 2020 petition from a group of disgruntled Muslim student members of the Muslim Students Association (MSA):[1]

To the Muslim Students Association,

Oh ye who believe! Stand out firmly for justice, as witnesses to Allah, even as against yourselves, or your parents, or your kin, and whether it be (against) rich or poor: for Allah can best protect both. (Qur'an, Surah An-Nisa 4:135)

"One ummah," "apolitical," "only a religious organization"—these are some of the many excuses our Muslim Students Association (MSA), and more broadly, many of our Muslim American communities, have used time and time again to stifle the voices of the marginalized. Our communities reek of anti-Blackness and unapologetic support of heteropatriarchy. Why do we constantly see claims to the

---

Dr. Nisa Muhammad is the assistant dean for religious life at Howard University. She is a graduate of Hartford Seminary's Islamic Chaplaincy Program, has completed a unit of Clinical Pastoral Education (CPE) through the Jewish Theological Seminary, and holds a DMin from Howard University Divinity School. She is the president of the Association of Muslim Chaplains and is on the executive board of the Association for Chaplaincy and Spiritual Life in Higher Education. Nisa is a wife and mother of five. She loves reading, swimming, and hanging out with friends.

---

blessed history of the life of the Holy Prophet Muhammad (Peace Be Upon Him), but both a passive and active refusal to follow in his role as a radical activist fighting for justice? Our own Muslim Students Association at this university reflects and further perpetuates the issues of many of our larger Muslim American communities, and we are tired of it.

The Black Muslims writing were tired of attending MSA programs and activities that reflected South Asian or Middle Eastern hegemony. According to the Black Muslim students I interviewed on various PWIs across the country, many felt the MSA to be a racialized organization where they often do not fit in. Many also felt their race came before their religion in the eyes of others, resulting in feeling invisible despite being the foundation for Islam in the United States, with roots that go back centuries.[2] When immigrants believe Black Muslims aren't "true" Muslims, it allows them to legitimize anti-Black racism[3] and effectively render Black Muslims invisible—both to immigrant faith communities and broader society. Consequently, Black Muslims must interpret everything through the lens and prism of the real and imagined expectations of immigrant and overseas possessors of "true Islam."[4] Yet Black people (not including those of Hispanic descent or mixed-race) make up twenty percent of the country's overall Muslim population.[5] This essay examines the challenges of being Black and Muslim on PWIs, being members of the MSA, and scrutinizes the questions of why some Black Muslim students (BMS) decide to leave the MSA to start different organizations, and how Muslim chaplains impacted students' lives with pastoral care and guidance. Being a Black Muslim within American Muslim communities means learning to navigate the precarious intersection of two marginalized groups, simultaneously fighting for respect from their Muslim peers and safety within a national system of violence. For many BMS, the fight becomes exhausting and unbearable; leaving the MSA and starting another organization that is culturally sensitive to their needs becomes the solution. The bridge to a safe haven for many Black Muslims is the Muslim chaplain on campus who unlocks the door to a peaceful transition to another way of life.

I got interested in this research when BMS would visit our MSA events from universities at Howard University, where I serve as a chaplain and assistant dean for religious life. Howard is a sacred space where it is empowering to be a Black Muslim. Everything is done to reinforce who you are, from Jummah speakers and event food to cultural, social, and spiritual events. In my conversations with the Black Muslim students from PWIs, I learned of their marginalization, feelings of isolation, and loneliness within their MSA. This intrigued me; I wanted to know more. In 2015, Howard hosted the Historically Black Colleges and Universities (HBCUs) MSA Conference for Black Muslim students from around the country. BMS from PWIs who attended spoke to me about their experiences at their institutions. The problems were severe and egregious. Students felt unwanted in the religious spaces, which they felt also belonged to them. They felt they were required to stand and deliver responses to a litany of questions at any given time, such as, "Are you in the Nation? Are you in the Imam's community? Do you know your prayers? Are you a convert?" It was an undressing that made the students feel uneasy and uncomfortable, especially the African students who have centuries of Islam in their lineage. After the conference, several students were empowered enough to return to NYU and start the Black Muslim Initiative, a campus group specific to BMS.

In 2020, I helped a group organize the first Black Muslim Students Conference that brought together BMS from HBCUs and PWIs. The conference featured a range of speakers that the students selected and were enthused to hear. It was the first opportunity for Black Muslim students from around the country to come together and share their needs and concerns regardless of the type of institution they attend. They were just Black Muslim students who could relate on so many levels. The students committed to return to their campuses and work to uphold the mantra that Black Muslim Lives Matter. They plan to have yearly conferences to celebrate their accomplishments. The conference drove home to me the importance of my research in this area, begun as part of my Doctorate of Ministry, which continues. I'm intrigued by the microaggressive language of oppression used to intimidate, hurt, and harm Black Muslim students and curious where young Muslims learn this. Further, I'm intrigued by how college spaces are microcosms of the larger spaces of masjid life off campus. Today's campus leaders are tomorrow's Islamic center's board members.

There is scarce research on BMS and anti-Black racism in Islam in most of the studies about Muslim college students. However, some important things are known: BMS face intrareligious racism on campus from Muslim students, faculty, and staff.[6] They report being excluded from Muslim student organizations and facing pressures to choose between "being Muslim or being Black."[7] Additionally, they face a double jeopardy in being racialized as Black and Muslim.[8] As a result, Black Muslim students find solace in other Black student organizations on campus that become safe havens where students can feel comfortable with their Blackness but often not their faith.[9]

Based on my observations, in addition to NYU's above-mentioned Black Muslim Initiative, which was established to speak on the duality of being Black and Muslim, increasing numbers of BMS at PWIs are leaving the MSA to start culturally sensitive Islamic organizations. The University of Pennsylvania's Black Muslim Student Organization, Penn Sapelo, is dedicated to fostering dialogue, creating community, and engaging in service around the Black Muslim experience on campus and the broader community. Columbia University's Muslim Afro Niyyah Students Association (MANSA) provides a space on campus and the surrounding community for Muslims of the African diaspora. Muslim chaplains have played important roles on each of these campuses.

These are not the first BMS to do this. In 1976, the students at Howard University created a campus Muslim organization to provide Jummah prayer service. They officially formed in 1977 as the Muslim Students of Howard University and explicitly decided not to be a local branch of the MSA. They wanted to be independent, celebrate their identity, and voice concerns about racism in the MSA. Students were influenced by the Islamic Party of North America (IPNA), which Yusuf Muzaffaruddin Hamid had founded near Howard's campus in 1971[10] in response to the lack of immigrant organizations providing *daʿwah* (missionary activity) to the Black community. He was equally dismayed by the MSA National and the organizations that had grown out of it, all of which centered immigrant-Muslim experiences and needs to the exclusion of Black Muslims.[11] Hamid was encouraged by Malcolm X's last interview before his assassination in which he said, "Much to my dismay, until now, the Muslim world has seemed to ignore the problem of the Black American, and most Muslims who come here from the Muslim world have concentrated more effort in trying to convert white Americans than Black Americans."[12] The Islamic Party was active on the Howard campus, with many alumni assuming leadership positions, and members often traveled to MSA conventions and challenged their leadership to involve more African Americans in their organization, especially in decision-making positions.[13]

In addition to BMS-specific groups, on some campuses the Muslim student organizations are purposely not called MSAs to avoid that history. For example, DePaul University has UMMA. "UMMA is a spiritual, social and service-oriented student organization working to raise awareness about the multifaceted and rich heritage of Islam in the DePaul and broader Chicago communities," explains DePaul's Ch. Abdul-Malik Ryan. "In addition to being an acronym for the group, '*ummah*' is an Arabic word meaning 'community,' which we use as the basis of our organization." That language makes all students feel welcome and wanted, absent the exclusionary history of the MSA.

The next paragraph of the disgruntled students' petition at the beginning of this essay reads:[14]

> Muslim spaces in America, whether they're displayed in the media or reflected in the homogenous makeup of our Muslim Students Association's executive councils is dominated by South Asian and Arab Sunni Muslims. These groups, although also marginalized in the larger American context, conform to white supremacy when they oppress marginalized subgroups in our communities.

These feelings were echoed by the BMS I interviewed on one campus who described how the MSA's events had only catered to South Asian and Arab students. They explained to me how from the music played to the food served to students speaking other languages at social events, the Black Muslim students felt unwanted and unwelcomed. They also shared that when they decided to host their own events that included discussions that challenged white supremacist thoughts and white privilege expressed by other students, they were often verbally attacked. Furthermore, the other Muslim students in the audience failed to come to the BMS's defense, creating a sense that they cosigned with the attackers.

The BMS reached a point where they didn't want to be involved with the MSA anymore and took their problems to the Muslim chaplain. The chaplain provided a safe space for the students to vent and share their frustrations. According to the students who spoke to me, the chaplain "heard us and understood what we were going through," without minimizing what they were experiencing. The students reported:

> He asked us, "How do you feel about the Muslim community?" and we could express our frustration about the lack of representation and involvement. Having him gave us the space to have weekly discussions about what we are thinking, how we felt, and what we want to see. It was beneficial for getting the ball rolling on starting our organization. We talked about building community and what it takes to do that. Could we build a community within the current structure of the MSA? Our chaplain was necessary for that discussion.
>
> Just knowing that he's someone we can go to, he created an environment with open communication between the MSA leadership and us, which I appreciate. I feel like he gave us not only the physical space we needed but also the Islamic advice and perspective of someone who's an adult, looking inwards. He showed us how to leave the MSA but still leave the door open if we wanted to do any joint events.[15]

Before the start of their new organization, there were only five to ten Black Muslims involved in the MSA. Since the start of their new organization, they have close to forty members.

On another campus, in addition to a Muslim chaplain who has made students feel welcome and wanted, one student told me that the Black Muslims on this campus have a strong relationship with the other Black organizations on campus and the Black community near campus, including support from the nearest masjid with a Black imam who often does programs for them. The student I interviewed said, "It was important for the MSA members who are Black and Muslim to see that the MSA leadership was putting in the effort to make sure that their voices were not being undermined or diminished within our MSA. Over the summer of 2020 with the Black Lives Matter movement that was significant."[16]

Beyond listening and supporting students to create their own spaces, there are other important ways that chaplains can support BMS. Establish relationships with Black Muslim leaders in your local community, invite them to speak—to all of your students—along with nationally recognized Black Muslim scholars, academics, activists, and artists. Check in with student leaders to encourage that events (topics, food, music, traditions, etc.) not consistently be themed around one ethnicity. Educate yourself so as to incorporate teachings about the Black companions into your teaching activities with students. Notice who comes to events but also who doesn't—if you've got BMS not attending, reach out and check in, find out if there are things about the programming that are driving them away. Make sure that you educate yourself about the history of race and racism in America and within the American Muslim community. Chaplains can help lead students but only if they are equipped to do it themselves.

———

I stumbled into chaplaincy. Hartford Seminary offered a certificate program in Imam and Community Leadership that Dr. Jimmy Jones spoke about during a leadership training course he was teaching. I inquired about the program and was accepted, and was subsequently encouraged to pursue their Islamic Chaplaincy Program. I was dedicated and loved the classes, finishing the normal three-year program in two. My field placement was as Howard University's Muslim chaplain, a position that had been vacant for twelve years. It was love at first sight. That internship allowed me to grow in myriad ways. I did my CPE at the Jewish Theological Seminary, which gave me such an interfaith grounding as we shared our struggles, our highs, and our lows among classmates from other faiths. Our verbatims were instructive and deepened our understanding as we explored our feelings brought up by our work. By the time I was hired in 2017, I had just graduated and was ready to start as the new assistant dean for religious life.

As a Black Muslim woman, I already knew that being a Black Muslim within American Muslim communities means learning to navigate the precarious intersection of two marginalized groups, simultaneously fighting for respect from Muslim peers and safety within a national system of violence. My research has allowed me to better understand how this operates and see the ways the fight becomes exhausting and unbearable for many BMS, for whom leaving the MSA and starting another organization that is culturally sensitive to their needs becomes the solution. It has also given me confidence and authority to speak on topics related to racism within the Muslim community without being so easily dismissed.

Muslim chaplains have to see the need to focus on becoming antiracist individually and collectively. This issue needs to be taught and discussed in chaplaincy classes and curriculums. How to make Black Muslim students feel welcome and wanted on each and every campus has to be taught. The fact that they don't feel welcome and wanted on PWI should be disconcerting for chaplains and make them seek refuge in Allah for guidance and direction. White supremacy and its imposed racial hierarchy have no place in Islam. The Arab and South Asian hegemony must cease and desist. It's disastrous in so many ways both to the recipient and to the one imposing it. Chaplains must recognize these problems and acknowledge their lack of awareness. Black Muslim lives matter. I repeat, Black Muslim lives matter. Chaplains need to rise to the occasion that the Qur'an calls us "to stand firmly for justice as witnesses to Allah."[17] May Allah guide us to the light of understanding. *Âmîn.*

Notes

1. MSA Student Petition, 2020.

2. Muna Mire, "Towards a Black Muslim Ontology of Resistance," *New Inquiry*, April 29, 2015, https://thenewinquiry.com/towards-a-black-muslim-ontology-of-resistance/.

3. Mire, "Towards a Black Muslim Ontology of Resistance."

4. Sherman Jackson, *Islam and the Blackamerican: Looking Toward the Third Resurrection* (Oxford University Press, 2005), loc. 172–173, Kindle.

5. Besheer Mohamed and Jeff Diamant, "Black Muslims Account for a Fifth of All U.S. Muslims, and About Half Are Converts to Islam," Pew Research Center,

January 17, 2019, https://www.pewresearch.org/fact-tank/2019/01/17/black-muslims -account-for-a-fifth-of-all-u-s-muslims-and-about-half-are-converts-to-islam/.

6. Zeba Khan, "American Muslims Have a Race Problem," *Al Jazeera America,* June 16, 2015, http://america.aljazeera.com/opinions/2015/6/american-muslims -have-a-race-problem.html.

7. Aneesa Baboolal, "Diversity and Inclusion: An Intersectional Analysis of the Experiences of Muslim Students After the 2019 Presidential Election—ProQuest," Ph.D. diss., University of Delaware, 2019.

8. Omar Etman, "For Black Muslim Students, a Two-Pronged Fight for Solidarity," *PBS NewsHour,* August 13, 2016, https://www.pbs.org/newshour /nation/black-muslim-college-students-issue-call-allies.

9. Keon McGuire, Saskias Casanova, and Charles Davis, "'I'm a Black Female Who Happens to Be Muslim': Multiple Marginalities of an Immigrant Black Muslim Woman on a Predominantly White Campus," *Journal of Negro Education* 85, no. 3 (2016): 316–329.

10. Muhammed A. al-Ahari, *Taking Islam to the Street: The Da'wah of the Islamic Party of North America* (Lulu Press, 2013).

11. MSA National was founded in 1963 at the University of Illinois at Urbana-Champaign (UIUC) predominantly by South Asian and Middle Eastern visiting students. The Islamic Circle of North America (ICNA), Islamic Medical Association of North America (IMANA), and later the Islamic Society of North America are a few of the organizations that grew out of it. Altaf Husain, "MSA: For 50 Years, 'Students' Has Been Its Middle Name," *Huffington Post,* January 2, 2013, https:// www.icna.org/msa-for-50-years-students-has-been-its-middle-name/.

12. Yvonne Yazbeck Haddad and Jane I. Smith, eds., *Muslim Minorities in the West* (AltaMira, 2002).

13. al-Ahari, *Taking Islam to the Street.*

14. MSA Student Petition, 2020.

15. Samimah Miller, 2020 interview with Nisa Muhammad.

16. Hanif Muhammad, 2020 interview with Nisa Muhammad.

17. al-Nisâ'/4:135.

And Then We Were One Before The One

TAQWA SURAPATI

FOR MORE THAN FIFTEEN YEARS, I have volunteered and worked in the healthcare setting, using a language that is not my mother tongue to discuss sensitive matters of life and death, mostly with individuals outside of my faith, in a country that wages wars with people who practice religion like me. The potential for mistrust and miscommunication is huge. Before each knock, right after I wash my hands or rub antiseptic gel on them, I focus my mind and heart with a ready supplication on my lips: "*Rabbi shrah lî sadrî, wa-yassir lî amrî, wa-hlul 'uqdatan min lisânî, yafqahû qawlî*—My Lord! Expand for me my breast! Make my affair easy for me, and untie a knot from my tongue, that they may understand my speech."[1] I believe in the One God who answers the prayer of anybody who calls on Him, and I strive to serve all people authentically and consistently. All the stories below capture sacred moments I shared with

---

Taqwa Surapati served as a spiritual care volunteer for nine years before she relented to her calling and enrolled in Clinical Pastoral Education (CPE). Ultimately, she completed five units, Hartford Seminary's graduate certificate in Islamic Chaplaincy, and completed her MA in Theology and Religious Studies with a concentration in Islamic Studies from the Graduate Theological Union. Taqwa is a member of the Association of Muslim Chaplains and previously served as a member of the Community Advisory Board for Bay Area Muslim Mental Health. She is an oncology, blood marrow transplant, and hematology chaplain in Northern California. Taqwa is married to a wonderful, supportive husband of twenty-seven years; together, they care for and love their two adult sons, one daughter-in-law, seven chickens, and a cat. Taqwa often dreams of visiting her family in her native Indonesia.

---

strangers who became friends and care recipients of my spirituality. These moments made me feel that even though careseekers and I came from different backgrounds and faiths with varying degrees of spirituality, we were one in front of God, experiencing the fullness of *tawhîd* (divine unity). May it be so. May He accept. *Âmîn.*

> *That is God, your Lord; there is no god but He,*
> *Creator of all things. So worship Him.*[2]

The room was dark, but my eyes adjusted quickly to make out the silhouette of the patient lying in bed. Rays of late afternoon sunshine peeked in through curtains not entirely closed. "Ms. Lysa?" I retain the old tradition of prefacing women's names with "Ms." I like how it sounds; to me, it conveys politeness and respect. In my Indonesian culture of origin, we never use only a person's name, it is always prefaced with an honorific term, and a similar practice is found in many Muslim cultures. The figure in the bed stirred at the sound of my voice and gave permission for me to proceed. She's white, in her early thirties, and a mother of three small children, the youngest being only eighteen months old. The hospital room walls were decorated with her children's drawings, notes, and other get-well wishes. This was only her first few days at the hospital, but she would require weeks of inpatient treatment.

"I don't want to die. I will fight for my children. My baby, she's so young." She pulled the furry pink blanket she'd brought from home closer to her chest. We talked about family, how the baby had to fight her own medical condition after birth for months at the hospital before being allowed to go home. "If she can do it, I can do it. She's shown me how." We talked about God. "I was never brought up with religion. I consider myself a Christian. I don't know how to talk to God," she shared. We agreed that God is the Creator, that God is loving and kind, that God listens and knows her heart and its wishes to get healed. Lysa seemed to gain energy in talking about this—how to connect with God—demonstrated through her smiles and nods. I concluded the visit with a prayer for God to continue healing for her, to support her, to protect her children, "the jewels of her heart." Lysa smiled broadly after the prayer, saying she liked the expressions, calling her children the jewels of her heart.

It has progressed. Despite the transplant and all the medications and treatments, there is always a risk of complication to the process. Her body was continuously weakening, her skin developed rashes, her gut could not process anything and was endlessly giving her diarrhea. The medical team talked about her in discharged rounds, how worried they were about her condition. During one of her good days, I visited her again. This time, she was more solemn as she told me that she was thinking of death. Lysa questioned God's wisdom in allowing her to deliver a daughter who was able to get better, only to take that baby's mother. I explored and asked questions of her beliefs: what does she believe about suffering, about trusting a loving God when all else seems dark? She cried quietly, expressing grief when considering that her time was shorter than she would like it to be. I stayed by her side, steady in accompanying her tears with a few of my own.

After a while, she wiped her eyes, blew her nose, and asked me with more curiosity than bitterness or anger, "Please tell me what your religion says about this." I was surprised; I am aware of the professional boundary of not prose-lytizing. But Lysa was persistent. I clarified her wishes, and she confirmed them. I made it clear to her that I was *not* trying to change her faith. I felt a bit awkward and fussy saying all that, but Lysa just nodded and smiled, looking at me. I began with the big picture, that God created us all, that the prophets were sent to remind humankind of the One God, that God loves us so much, and that life is a journey: a test for the believers, an opportunity to get closer to Him when times are tough. I tried to convey this simply, with short sentences, in a comforting voice and not in a rushed state. I felt so much pride in the teachings of Islam that I uphold to be true, yet so much humility knowing how special it was to share this with her. Every now and then she murmured, "That makes sense." We pause along the way, allowing her to ponder or ask questions. We smile at each other. I leave her after we pray that God would give her strength and courage whatever lies in the road ahead.

I cared for Lysa until she died, about two weeks after that conversation, the longest that we had. She went to the ICU, was intubated, and required a dialy-sis machine. While she lay there unconscious, I supported her mother: I heard more about Lysa's childhood, her loving and strong-willed character, her mother's struggle to provide a living. I also heard Lysa's husband's rough expressions born out of the fear and anger of losing her. "I tell yah, yah better wake up and come home. I don't know what I'll do with them kids at home." After some grueling time in the ICU, she passed away.

It was the first time that I conveyed Islamic teachings explicitly to a criti-cally ill patient as they considered their death; I gained clarity and confidence from this experience. My intention is always to care wholly for patients and to walk alongside them. When lucid patients insist on wanting to learn more about Islam and declare it clearly to me, I will tell them about it, but I will not do so without first meticulously delivering pastoral care needed at the moment.

To accomplish this, I conduct a spiritual assessment, which is an approach chaplains are trained in that can take several different research-backed forms, but that all ultimately help chaplains evaluate the needs and resources a patient has through observation and inquiry.[3] By asking about and honoring what the patient believes in, exploring their spiritual pain and distress, facilitating their emotions and working through them, a chaplain begins to recognize the tools the patient has as well as the struggles they need to address.

There is wisdom in this assessment process, and thus I will continuously practice it as a professional chaplain. Doing otherwise might harm patients by violating their trust, abusing my authority and power notably in a time of vulnerability, overstepping my duty and role as a professional chaplain, and disrupting my chance to continue to work as a chaplain, which I love and thrive at. A healthcare chaplain cannot proselytize to one's patients; it is an offensive violation of ethical guidelines that risks terminating one's job. Codes of ethics for chaplains require us to demonstrate respect for the cultural and religious values of those we serve and block us from imposing our own values and beliefs in caregiving. Chaplains are mindful of the imbalance of power in the professional/client relationship and refrain from exploiting that imbalance.[4] "Do no harm" is one of the Islamic legal maxims in practicing care, which is compatible with the ethics of conduct to maintain a high standard in patient care.

Whatever good you send forth for your souls,
you will find it with God better and greater in reward.
And seek God's Forgiveness. Truly God is Forgiving, Merciful.[5]

Around the same time as Lysa's hospitalization, there was an older white gentleman in his late sixties, who had been an inpatient for more than fifty consecutive days. He was able to be discharged, only to return three days later due to pain. The medical term that was used to describe him was "failure to thrive." In other words, he was not getting better but not declining fast enough to call it an immediate crisis, but in this patient population of blood transplantation recipients, a prolonged failure to thrive was a slowly lurking death sentence. He must have sensed this. He was a proud man, declaring politely that, "I do not have any need for your service," the first time I introduced myself to him. I nodded my head in agreement before extending my welcome with my quick "one-two jab" that I use as part of my introduction: "My role as a chaplain is to offer support emotionally and spiritually, wherever you get your spirituality from. I am not here to change you or sell you anything. I wish you healing for the physical body, for the heart, and for the mind." I gestured to his frail body as I said that and lightly touched my heart and my head. He listened thoughtfully and a small smile broke onto his face. This was always a critical point in any visitation: either the patient decides to extend enough trust to give you a chance, or they deny you that. In my census list, he was listed as NRP: No Religious Preference. "I'm sure you're able to give people comfort. But maybe not now for me. I'm waiting for a physical therapist person to come." This answer is enough for me: he didn't say no as in never; rather, he said, "Maybe not now," keeping the door open a crack and granting me entrance! I wished him a good session with the physical therapist and framed my next visit loosely, "Maybe I'll come by again in the future." He nodded and bid me farewell.

A social worker had referred him to me because she thought a visit might be good for him, but she warned me, "He might not want to talk to you." I continued to check on the gentleman regularly, each for a short time. Then one day he told the nurse that he wanted me to visit him. I was happy to hear the request from the nursing staff. He prepared himself well, sitting on a chair, facing the big window in his room overlooking the garden. I sat next to him. We admired the garden. The conversation was flowing, but every time I got close to learning something valuable about him, he would evade my questions. He would give me a "yes and no" answer, without any definitive mark. I let him be and did not press. At times, we laughed; I think we were talking about songs, and I admitted that I learned English in Indonesia from my cousin's Beatles cassettes about love, utilizing the chaplaincy tool of a small self-disclosure with the intention of building rapport. It worked. He told me that, while he did not wish to be rude, his life experiences with people of faith were disappointing.

He went on to share that he felt religious people were always pushing their beliefs. He rejected the notion of God, religion, and other aspects of faith for a long time. He was very practical and rational, a thinking man; yet, now when he must contemplate the end of his own life, he found himself struggling to make decisions and to figure out what mattered most to him. I asked him about his life task, his purpose in life. He briefly shared that he hoped to get better, to "continue what I can in doing good in this world." He declined to say more about it, though. I did this push and pull, prodding him and then letting him go, not answering something that I knew would reveal more.

His health continued to teeter; he ate sparingly—not enough to maintain his body weight, he walked gingerly with a walker—not strong enough to stand on his own. He refused to go home with hospice or even have a conversation about death as he still hoped that he would live longer. This type of situation is devastating for staff members who have seen enough patients and cases that they know what comes next. Staff members wanted him to have some time at home while he still had some life in him rather than spending it at the hospital.

It was under these circumstances that I saw him again. After our usual banter, he told me that he was contemplating his life and, subsequently, his death. I listened deeply. He asked, "What would you do in my place?" I continue to be startled when patients ask this question of me as they do from time to time. I asked for clarification. He told me that he was interested in my answer, as if I were in his shoes. I took a deep breath. I said that I would ask for and give forgiveness—to ask forgiveness from family members and friends, the people that I've hurt. I would ask forgiveness from God. I would try to forgive people who wronged me, and I would try to forgive myself for things that I did in the past, not knowing any better. I would do all that because I want my slate to be clean in front of God during judgment time. He had a knowing look. He was frailer than before, but a determined look appeared on his face. "Maybe I could do that. I could ask for forgiveness." He went home with hospice not long after and died there with his family.

Despite our differences, me, a hijab-wearing practicing female Muslim chaplain, and he, an older white male without religion, we established understanding and trust. His brother was there during that last conversation and witnessed what the patient said. Later, I learned that the gentleman had an estranged son. I do not know if he had the opportunity to meet his son before his death or to seek and offer forgiveness with him, but I think perhaps our conversation opened up a place for healing in his own heart. This gentleman struggled to prolong his life to the point that he did not know what he would want to do with his extra time on earth; existing for the mere sake of existing is not life. I hope God will give him forgiveness as vast as His mercy as this person deserved and more.

---

*The revelation of the Book from God, the Mighty, the Knower, Forgiver
    of sins,
Acceptor of Repentance, severe in retribution, Possessed of Bounty.
There is no god but He; unto Him is the journey's end.*[6]

I saw him in a patient room in one of the emptying nursing units. He was wearing street clothes, and for a while I thought he was a family member instead of a patient. I introduced myself; he wanted me to look at his discharge papers as he was worried about how and where to get his pain medications. He shared that he suffered a lot of pain and drove six hours for checkups and prescriptions. This time, his pain was so excruciating that he had needed to be hospitalized two nights ago. He had a pensive look. I asked what worried him, and the answer came lightly at first, but it got heavy fast. "I don't know if I'm ready to be home with my mother, my brother, my niece and nephew. They looked up to me." It turned out that he was a soldier who had done a tour in Afghanistan and was living on his own but due to his illness now needed to move back with family. He was Latino and a Catholic. "I'm not who they think I am; it's very hard for me." Perched on the edge of his bed, he slumped forward. I kneeled by his side, sensing his pain. "I kept having this dream of children . . . dead." Silence hung in the air as tears flowed.

He went on to say that while he was in Afghanistan, he'd been one of the last to board a chopper when they suddenly took fire. His officer ordered him to return fire and to keep shooting at a structure near them, where they thought the shots were coming from. Later as the helicopter was taking off he saw that there were children in the building. My heart sank and we cried together. Something moved inside me, and as I wiped my tears, I recognized that I felt a strong desire to pray for the victims. I offered that, if he would like, we could together pray for the children. He cried even harder, and seeing him tormented like that, I thought about my own faith's teaching around seeking forgiveness. Knowing my faith was likely also the faith of the children he'd inadvertently killed, I offered the practice of reciting *astaghfirullâh al-'azîm* (I seek forgiveness from God Almighty) for him to consider sensing that the connection between he and I, and I with the children, might provide a bridge for healing. He welcomed it, and I guided him through the words, breaking them down slowly for him. His voice trembled and halted as the words were foreign for him, but the effort and the heart he placed into them made it sacred. There was a strong connection between us at the end of the prayer as we both fell silent. When we resumed talking, his mood was lighter, and it was as if I could see a reduction in the burden he was carrying. We talked about his plans moving forward, and I encouraged him to continue seeking opportunities to talk to others closer to home, maybe a therapist. We said goodbye.

Leaving his room behind me, my steps were steady, but my heart was not. I pondered the fate of the children and other victims of war as lives lost unjustly. I thought about how men became soldiers; soldiers followed orders but became scarred and suffered as human beings. This man was feeling guilty and could not face living with his own niece and nephew. This was also the first time for me to knowingly be a chaplain for someone who had killed. And specifically, he killed Muslim children, whom I did not know, yet to whom I feel bonded all the same. Can I forgive him? Should I? I allowed the uneasiness in my heart to continue. In the days following this encounter, I turned to writing a verbatim as a way for me to process the complexity of my feelings.[7]

While I continue to develop my comfort with use of self as a pastoral care technique, I also recognize that by simply visiting with patients as a Muslim, I present an opportunity for people to begin healing from the toxicity of fear that grips so many when it comes to Islam. It was healing for me, as I hope it was healing for the others. I visit people as they fall ill as my own way of thanksgiving, of serving. Along the way, not only have I found God, I found one more elusive: myself. In those times, my patients and I are all children of Adam. We were one before the One.

Notes

1. Tâ Hâ/20:25–28.
2. al-Anʿâm/6:102.
3. Spiritual assessment is a tool used to evaluate a careseeker's spiritual wellbeing through noting their meaning-making sources and support network. Fitchett's 7×7 and Spiritual AIM are two commonly used models.
4. Council of Collaboration, "Common Code of Ethics for Chaplains, Pastoral Counselors, Pastoral Educators and Students," 2004, sections 1.3 and 1.4, https://spiritualcareassociation.org/code-of-ethics.html.
5. al-Muzzammil/73:20.
6. al-Ghâfir/40:2–3.
7. A verbatim is a writing technique used in CPE wherein the student writes as many of the details from the visit as they can recall, including the dialogue line by line, any observations about the physical space, and what they were thinking and feeling throughout the encounter. Many chaplains return to this tool from time to time as a processing technique that allows for reflection and, when one chooses, the opportunity to seek feedback from colleagues.

Drawing from the Five Pillars

A Chaplain's Guide to Providing Meaningful Spiritual Care

SONDOS KHOLAKI

SINCE I BEGAN serving as a hospital chaplain, I have awakened to a renewed appreciation of Islam's five pillars as the building blocks necessary for my effective provision of spiritual care.[1] Offering accompaniment in the midst of death, cradling the crestfallen, and sitting in helpless discomfort in the face of overwhelming suffering have informed anew my interactions with the five pillars of witnessing, ritual prayer, almsgiving, fasting, and pilgrimage. These rituals I once compartmentalized now prove intimately indispensable to my professional and personal growth in cultivating humility, presence, compassion, and patience through the muting of the ego—all of which enhance one's ability to hold space for others, a key function in chaplaincy.

Sondos Kholaki was born in Damascus, Syria, and raised in Southern California, where she currently serves as a hospital staff chaplain. She is board certified with APC and holds an MDiv in Islamic Chaplaincy from Bayan Islamic Graduate School, where she earned the Fathi Osman Academic Excellence Award. Sondos completed five units of Clinical Pastoral Education (CPE) and acquired certification in palliative care and in bereavement facilitation. She serves as the vice president of healthcare chaplains for the Association of Muslim Chaplains. Sondos is the author of the book *Musings of a Muslim Chaplain*. She enjoys sipping a cup of perfectly brewed black decaf coffee, listening to Qur'an recitation by Turkish reciters, and singing her heart out at spiritual gatherings in praise of the beloved Prophet ﷺ. She lives with her husband and two teenage children in Orange County.

Shahâdah *(Witnessing)*

The *shahâdah*, the Muslim attestation of faith, translates to *witnessing*. Muslims intentionally recite the *shahâdah* at specific milestones that merit notice, such as the beginning of one's spiritual journey into Islam (whether this occurs as a child or later in life), in the call to prayer, after the ritual washing, and at the final moments before death. Years ago, Ch. Dr. Kamal Abu-Shamsieh taught me a key insight into this oft-uttered creedal phrase. Leaning in, he said, "The *shahâdah* begins with a negation. One must empty oneself to create space for what can be. To meet people where they are at, leave your assumptions and judgments behind and let God do the rest." From the *shahâdah*, I learned that witnessing requires humility and a suppression of the urge to "fix" immediately the perceived disruption.

Chaplains journey alongside those in crisis who may experience heartbreak and emotional and spiritual disintegration. Often, bearing witness to another's pain remains my most important task in those moments. Early on in my chaplaincy training, I could rise to this task but, instead, I found any excuse to run out of the room—to fetch someone water, a blanket, a nurse, anything to get out. Gradually, with more experience, I learned to empty myself of my own discomfort, sit still, and hold space for the pain to unfold. This witnessing, followed by the engagement of meaning-making, wherein the careseeker evaluates a crisis through their belief framework and spiritual truths, proved transformative in sacred ways. I sat with a patient's family member whose own personal burdens drove them to confide in me in a hallway for over an hour. In previous days, this family member had lashed out verbally at the staff and displayed an overall volatile state. Following our hallway conversation, in which I spoke no more than a handful of words, I walked this individual back to the patient's room where other relatives stared at their loved one in surprise. "Your face . . . it looks different; more peaceful," one of them noted about the individual, who smiled softly and replied, "That's because I *feel* more peaceful."

The healing cultivated in the pastoral encounter stems less from what we say and more from how we make others feel—seen, understood, and loved. When people request prayers from the chaplain, for instance, often they're not only asking to be witnessed by God but also by the designated one summoning Him. For me, that means the difference between perfunctorily reciting a memorized prayer—whether with a patient or in personal worship—and emptying my mind and heart of distraction to offer full presence. When we offer full presence in this way, we may see beyond the presenting narrative, wherein one sees new meaning through a different perspective, termed a "reframe." Mystic saint Rabi'a al-'Adawiyya demonstrates this beautifully through her reframe of the function of the Angel of Death when she responded to him as follows:

"I am the murderer of joy," said the Angel of Death. "The widower of wives, the orphaner of children."

Rabi'a replied, "Why always run yourself down? Why not say instead: 'I am he who brings friend and Friend together'?"[2]

Like the negation at the beginning of the shahâdah, we bear witness when we can empty ourselves of ourselves.

In chaplaincy, we learn that every individual is an expert of their experience, and thus, we aim to approach all souls with the posture of a curious learner to help the careseeker discover their meaning-making process. The Islamic tradition emphasizes that one gleans knowledge not from lines on paper alone but also in the silent, sanctified exchange between hearts and souls. Witnessing the pain of the bereaved softened and humbled my heart in a way that decades of courses, texts, and sermons could not. This notion of learning through storytelling appears in the Qur'an, too, when God states that believers will find lessons and reminders in stories (Hûd/11:120, Yûsuf/12:7, 111). Then, every ennobled soul with whom we cross paths is sent to teach us something about ourselves in relation to the Divine.

Salât *(Ritual Prayer)*

Salât, the ritual prayer, encapsulates the foundational skills necessary for chaplaincy: intentionality, active listening, and full presence. Once, I prepared to join one of my spiritual teachers for *salât,* but my teacher hesitated and then gently advised that I proceed on my own, explaining, "Some people feel that I take too long in prayer, so I don't want to burden you with my slow pace." Knowing my limits, I thanked him and performed the *salât* by myself. Afterward, I watched my teacher with curiosity. Eyes closed, body relaxed and completely still, he lingered in and savored every movement. Watching him helped me rethink my approach to this sacred space, where a Muslim carves out time to recharge via this intimate conversation with the Beloved. In the Qur'an, God instructs believers to "be continuously mindful of prayers and of praying in the most excellent way."[3] At the hospital and at home, where quiet time exists in limited quantities, *salât* offers me a consistent space to self-care through union of my body, mind, and soul. In my reading on trauma, I discovered a fascinating connection between *salât* and clinically proven healing practices such as music therapy, synchronized group movement, and physical activity that links the mind and body. In *salât*, we benefit from all these techniques from the melodious recitation of the Qur'an to the synchronized motions of congregational prayer, to the mind-body(-soul) connection of the mindful bowing and prostrating.

Neither chaplains nor those approaching *salât* move into the sacred space without intentionality. Approaching *salât* requires a specific physical and mental state, not unlike the process each chaplain adopts for himself or herself through words of prayer or some other ritual meant to ground one in the moment before a pastoral encounter. Before *salât*, Muslims perform a ritual washing called *wudû'*, a spiritual and physical *tahârah* (cleanse). As chaplains, we aim for a similar process of internal purification through pausing before and after the pastoral encounter, recognizing that conversation between souls creates sanctified space.

Sacred conversation necessitates active listening, or listening to learn. In the Qur'an, God directs believers to "appreciate and listen quietly when the Qur'an is recited,"[4] thereby underscoring the connection between that which is deemed sacred and the respect it is due. In chaplaincy, one trains the mind and soul in stillness and presence such that one's entire being focuses on the words, body language, and energy of the careseeker. A Muslim deems the ritual prayer conversation with God so sacred that, out of respect, one strives to hold oneself in *hudûr*—complete presence and stillness of mind and body apart from the prescribed movements. One's *salât* involves "being" with God rather than a "doing" on one's checklist, just as a chaplain aims to "be" with a careseeker versus "doing" tasks or "fixing" the challenge.

Once, I sat in full personal protective equipment for over an hour at the bedside of a paraplegic patient who had recently lost all sensation in his lower body due to a rare cancer. Together, we grieved his independence, his work, his mobility, his relationships, and his basic bodily functions. After receiving his story while trying to regulate my physical discomfort under the weight of the mask, gown, and gloves, I asked what I could do to support him during his hospitalization. The patient thought for a moment and said, "My family members just want to talk to me about their experience of my diagnosis, and that puts a lot of pressure on me. I've never had anybody just be fully present."

Zakât (*Almsgiving*)

The Qur'an often mentions *zakât* in tandem with *salât*. In exploring the connection between these two rituals, we discover a breathtaking meaning: as one builds a relationship with their human family, one builds a relationship with the Lord of that family. Cultivating an awareness of the needs and suffering of others remains central to the religious life and duty of a Muslim, as well as to the role of the spiritual caregiver.[5] *Zakât* underscores the importance of the health of the wider community over the self; the Prophet ﷺ taught that one should not eat to satisfaction when one's neighbor goes hungry.

Notably, the concept of *zakât* extends beyond finances; Muslim scholars often remark that their efforts in teaching manifest symbolically as a *zakât* on the wealth of knowledge and experience they acquired. So too, if God blesses us with the gift of empathy, we must pay that forward as part of the purpose of *zakât*. All humans suffer loss of some kind, as foretold by God in the Qur'an, "And We will certainly try you with fear and hunger and loss of wealth and crops."[6] Through the skill of "use of self,"[7] the chaplain recalls their own experiences of joy, grief, fear, and so on to empathize with the emotion of the careseeker, thereby enhancing connection. Once, I sat with a physician who struggled with a recent loss. As he described his grief, I remembered a season of my own grief and felt deep resonance with his pain—an application of "use of self"—whereby my eyes welled up with tears. Concerned that my tears might distract from *his* pain, however, and aware of my tender spiritual and emotional wounds that may eclipse the distinct experience of the careseeker and result in transference, I apologized to him. He paused before saying gratefully, "Your tears remind me that you know what it's like to be human."

When considering the meaning of the Arabic word *zakât*, "that which purifies," the Islamic spiritual refinement process known as *tazkiyah* comes to mind, a practice of the purification of one's heart. Neglecting this practice, rooted in self-assessment, risks putting the spiritual caregiver in a place of self-contentment and spiritual complacency or, worse, arrogance. Even the spiritual caregiving work itself may threaten to prompt the ego into an exaggerated sense of its importance or ability when we serve to convince ourselves that others need *us* to heal when it is God who heals.

Siyâm *(Fasting)*

The Islamic fast requires one to refrain from drinking and eating, engaging in intimate pleasures, succumbing to anger and cruelty in word and deed, and generally capitulating to one's base desires. Muslims observe this ritual during daylight hours in the month of Ramadan but also at different points throughout the year, such as the prophetic practice of fasting on Mondays and Thursdays. Fasting inculcates a recognition of our vulnerability, fragility, and humility as human beings in a very stark way, which many careseekers also deeply experience. In fasting, one empties oneself of physical matter and worldly distractions such that one may hold space for others.

As a chaplain, I appreciate my experience in Ramadan for this very reason as I connect to myself in new ways and deepen my practice of self-awareness. For a whole month, I consciously break my usual patterns and routines of convenience and comfort, allowing new meanings and spiritual understandings to emerge. When I better understand myself—my triggers, traumas, and wounds—so grow my understanding of and connection to others. Without this annual, welcome interruption, I may settle deeper into my patterns, habits, and assumptions without creating the space necessary to consider new ways of being and doing. When sitting with a careseeker, I utilize this training to let go of what I find convenient so as to open myself to new practices, such as a time when I tended to a young woman in her twenties having a panic attack in the ER. Drawing on the practice of co-regulation, something I had recently trained in but remained skeptical of, I asked the patient's permission to place my hand over her heart and then guided her hand to rest over my heart. After several minutes, her ragged breathing synced to my deeper breaths, and her panic was subdued in the presence of my calmness. I had never used this technique before but felt grateful to God for helping me try something new and beneficial.

To endure a month of hunger cultivates a comfort with discomfort, an embrace of suffering and pain, and a renewed appreciation for satiation when the fasting day comes to an end at sunset or even at the end of the month (just ask a coffee lover how the first sip tastes on Eid morning!).[8] Similarly, chaplains train to achieve these goals given that many pastoral visits involve facing the unknown of the future and a wistful appreciation for "better times" as opposite seasons spark reflection and sincere gratitude. I remember spoon-feeding ice chips into the parched mouth of a patient who had been prohibited for days from consuming anything substantive. The patient let out delighted cries with every spoonful and smacked her lips: "These taste like cookies to me; water cookies!" Having endured a parched tongue for a month, I could appreciate the patient's joy and gratitude in every spoonful.

Hunger also serves as a slowing mechanism—without constant fuel from food and drink, one develops an acute self-awareness and groundedness of the body. As such, inward soul healing informs outward bodily healing. God says in the Qur'an that He changes the condition of a people when we begin the hard work of improving ourselves (al-Ra'd/13:11). A resolute peacefulness settles in the mind, body, and soul, and this tranquil state creates room for reflection and gentleness in word and deed. As chaplains, we employ an action-reflection-action process around our work; the ritual of fasting drives this process as we complete a task, take a much-needed rest to recuperate, and move again.

Furthermore, controlling base desires invites a personal aim of setting boundaries and limits. Many spiritual care professionals struggle with this ethical practice of setting boundaries because chaplains desire to love and serve—often to their own detriment. The practice of fasting helps us prove to ourselves that we can, indeed, exercise control, choice, and agency over our situation, particularly when rooted in spiritual goals. Instilling a practice of delayed gratification spends on one's cultivation of patience, a most valued quality of any spiritual caregiver. A chaplain recognizes that they cannot rush a careseeker's journey. As Imam 'Ali said, "Your sickness is from you, but you do not perceive it, and your remedy is within you, but you do not sense it." A chaplain accompanies the careseeker with patience, gentleness, and wisdom as the chaplain assesses the source of distress and works with the careseeker to find the answer within.

For many, the most anticipated part of fasting is *iftâr*, the meal at sunset, with family, friends, and community. One of the foremost principles of chaplaincy is this concept of hospitality. The chaplain embodies the role of the host in transforming a space into one that is warm, safe, and welcoming such that the careseeker feels able to set down their burden, even for a brief time. The chaplain also embodies the role of humble and grateful guest when invited into a space by the careseeker. As such, I make it my personal practice at the end of every pastoral conversation to thank—with deep sincerity—the careseeker for trusting me with their story and journey. The invitation into the pastoral visit and space remains a privilege and honor not to be taken lightly or for granted.

Hajj *(Pilgrimage)*

The pilgrimage to Mecca that Muslims are called to perform once in a lifetime involves a series of rituals that capture the journey and legacy of Prophet Ibrâhîm (Abraham) and his family. The first step of hajj is to observe an inward and outward state of *ihrâm*, ritual sanctity. The inward state of *ihrâm* requires a commitment from all pilgrims to do no harm, even to the point of avoiding cutting one's fingernails or hair. Observing *ihrâm* necessitates a diligent self-awareness, *murâqabah*, wherein one guards one's words, actions, and intentions to fulfill the promise of "do no harm." When I enter into a pastoral visit, I strive for a similar state—I am sensitively aware of my facial expressions, words, and overall message so as to avoid harming the careseeker emotionally, spiritually, or intellectually. In Islam generally, at the minimum, one does not bring harm to others and, at best, one seeks to leave every person one meets in a better state than before.

The outward manifestation of *ihrâm* is two white, unstitched pieces of cloth for men and simple, modest clothing for women. This humble uniform serves as an equalizer: whether rich or poor, privileged or not, educated or illiterate, pilgrims avoid seeing themselves as better than their brother and sister. *Ihrâm* strives to unite humans at their essence—the spiritual soul—and move away from worldly variance. As a hospital chaplain, I see this spiritual lesson of *ihrâm* manifest in the simple gown all patients wear, such that one cannot tell the company CEO from the unemployed. The chaplain plays an integral role in sustaining the due respect and dignity for all patients when they are stripped of all outward titles, labels, and expressions.

At hajj, Muslim pilgrims from every corner of the globe gather at the Kaaba in unified worship of God. Once everybody gathers side by side to bow and prostrate in unison and recite the same litany in the same sacred language, a soulful community based on worship of the One emerges. Languages, customs, cultures, and colors of varying hues beautify the sanctified space as the shared speech of divine connection releases an inimitable sweetness. Amid this precious diversity, we may also come face to face with our own implicit (and explicit) biases. For the spiritual caregiver, this discovery proves even more necessary to name and overcome for comprehensive and sincere service to all. The diversity of the human family requires that a chaplain ask the careseeker questions to assess spiritual needs, worship rituals, and traditions. With this understanding comes a responsibility for the chaplain to discern the perspective of the careseeker rather than force the chaplain's own faith tradition or expression of belief. By remaining curious, open to learning, and maintaining cultural humility, the chaplain approaches every careseeker with appreciation and awe.

One careseeker called me during my community chaplaincy office hours to explore her spiritual wayfaring. Having recently converted to Islam and moved away from home to a new state, she felt isolated and insecure. In seeking self-worth and belonging, I helped her unpack the changing definitions of "home" and "community" as she integrated her identities into that of a Muslim. Eventually, we reached a point where that had been achieved and she no longer needed to process what she was experiencing in the same way. Our journey together had ended, and, providing a gentle reminder that the space remained available should the need for companioning arise again, I bid her *salâm*.

Conclusion

I grew up with a cursory understanding of Islam. Religious studies consisted of learning the mechanics of *salât*, proper recitation of the Qur'an, and so on. While such scrupulous practice cultivated important self-discipline, the potential for a deeper understanding of God and practical application of connecting to the sacred remained dormant within me. Engaging with these fundamentals of practice comprehensively as a chaplain has enriched their meaning in my personal life while also cultivating my ability to sit with others and with God with full presence and compassion. While I often serve individuals who are not Muslim and meet them where they are on their own meaning-making journey, I do so deeply rooted and informed by my own.

Notes

1. Some Shi'a denominations have additional pillars, including *walaya* (devotion to God).

2. Charles Upton, *Doorkeeper of the Heart: Versions of Rabi'a* (Pir Press, 2004), 53.

3. al-Baqarah/2:238.

4. al-A'râf/7:204.

5. The Prophet Muhammad ﷺ identified the rights a Muslim has over another Muslim as: returning the greeting of peace, visiting the sick, following the funeral procession, accepting an invitation, blessing the one who sneezes, and giving advice when asked.

6. al-Baqarah/2:155.

7. Catholic theologian Henri Nouwen coined the term, "wounded healer," to mean that one learns from one's own experience of suffering. Rabi'a hinted at this when she said, "If You hadn't singled me out to suffer Your love, I never would've brought You all these lovers."

8. Ch. Omer Bajwa taught me that an Arabic word exists for this blissful experience: *Marqaha*!

21

Duʿâ

The Heart of Chaplaincy

KHALID LATIF

THE PROPHET MUHAMMAD 鬒 said, "Supplication is the essence of worship."[1] When we beseech Allah, we affirm our own powerlessness, and it reminds us of our relationship with Him, that we are absolutely dependent on Him as our Lord. Yet *duʿâ* (supplication) is also empowering because it teaches us to rely solely on Allah and not on creation or created systems. By praying to Allah, we affirm that we understand, physically, psychologically, and spiritually, that nothing is either too big or too small for the One whom we are asking.

Allah describes the power of *duʿâ* when He informs the Prophet 鬒, "When My servants ask thee about Me: truly I am near. I answer the call of the caller when he calls Me."[2] *Duʿâ* is a conversation with Allah, our Creator, our Sustainer, the All-Hearing, the All-Seeing. In our tradition, *duʿâ* is an inspiring, liberating, and transformative conversation with the Divine. Only He can alleviate our suffering and resolve our problems. In *duʿâ*, we open our hearts to describe our difficulties to the One who can truly help us.

Khalid Latif serves at the Islamic Center at NYU where he helped found the first Muslim student center at an institution of higher education in the United States. His exceptional dedication and ability to cross interfaith and cultural lines on a daily basis has brought him recognition throughout the city, and in 2007 Mayor Michael Bloomberg nominated Khalid as the youngest chaplain in the history of the New York City Police Department, at the age of twenty-four. He is also cofounder of Honest Chops, a whole animal zabiha butcher shop, and Muslim Wedding Service.

As chaplains, we may expect to be called upon to make public prayers and to provide *du'â* for those who seek our care. While these *du'â* should include the familiar (and comforting) Arabic litanies in the Qur'an and modeled for us by our beloved Prophet ﷺ,[3] we also aspire to lift up the spoken and unspoken burdens on peoples' hearts—and on our own. As chaplains, we learn to listen deeply to what careseekers and our community are experiencing. What is troubling them? What do they want from their Lord? What will assuage their anxieties? Providing resonant *du'â* is an act of reflective listening.

As a Muslim chaplain, I regularly offer public prayers in English at various events. Here is an example of a *du'â* that I delivered at the 2015 "Reviving the Islamic Spirit" convention in Toronto, Canada:

Ya Allah, our Lord, Most Merciful of those who show mercy, instill within us courage as we start this day. Our struggles are real, but Your Promise is true. Indeed, with hardship there always comes ease. Remove from our hearts any fears or inhibitions, and replace them with an ever-increasing boldness to live each moment as best as we can.

Grant us the courage to express our feelings, to let those that we love know how valuable they are to us, to seek forgiveness from those that we have wronged, and to exert mercy towards those who have wronged us.

The burdens of life sometimes seem too heavy to bear. The anxiety and anguish that sits inside of us feels bigger at times than the world around us. Give us audacious hearts that can overcome that pain inside—hearts that help us to carry each burden with ease, regardless of how heavy it seems. Make us not from amongst those who are sheltered from life's realities, but rather amongst those who are not afraid to face them.

Bring people into our lives that we love so much that our love for them moves us to be courageous but not foolish. People who we love so much that our dedication to their well-being is rooted in wisdom and mindfulness. Make us people who find strength through selflessness not selfishness, sincerity not self-centeredness.

Grant us the courage to stand again after we have fallen, to find meaning in our failures, and to keep moving forward no matter what is trying to push us down. Grant us the courage to put our trust in You, whether we understand or not, and the courage to recognize and feel the depth of Your Love. Help us to harness that Love and utilize it to illuminate the darkest of places we might have to venture in, both in the world around us and the world within us.

Grant us the courage to live our own lives, to understand our role in the writing of our own stories, to make decisions with foresight and insight, and before each step we take in this world, to remember we will have a life in the world beyond this one.

Grant us the courage to forgive ourselves and to live a life in pursuit of true contentment, the courage to ask You to remove from our lives anything that distracts us, gives us only complacency, or satisfies only our wants at the expense of our real needs.

Love Your creation through us. Be gentle to them through us. Increase them in strength through us. Give them courage through us. Help them grow through us. Endow them with confidence through us. Fill them with sincerity through us. Protect them through us. And us them. Bring good and benefit to the rest of us and this world—Most Merciful of those who show mercy.

Let our anger be only at injustice, oppression, and exploitation of people so that we will work for justice, equality, and peace.

Let our tears shed only for those who suffer from pain, rejection, starvation, and conflict, so that we will reach out our hands to comfort them and change their pain into joy. And let our successes be many as we make a difference in this world by doing the things which others say cannot be done.

You are with us always, Ya Allah. Help us on this day to recognize Your Presence, and through it give us the courage to meet the challenges of this day and those of every tomorrow that we will see.

Protect us always from hearts that are not humble, tongues that are not wise, and eyes that have forgotten how to cry. Forgive us for our shortcomings, and guide and bless us all. *Amîn.*

Notes

1. al-Tirmidhî, *Sunan* 3371.

2. al-Baqarah/2:186.

3. I think often, for instance, of the powerful *duʿâ* made by the Prophet Muhammad ﷺ after his abuse at the hands of the community of Ta'if, when he felt betrayed, alone, and rejected, and the *duʿâ* of Prophet Mûsâ as he received Allah's command to confront Pharaoh.

Sister Padres

Canada's First Female Muslim Military Chaplains

BARBARA LOIS HELMS AND SERAP BULSEN

I LOWERED MY head to shield my face from the biting, subzero winds. *Just concentrate on the path*, I reminded myself, making sure I balanced the weight of my heavily loaded rucksack while stepping evenly on the military-issued

---

Captain Barbara Lois Helms is a registered psychotherapist with the College of Registered Psychotherapists of Ontario and a Canadian Certified Counsellor. She holds a BA in Religious Studies and an MA in Islamic Studies from McGill University, as well as an MA in Counseling Psychology from Athabasca. Currently pursuing a DMin with a focus on Muslim Chaplaincy through Emmanuel College, she is a unit chaplain with the Canadian Armed Forces (30th RCA) and a civilian officiant with the Canadian Forces Support Group (Ottawa-Gatineau). She holds endorsement from the Interfaith Committee on Canadian Military Chaplaincy and Cordova Spiritual Education Centre. Raised primarily in Princeton, New Jersey, Barbara returned to her native Canada for university where she embraced Islam in 1987. The proud mother of six children, Barbara practices self-care through exercise, time in nature, Tai Chi, and classical music.

Captain Serap Bulsen's childhood fascination with religion and spirituality in Turkey led her to enroll in the University of Toronto for a BA in Near and Middle Eastern Studies, and subsequently an MA in Arabic and Ottoman Studies. Serap has held various roles in nonprofit Islamic organizations and was supported by the Royal Canadian Chaplain Service to pursue a master of Pastoral Studies (Muslim Stream) at Emmanuel College before being posted to Kingston, Ontario, to be a unit chaplain. She currently lives in Kingston with her husband and two teenage children, and enjoys reading, cooking, and spending time with her family and friends. She regularly goes on nature walks where she finds mental tranquility and peace. Another passion of hers is the Islamic art of Ebru; she always seeks opportunities to learn new techniques of this beautiful art form.

---

snowshoes lashed to my feet. As a fifty-nine-year-old grandmother, I had not envisioned this future, yet I was now fully engaged in an adventure of a lifetime.

Neither I nor my Sister Padre, Capt. Serap Bulsen, anticipated careers as the first female Muslim chaplains in the Canadian Armed Forces. Yet we had already spent much of our lives on journeys of preparation for this unique vocational calling. Our paths had been marked with difficult challenges but also exhilarating moments of joy and transformation as we found the courage needed to break new ground.

Padre Barbara Lois Helms: Warrior Mother

In 2017, I enrolled in 30th Field, Royal Canadian Artillery as a chaplain—more affectionately known within the Canadian Armed Forces as a "Padre" (Father). Although I had successfully accumulated all the prerequisite education and training necessary to become a Direct Entry Officer, by the time my long and circuitous path to military chaplaincy combined three parallel careers with over three decades of community service, at fifty-five, I was too old to be eligible for the Regular Forces I had applied to. I nonetheless enrolled as a captain in the Primary Reserves, and within two years completed my Developmental Period 1, including boot camp, trade qualification, and the Chaplains' Ethics, Counselling Skills, and Deployed Operations training. As a result, I was also hired as a full-time civilian unit chaplain with Canadian Forces Support Group (Ottawa-Gatineau), and through the combination of these roles I served both Reserve and Regular Force members, as well as their families.

My academic training included a bachelor of religious studies and a master of Islamic studies (from McGill University), a master of counseling psychology (Athabasca University), and a doctor of ministry degree, specializing in Muslim chaplaincy (in progress at Emmanuel College).[1] However, my vocational path reaches back much further, to my youthful search for authenticity, meaning, purpose, and connection, which originally influenced me to pursue Christian ministry before my spiritual journey led me to Islam. My drive for an authentic life, engaged in compassionate service, has also continued, finding meaningful expression in the transformative interactions that are connected to the vocation of chaplaincy. Of the life experiences that have shaped me for military chaplaincy, none is more important than my experience as a mother—to my own six biological children as well as to my "adopted children," those many youths whom I mentored in educational, community, and interfaith settings. As a mother and nurturing mentor, I have had to find the strength to overcome challenges to care for those in my charge and to create environments in which they could grow and thrive. It has been the courage of motherhood that has propelled me through many daunting circumstances.

One of these many daunting challenges occurred six months after my military enrollment, while attending Basic Military Officer Qualification (a.k.a. boot camp) at the St. Jean Garrison. I was almost a decade older than even my most senior platoon mate, and two to three decades older than our sergeant and master corporal instructors. As a platoon of chaplains and medical officers whose median age was above the norm, we did not face quite the same rigors of regular infantry soldiers. However, the training was designed to make us suffer—and we did—so that we would better understand the hardships faced by the members we were to serve, and to understand how we reacted in "artificially created stress environments." I was up before 5:00 a.m. every morning, running throughout the day, marching in ranks, attending classes from morning until night, climbing multiple sets of stairs while carrying full equipment, and crawling in fields wearing camo paint. Our access to cell phones, computers, visitors, and leaving the base were restricted, especially during our indoctrination period. We learned to stand at attention, salute, and address our instructors with proper decorum. We practiced drills, learned to read maps and unload rifles (Canadian military chaplains do not carry arms or learn to shoot). We learned to pitch tents and cook outdoors, administer first aid, identify unexploded ordnance, and handle fire extinguishers, culminating in a final field exercise in which we would each lead our section on a successful mission following specific required battle procedures.

My initial reaction was one of disorientation; I had not understood the nature of the training. I was unfamiliar with my gear as well as the most basic military routines and was generally unprepared. Yet soon into the training, I found that another sense kicked in, and I started to have a heightened awareness of my environment. I learned to anticipate expectations and proactively prepare myself and then be on alert to help fellow platoon members if needed. I felt very alive and connected to my team. The turning point in this experience of "being switched on" was the night before we were to dip our uniforms in a repellent, in preparation for our field exercises in wooded areas infested with Lyme disease–carrying ticks. We had been instructed to sew name tags into our uniforms if we wished to have them back after the dipping. As one of the few platoon members with sewing skills, I stayed up all night attaching name tags onto the uniforms of my companions. I realized that this would negatively impact me the next day, yet it was clear to me that I would not put any of my companions at risk as they crawled on the ground among the ticks.

Hence, I was prepared to take my chances even if this meant failing my upcoming room inspection. That morning, as I tried to organize my locker and lay out my gear, I felt completely confused. Miraculously, several platoon members came to my rescue, ironing and folding my T-shirts with geometric perfection, hanging my uniforms in perfect alignment, arranging my locker, making my bed with precision hospital corners (which the inspecting officer measured to the millimeter), and leaving my room in pristine order. This was a powerful lesson in teamwork: I not only passed inspection, but I also discovered the importance—even sacredness—of bonds that are forged when people join to face a common challenge. Inspired with this new insight, I recognized I could also draw on my previous experiences facing challenging situations, especially as a mother of six, and learning to exercise decisive authority. Instead of the out-of-place, somewhat intimidated middle-aged woman, I rediscovered myself as the warrior-mother-leader who could manage a chaotic one-room schoolhouse while breastfeeding an infant, or transport six children with diaper bags, car seats, and snowsuits, within a designed timeline, or write a publishable master's thesis with one hand while cradling an infant shortly after giving birth. Any remaining self-doubts were replaced with a firm and confident inner voice: I was exactly where I needed to be and exactly the right person for the task at hand. As a courageous mother-warrior, now with team support, my capabilities expanded exponentially. During our group challenges, I found myself relaxing into the wonderful experience of team trust, allowing myself to be hoisted, thrown, carried over and around multiple obstacles, trusting God and relying in full confidence on my teammates.

During our final, cumulative task of leading our sections on field missions, I committed fully to the experience, as a loyal subordinate, as an efficient second-in-command, and as a capable section leader, realizing the truth that only good followers can make good leaders and knowing that we either fail or succeed as a team. I excelled in the exercise, demonstrating excellent leadership skills, and feeling exhilarated with both the personal challenge and the teamwork experience. I not only passed this course but was voted by my platoon as the most improved candidate. I felt great respect for the staff who trained me, most of whom had served in Afghanistan but were the age of my sons. I appreciated that they took me seriously and treated me like other candidates, yelling at me when appropriate or giving me disciplinary tasks—like push-ups—for such offenses as failing to fill my water canteen to the very top. In turn, my sincere efforts gained their respect as they recognized my physical and mental resilience and my commitment to learning and to teamwork.

It has taken me many decades of intense effort, facing multiple barriers and many closed doors, before reaching my current vocational and career establishment. I have had many heartbreaks, but no regrets. My original calling to a life of ministry has reemerged in a more vibrant and mature form, integrating my accumulated experiences. In terms of our expectations for Muslim women, my life challenges and my vocation as a military chaplain have required me to step beyond traditional domestic and gender roles. However, it has been the strength of these roles, especially the courage of motherhood, that has informed and empowered my calling and given me the motivation to persevere.

Throughout my relatively short yet highly condensed military career, I have heard my senior chaplains comparing my journey to that of Moses, who led his people through the desert but could not enter the promised land. Others have described my groundbreaking role as laying tracks for those who come after me, while not being able to ride on the train. I accept my destiny, even not being able to enter the promised land or ride on the train. Yet, with courage and gratitude, I will make the most of this journey for as long as God grants me the strength to break ground, looking forward to meeting in another promised land that has no age barriers.

Padre Serap Bulsen: Connecting the Pieces to Care for All

My journey to becoming a military chaplain might be best characterized as a puzzle. As a child, I was drawn to the mystical world of discovery, the knowing of the unknown, which inevitably raised my interest in religious knowledge. The first puzzle piece entered my life while attending high school in my native country of Turkey as I struggled to understand and practice my faith. I had so many questions about Islam and other beliefs; ultimately, the quest for answers was leading me to find my calling. An influential religious teacher with whom I studied in high school encouraged me to study theology, but my national exam results tracked me toward healthcare. So I found myself enrolled in physiotherapy studies when the government banned hijab from all public institutions. Hijab was an important part of my faith practice; as such, this was a big conflict for me. Ultimately, rather than take off my hijab, I chose to follow my heart and left school. All the years of prioritizing my academics suddenly seemed so futile. As painful as it was, now I clearly see this was another puzzle piece put in place.

Although it took me almost two decades to seriously consider my former teacher's encouragement, my interest in theology always remained. After immigrating to Canada and enrolling at the University of Toronto, I decided to take some courses on Islam. Intrigued by the content of the courses and enjoying the lively discussions, I changed my major to Near and Middle Eastern Civilizations. While it did not occur to me then, I had put another piece of the puzzle in place.

As challenging as it was with two young children and working for an Islamic nonprofit organization, I started to get involved tending to the spiritual well-being of my faith community. Interfaith work was also an important part of this time for me—service and dialogue. These experiences were challenging in new ways and taught me many valuable life lessons about myself and others. Often, I felt I knew little, but I seized the opportunity to learn and grow while working on my own spiritual development, reminding myself of the common Muslim saying, "Whoever knows herself knows God."

One day, I heard a hospital chaplain speak about his work at a retreat my faith community held over Christmas. As he spoke, I thought, *chaplaincy is something I want to pursue.* A little research about chaplaincy showed that to pursue my goal I needed to have a master's degree. For that reason, after finishing my bachelor's, I did an MA at the same department focusing on Arabic and feminist interpretation of the Qur'an. As I neared completion and began to look at chaplaincy applications, I found most were for men to work in men's prisons. Others were for volunteers, but after over a decade of volunteering I knew I wanted a professional chaplaincy career. Then I read an interview with Wafa Daddagh, the first hijab-wearing Muslim woman to serve in the Canadian Armed Forces (CAF). Her story touched my heart, giving me a new direction and leading me toward military chaplaincy.

I remember vividly that it was after my morning prayer when I decided to complete a chaplaincy application for the Canadian Armed Forces, having no idea how long the application process would take or that there were no female Muslim chaplains in the CAF. One of the biggest challenges for me during my application process was translating my experience and style of religious leadership to meet the application requirements. "Pastoral Associate" sounded close, but it turns out that is specific to Catholics. In addition to the absence of relevant language, I had served *fî sabîlillâh* (volunteering for the sake of God), as women so often do. I ran specific programs and classes, but I also responded to a multitude of needs ad hoc as they arose under no specific title. Through each, I mastered different skills and learned things that benefited me as a chaplain, but there was no easy way to give voice to that. Furthermore, with so many of our religious institutions being founded by immigrants, they lacked the financial resources, organizational structures, or governing bodies that more established Canadian religious institutions have.

While waiting, I sought out the senior CAF Muslim chaplain, Padre Suleyman Demiray, to learn more. His support gave me hope and while my application was still pending, I enrolled in Emmanuel College's Master of Pastoral Studies program at the recommendation of my recruitment officer. During my application process, my spouse was very supportive, although he was initially hesitant about my decision to become a military chaplain. His main concern was the challenges that military life could bring, and he was not sure if we were ready for this. Eventually, he became my biggest supporter. Contrary to what many assume, my own faith community and friends supported me greatly since the beginning of my application and throughout the challenges that I faced balancing family life, school, and military training. They made sure I was constantly reminded of how proud they were of me. I even heard from other Muslims how I have inspired them to consider military careers. I was eventually accepted by the Royal Canadian Chaplain Service, and after several internships, posted to CFB Kingston Ontario.

In the decade since I started the journey, my life has been filled with countless exams, trainings, Clinical Pastoral Education, deadlines, Basic Military Officer Qualification (BMOQ) training, a knee injury, sleepless nights, tears, and so many social invitations I've had to turn down. Throughout writing this essay, I revisited each step of the process—pausing to reflect about it for the first time. In that reflection, I also see how my days have come to be filled with determination, hope, prayer, reflection, and contemplation. I clearly see "For truly with hardship comes ease!"[2] manifest in my journey as my puzzle has come together. I've come to understand that each part of the journey that brought me here prepared me for the work I am doing right now. As the thirteenth-century Muslim poet Rumi says, "Don't grieve, anything you lose comes round in another form." Even through challenging times, I have never considered a different career—I love my job. My experiences as a Muslim woman, a mother, and a visible minority help me connect to the people I am serving.

As a Muslim woman, I used to think other people's assumptions and biases toward my appearance and identity might hinder my chaplaincy service. However, I am pleased to say I have met many great souls who value my identity and presence regardless of their own background. Every day I serve people from different walks of life, and time and time again I see the ways that my appearance and identity are actually an asset to this work. As a human family we are all interconnected; this connection is an important aspect of my chaplaincy. As the Royal Canadian Chaplain Service motto says, *"We minister to our own, we facilitate the worship of others and we care for all."* Service to humanity is a core Islamic value that continues to inspire me daily. There is a saying attributed to the Muslim scholar Saʻdi (d. 1291) that guides my work:[3]

Humanity are members of one body
created out of the same essence.
When one member of the body feels pain,
others remain distraught

Muslims make up only a small part of my care; the majority is spent with "care for all" regardless of faith, race, sex, gender identity—and I love that. I often reflect on the verse, *"O Mankind! Truly We created you from a male and a female, and We made you peoples and tribes that you may come to know one another."*[4] Contemplating on this verse, I see how little we actually know about each other. No matter how close we are physically, unless we meet and engage, sharing the morals and wisdom from our different traditions, we miss great opportunities to learn and grow—as individuals and as a united humanity. Interfaith work for me reflects the idea that every human being is carrying a universe within them.

Conclusion

We realize that despite the geographical and time differences in our journeys, we have encountered many of the same barriers and shared many of the same joys in serving and caring for all. Initially propelled by a hunger for meaning and purpose, we have accepted the call to step into unknown and uncharted territories, requiring us to move out of our personal comfort zones as well as challenge community norms for women. Yet we have learned to draw on our courage as Muslim women and mothers so that we could move forward despite daunting challenges. We have learned the value of teamwork and now, working together as Sister Padres, we continue to blaze this path, and we stand by to support others who are inspired to follow us.

Notes

1. This program is offered as a partnership with Toronto School of Theology and the University of Toronto and is, at this point in time, the only accredited graduate program for Muslim chaplains in Canada.

2. al-Sharh/94:5.

3. Omid Safi, *Radical Love: Teachings from the Islamic Mystical Tradition* (Yale University Press, 2018), 213.

4. al-Hujurât/49:13.

23

Paradise Beneath Her Feet

Chaplaincy in Birthing Spaces

JAYE STARR

MY FIRST CLINICAL PASTORAL EDUCATION (CPE) placement was in a small Catholic hospital where I and one other first-unit CPE student were typically the only chaplains on site. During our orientation, the labor and delivery (L&D) unit had been casually dismissed from afar with the explanation that chaplains rarely went there "unless there was a fetal demise." Inquiring further, I was told there was blessing oil in the office if needed. Self-conscious about being the first Muslim student and wanting to appear capable of fulfilling the role, I didn't confess that I had no idea what to do with it. Subsequently, I learned a lot about the L&D unit through my own two births as well as the neonatal intensive care unit (NICU), where my daughter would spend the first weeks of her life. Residency four years later took me back to the hospital of her birth where I was delighted to receive a placement that included the "birthing floor"—L&D, NICU, and postpartum.

Jaye Starr is an aspiring healthcare chaplain, board member with the Association of Muslim Chaplains, and ethics committee member at a large research hospital. A graduate of Hartford Seminary's Islamic Chaplaincy Program with three units of Clinical Pastoral Education (CPE), Jaye also studied with the Fellowship at Auschwitz for the Study of Professional Ethics and as a Luce Fellow at Gadjah Mada University (Indonesia). She is a white convert to Islam living in Michigan with her husband, a fellow chaplain, and their two small children. Jaye loves gardening and finds geeking out over Islamic studies and bioethics strangely rejuvenating.

CONTENT WARNING: *Perinatal loss and birthing trauma*

On my first day shadowing on the floors, we received a call that a mother in labor would be delivering a baby expected to die soon after birth. The mother, a patient in our palliative birthing program, had known in advance and planned to spend the family's brief time in this world together with her other children present with a photographer, to bathe and dress her baby, and to have her baptized. Despite her long labor, the mother looked radiant, her loving family encircling her as she held her beautiful newborn. The chaplain I was shadowing navigated the space skillfully, engaging the mother and the family in a way that celebrated the baby's birth even as she honored the start of the dying process. I felt totally calm and utterly grounded. This was where I wanted to be.

Rounding as it occurs on other units, with a chaplain walking from door to door inquiring if inhabitants would like a visit, does not occur on the birthing floor. When I first started, the nurses' station was an intimidating space. Monitors filled the room with endless streams of information, and people seemed to speak in code. However, I slowly learned that stopping by often yields patients: oh, there is a mother preparing for a cesarean who might like a prayer, a woman whose induction is taking forever is growing anxious, a distressed grandmother in the waiting room, a terrified husband in the hall. Once accustomed to my presence charting in the lounge, staff seek me out for their own spiritual care.

It is also in the lounge that I begin my spiritual assessment, specifically with the giant whiteboard that holds a plethora of information: previous births versus pregnancies, twins, NICU standby, cesarean prep, and so on. While this information doesn't tell me about spiritual states, it gives me context. Questions like "Is this your first?" are ambiguous: *Yes, this baby in the isolette is my first to make it this far, but no, this child is not my firstborn.* "Do you have other children?" is present tense. The context isn't necessary, but it aids in my capacity to interpret what I'm hearing. It can also help me create space for a person to explore the intersections of pain they are encountering.

The nurses graciously provide me with other helpful context such as the language a patient is using so I can mirror that in my own conversation. If a woman isn't using "baby" or if she is seeking validation in her identity as "mother," I want to meet her where she is. If she is using a name, I want to honor that with my words as I mirror her tone. After several visits I add a question: What does the baby look like? Babies born too early into this world don't look like the misleading gestational week-by-week baby images on the Internet. In training, I learn to draw the parent's attention to humanizing details with affirmations. Yet I naturally find myself saying silently *subhânallâh* over and over again as I find the beauty of The Merciful's creation in every detail, *âyât* (signs of Allah) in and of themselves.[1]

<hr />

When babies are born with medical complications or already dead, it is common for families to request, or staff to offer, a chaplain's visit for the purposes of providing a blessing or baptism. Most chaplaincy students at some point will have to wrestle with what their role is in facilitating baby blessings and baptisms for families, especially outside of their own faith traditions. I learned how to navigate blessings from my Baptist mentor, while a Baptist cohort mate was very clear that he would never baptize a baby as his tradition believed in only adult baptism. Muslims have a similar diversity of approaches and practical theologies. For myself, I draw from the hospitality that Prophet Muhammad ﷺ provided to the Christians from Najran when he invited them to make their prayers in his masjid. What does it look like for me to bid the Other welcome with hospitality? What can I provide them with to make their stay more comfortable? I cannot say their prayers for them, but I can provide for them by creating the space.

I believe that rituals can be like bookmarks laid between chapters, helping us to break life's joys and tragedies into manageable units to reflect upon and in doing so to aid in transitions.[2] Growing up in the Unitarian Universalist tradition, I was imbued with a more fluid idea of rituals than most as rituals were in a constant state of development and evolution made sacred by the moment unlike the rituals of most religions made sacred by their repetition. Now Muslim, my use of ritual is still informed by that fluidity and by my past studies of theatrical design. Coming into a call for a blessing, I seek to understand what a family means by that request as a designer seeks the understanding of the director's vision. Do they need a connection to Jesus? Are there specific actions such as a baptism that they desire? Are they without a tradition and reaching out for something to try to help make order in the absence of any? People in this moment are vulnerable, suffering, and often exhausted by labor—it isn't the time to go through a menu of options. Rather, I attempt to discern what is important and then seek confirmation or clarification.

When someone is seeking something traditionally Catholic, I turn to a generic prayer card in the office closet. When there is a greater seeking, I turn to the tradition of poetry so central to my Islamic faith, pulling the blessing prayers from my conversations with parents. I incorporate the hopes and dreams families had for their baby, conversations that are like eulogies for lives never lived, for when a desired baby dies, so too does the imagined toddler, kindergartener, teenager, and future adult.[3] I've written in dreams of fishing, reading favorite stories, and singing family lullabies, along with *Star Wars* viewing and listening to Beyoncé, because those were what was important for parents. My blessings often take the form of first honoring the dreams for the baby, followed by a formal blessing/baptism/honoring for those who desire it, and concluding with a prayer for the parents. For the blessing or baptism of a Christian baby, I invite the parents to perform the formal ritual by marking the sign of the cross with oil or water and repeating the words after me—as simple as they are, they are easy to forget in the midst of grief. I include the parents in this way because I feel it is cathartic for the healing process, but also because baptisms and blessings in this form are in conflict with the *tawhîd* (monotheism) central to my faith. Providing them directly feels like an inauthentic honoring of the parents' beliefs, just as a Christian whispering the *âdhân* in my own baby's ear would have felt. I dread the thought of someone recounting their experience after saying "and then this Muslim chaplain came and preformed the baptism" only to have the listener inform them that Muslims don't believe in the Trinity, leaving the parents to feel that it was invalid and inauthentic.

In some ways it is the *'urf* (customary tradition) of chaplaincy to provide blessings for families when situations require it, but that is insufficient for there are other careers one could pursue. Through much soul searching, I have come to believe that this is an invocation of the mercy and compassion central to my practice of Islam. Women experiencing loss often still undergo labor—the pain, the hormonal shift, the engorgement of breasts, the exhaustion, the need for physical and mental recovery time. This is the space I arrive at when I attend to families. So sacred is the space to me that it has always seemed I ought to be removing my shoes when entering into the hallowed ground of a labor and delivery room. Instead, as I sanitize my hands outside the door, I pause, whispering *bismillâh* before knocking. When I enter, the typical room configuration appropriately places me at the feet, reminding me of the Prophet's ﷺ teaching, "Paradise is at the feet of the mothers." If the cloak of these words of blessing can provide comfort to a family in the midst of so much pain and suffering during a woman's liminal and heartbreaking entry into this space of motherhood, then I am willing to provide them, inclined that the Merciful understands my intentions.

Blessings and baptisms are only a small part of what I do in the units. Much of my time is spent around birthing trauma.[4] The metaphor of chaplaincy that resonates most deeply for me in attending to any trauma is the beading together of *misbahah* prayer beads on a string. I think of the experiences and the emotions that surround them in people's lives as individual beads that can both complement and jostle other beads. Usually when we go about our day-to-day life the beads all string into place, but sometimes they come too quickly and from unexpected directions, resulting in a pile of beads tumbling around in a person's heart stripping them of their capacity to string them. When I enter into companionship with a patient, I am inviting them to tell me about the beads one by one, and in doing so we become the craftsmen whittling down and polishing away the distress tarnishing them, so that the patient can slowly begin to bead them onto the string.

I recall one father who stood in the operating room thinking he was losing his wife and son as he witnessed a traumatic cesarean birth that included substantial hemorrhaging. He'd been completely overwhelmed by what he'd felt, seen, and heard. When I encountered him the following day, I could tell from the scattered way he spoke that he had a lot of beads jumbled up. I sat and listened as he worked his way through naming the beads—the blood, the lifeless lines on the monitor, the constant beeping of NICU machines, the words he'd heard the team say, the ashen look of his son's face, the unknowing. This initial naming wasn't sufficient to begin stringing the beads back together, it was merely taking inventory. The next day, I visited again and we talked through his experiences in greater detail, releasing some of the emotional weight they held.[5]

The third day, I received a call from the nurse asking if I could visit again as they were planning to discharge, but she wasn't sure he was ready. In our conversation I said very little beyond asking the occasional question to help him dig deeper and give voice to what he was feeling. I affirmed his tears, and I listened. As we talked, he started to settle, to breathe more calmly, and to ease into his new normal. When it was time to part ways, I could see that he was ready—so could the nurse. At the conclusion of each visit, I guided him in a grounding exercise. For me, this is when we put down the string for the time being and acknowledge that the beads on there are okay, even though there is more polishing and more stringing to come. As is so often the case, I'd done little more than provide a calming ministry of presence that allowed him to work through the stringing of his own beads.[6] Like so many of the people I've found most seeking what chaplains can provide, this father was not a man of faith. Had I not encountered him in the NICU it is unlikely he would have requested a chaplain visit.

I don't look like what most people expect a chaplain to look like. I'm a middle-aged woman wearing a headwrap pinned to a turtleneck. I tend toward loose flowing natural fibers, long skirts, and abaya that I believe help to distinguish me from my social work colleagues. In interdisciplinary units like the NICU, it is common for colleagues to suggest a chaplain's visit to a patient. Even when I hear that someone isn't interested, I still stop by to introduce myself—not in a pushy way but simply to let them see me so their decision can be informed by the reality of me rather than the idea of me. More often than not they do welcome me in. When they don't, I endeavor to offer the same concern for well-being and warmth Prophet Muhammad ﷺ is said to have continued to provide to a woman who threw trash onto his path daily.

In rounds one day, discussing a baby anticipated not to survive, my social worker colleague informed me she'd already asked: the parents were not religious and didn't want a chaplain. I made a mental note to be particularly sensitive to any indicators of disinterest they might express but still introduced myself while rounding. We ended up spending an hour together during which they voiced their certainty that the baby would survive. It wasn't my place to persuade them otherwise. I honored their hope and encouraged them to give voice to all of their dreams for him. When their son's health began to more visibly deteriorate the next day, I was able to be a supportive presence because of that relationship and trust we'd established. When they came to terms with the need to stop artificial breathing, they requested that I facilitate a ceremony and a blessing before the equipment was removed.

When I was new to Islam and first heard the story of Mûsâ and Khidr,[7] one of the ultimate theodicy stories in the Qur'an, I was appalled. The seemingly random and horrific nature of what transpires, especially the murder of the young man, unsettled me. It is only over time as I've witnessed so many seemingly random and horrific things that I've come to fully appreciate the story and lean into the details. I can recognize now that nothing in the story shies away from the horrific nature—indeed, Mûsâ's own aghast response affirms it. Yet in the Qur'an's telling of it I am reminded that there are reasons things happen that remain entirely beyond my grasp, and that there is good in all things from Allah—even though I, like Mûsâ, may not be able to recognize it in the midst of tragedy. Part of chaplaincy is providing people with the space and support to do the meaning-making work of grief; I often think of myself as the companion shining the light so that they can look around inside their own heart. In the meaning-making process, a person becomes their own Khidr to their aghast and confused Mûsâ within, holding up their own light and allowing them to reconcile the suffering in this world with the Mercy of Allah. I rarely give this story to those I care for, but it is the story that helps me hold space for meaning and good in the countless tragedies I encounter in my chaplaincy work. The ability to know why tragedies happen lies beyond the river of my human knowledge; I can only respond with *sabr* (patience), *taqwâ* (God consciousness), *tawakkul* (trust in God), and steadfast prayer.

Notes

1. England's resources outpace those of the United States with Muslim Bereavement Services (volunteers specifically trained for perinatal loss), Children of Jannah (providing Islamic resources on pregnancy loss), and Ibraheem's Gift (providing comfort baskets containing two small shrouds for burial, a hat and blanket, a bottle of attar oil, prayer beads, and *A Gift for the Bereaved Parent: Remedy for Grief from the Islamic Perspective*, by Ch. Zamir Hussain).

2. Rituals in my context extend beyond baptisms and include blessings for things such as the transition of a baby between a birthing parent and an adoptive family, or for a birthing family reluctant to leave as the Child Protective Services' appointed foster parent awaits discharge, to celebrate a discharge following months in the NICU, or when a baby is born after a journey with infertility or previous loss, which can often be a difficult, apprehension-filled transition.

3. My pastoral care has been significantly informed by Julia Bueno's *The Brink of Being* (Penguin, 2019).

4. Racism is one significant contributing factor to birthing trauma that can't go unmentioned. In the United States, Black women are significantly more likely to die during childbirth or recovery than white women, often because providers' implicit bias results in a failure to respond to early symptoms. I believe that well-embedded chaplains can help address this problem.

5. During traumatic experiences, the brain's operational command center switches from the prefrontal cortex, where it usually resides, to the amygdala. Rather than sequential "beads on a string" memories like the prefrontal cortex supplies, the amygdala forms fractured memories—beads on the floor. My talking through them in detail is an intentional process aiming to aid the fragmented pieces to begin being (re)membered in sequential order toward alleviating the emotional distress around them.

6. As Reesma Menakem points out in *My Grandmother's Hands*, the settled calm of one body can also help to settle another simply through presence (Central Recovery Press, 2017).

7. This story comes from Qur'an 18:65–82 where Mûsâ, desiring to learn of God's wisdom, is given the opportunity to accompany a mysterious figure known as Khidr if he agrees not to ask any questions about what he sees as the actions will be beyond Mûsâ's comprehension. As they journey, Khidr proceeds to undertake actions that overwhelm Mûsâ, leading him to ask why. Khidr then reveals the unimaginable good that will come of the actions in the future.

24

Oh Allah, Thank You for Your Service

JAMAL BEY

WHEN I FIRST JOINED THE MILITARY, initially as a soldier at thirty, I already had a lot more life experience than many. I was, at that time, not the best example of what a Muslim should be even though I was born Muslim, went to an Islamic private school until high school, and was raised by Muslim parents. Both my father and my grandfathers served, and I'd come to believe that enlisting for the structure, discipline, and physical demands military life offered was the only way that I could improve myself.

When I got to basic training, having set my intentions upon enlisting to improve my spiritual life as an important part of getting my life on the track I wanted, I made it a point to read at least one Qur'an verse every night. Absolutely exhausted, I would make my prayers lying in my bed at the end of the day, but at least I was making them, it was a start. Still, I did not openly express my religious identity, not out of fear of being found out to be Muslim— my dog tags stated that I was—but because I lacked the ability to fully communicate and advocate for myself and my religious needs. I was still unfamiliar

---

Captain Jamal Bey, a native of Houston, Texas, currently serves in the United States Army as a chaplain, having previously served in the army's Chaplain Candidate Program. Jamal has a BA in Communications and an MBA in Finance, both from Texas Southern University. Jamal is also a graduate of Hartford Seminary's Islamic Chaplaincy Program and a member of the Association of Muslim Chaplains. A former member of the United States National Karate Team, Jamal enjoys running marathons and practicing several martial arts in which he has a black belt.

with military ways and unaware that there were any chaplains who would advocate on my behalf, let alone Muslim ones.

After ten weeks of basic training, I moved to advanced individual training. I arrived shortly before the start of the Ramadan fast. Despite my earlier struggles to live in accordance with the faith in full, I had fasted for at least twenty of the previous years. That July, Ramadan was just beginning, and I wanted to participate as I had in the years prior. Especially given that while undergoing boot camp, I'd been putting myself through an additional boot camp: a spiritual one reconnecting to my faith, and as such I'd became more aware of my role and obligations as a Muslim in Ramadan. However, my sergeant told me that I could either stay and train or go home and fulfill the requirements of Ramadan.

After all the spiritual struggle and growth I'd gone through, to be told that I could not do what my Creator instructed me to do was deeply disappointing. At the same time, the reason I could not do what my Creator instructed me to was because I was in a place that I thought would improve my life and my *dîn* (faith). I was torn trying to understand what was the right path forward: which of my commands was I to follow? After a call home to help me think through it with family, importantly fellow Muslims, I determined that I would make the days up. I have always questioned myself on whether that was the right decision. *How will Allah judge me for putting a job ahead of my Ramadan obligations?* I never had the opportunity to revisit the topic with my former sergeant; he died in a car accident the following weekend, leaving me to wonder how his command will weigh on the scale at the Day of Judgment. The experience left me feeling isolated—I felt disconnected from the rest of the *ummah* (Muslim community) but also from my unit. My heart was distracted with a longing to fulfill the obligation of the fast while serving.

While I carried the weight of longing for Ramadan rituals, I also struggled with the blatant misuse/mischaracterization of my other religious rituals. During the same training program, we were doing a drill where we were instructed to low crawl through sand carrying automatic rifles. While we crawled, there was live machine gunfire spraying fast-flying bullets just above our heads from the "enemy" bunker we were crawling toward. As we crawled, between the whizzing of the bullets, I suddenly heard the *âdhân* (call to prayer). When I first heard it, I was surprised that the time of prayer had come in already, but it slowly dawned on me that the timing wasn't right: the *âdhân* was being used as part of the battle scenario—a setting of the scene. It is my understanding that during this kind of training exercise, the military is attempting to create a soldier prepared to go to war and win the battles.

However, even though the U.S. military is currently heavily engaged in Muslim lands, it felt egregious for the *âdhân* to be playing, both for the sacredness of it but also because of what it implied: Muslims are the enemy. Some of our enemies may be Muslims, but Muslims generically are not; indeed, there are over 6,000 of us actively serving and sacrificing for our country. I began to worry that if my fellow soldiers heard me reciting the *âdhân* as we do before prayers, it might trigger "enemy" for them as a result of their training. Yet, I was not aware at that time how to advocate for myself. Between the fasting prohibition and the *âdhân,* I was wondering if Allah was sending me a message. Had I come to the wrong place to get my life in order? I began to experience self-doubt.

Eight years later, after completing my MBA while in service, I was contemplating a move toward the officer corps. A chaplain who had become a mentor pointed out that chaplaincy would be a good way to combine my love of God with my love of military service, and I decided to pursue it. Arriving at the army chaplain school, I was surprised to find myself the only Muslim in the room and disappointed to be the only Muslim that many of the other students had ever met. Many carried misperceptions that came up during the training. But nothing shocked me more than the attitude of one of the instructors, my assigned small-group leader, who was antagonistic throughout the training. The third week of class we were doing a course on what are known as "key leader engagements." This is where, when on deployment, a chaplain may be sent to speak to key community leaders, including religious ones. This instructor stated in front of the entire class that Muslim chaplains needed to be cautious that they not become radicalized by these engagements. I was disappointed by his words. Everyone heard him, and it felt like all of the eyes were now on me, trying to evaluate if I could be trusted: are you with us or are you against us?

In the military, there is a rank structure. It is unlawful for those of a lower rank to engage aggressively with those who are higher. They must always be approached with respect. In this instance, I was unable to have any respect for this instructor, but for the sake of myself and any other Muslim who might come in the future, I tried to respond to him with patience and gentleness so as to exemplify the model of our Prophet ﷺ. I did later address this situation through the appropriate chain of command, gaining the respect of my supervisors for it, which helped to affirm my sense of place as a Muslim among military chaplains. However, I was still faced with the challenge of finding my sense of place as a Muslim in the larger American Muslim community.

I come from the Warith Deen Mohammad community, a community born out of individuals who converted from Christianity to the Nation of Islam and from the Nation to a more Orthodox practice of Islam. It is an indigenous community to the United States. Unlike many immigrant Muslim communities where military service is frowned upon, military service does not hold the same stigma. Indeed, many have served honorably, so when I enlisted, I largely found collective understanding from those who had served and their family members. However, my journey has taken me into the larger American Muslim community where there is often a palpable disapproval of a Muslim's choice to serve. The impact of this judgment weighs heavily on Muslim service members: in military settings it can be hard to relax as we are viewed as potential traitors, yet solace in what should be the sanctuary of the masjid can be elusive as we are viewed there too as potential traitors. In both situations, this mistrust arises from people we consider ourselves to be one with. Once while attending an Islamic conference in uniform, I went to pray accompanied by another chaplain. When we arrived, two brothers had just begun praying together. I made our presence known by tapping the elbow of the person following as is the custom to initiate the fall back and formation of a prayer line in any Muslim community I've ever been a part of. This person glanced at us, and—I can only assume because of our uniforms—did not move to extend a prayer line. After waiting a couple of seconds, the other chaplain and I decided that it would be best for us to create our own space and pray together. I thought nothing more of it, until I concluded my prayer and saw a line of about eight individuals had formed where we had attempted to join. It was not only that there are additional blessings in making prayer in congregation, but this individual had decided to create a line for the other group of people but not for us. I cannot with certainty say that it was because of our uniforms or our race, but those were the only differences I could identify.

The above examples depict some of the different ways military life as a Muslim over the past decade has often left me feeling isolated, unjustly distrusted, and alienated from my Muslim community *and* my military community. During my time in service, I've seen in my own and in others' experiences, several themes that contribute to these feelings and sometimes even moral injury[1] for Muslims. A common source of isolation that I alluded to before is that the decision to join the U.S. military may not be viewed positively by the service members' relatives or community, an issue that has become heightened as the country increasingly engages in Muslim majority regions. While family may identify as American and be loyal to the nation, they may frame fighting against fellow Muslims as problematic vis-à-vis theological arguments. This pressure from family members and concern about community ostracization—with its implication for marriage prospects—can be difficult for the individual in light of the Qur'anic verses that speak to maintaining familial and communal relationships.

Muslim service members may also experience moral injury by observing the actions of residents where the U.S. military operates. The practice of those residents may be viewed as heretical or against what the service members view as a sound religious practice, such as suicide bombings, the use of civilian spaces (including masjids), schools, and hospitals for waging combat, or the prohibition of female students. Furthermore, they may be asked to answer for such behaviors by fellow soldiers who view them, as the only Muslim they may know, as a subject matter expert. Constantly needing to respond to Islamophobia in American society can leave Muslims feeling guarded and make it difficult for some to be vulnerable enough to share with unit members their own misgivings about the actions of other Muslims. Additionally, service members may not be recognized as fully Muslim by the local community—as is often the case for those of African descent deployed to the Middle East. This contributes to an isolating paradox wherein the service member is viewed as *not Muslim enough* for the locals, while being seen as *too Muslim* by fellow unit members.

I believe that the tools offered by the Islamic tradition can help to address the isolation, moral distress, and injury experienced by Muslim service members. For instance, the practice of fasting in the Islamic tradition creates space for one's purification and detoxification, both physically and spiritually. As a soldier who struggled to practice fasting during my first Ramadan in the military, I now serve as a chaplain who assists my fellow Muslim service members in maintaining this ritual that offers an invaluable opportunity for spiritual repair, growth, and a subsequent return to wholeness. The ability to maintain my fast through my subsequent years of service has been an important part of my own spiritual journey. After a decade in, I can see clearly how the structure and discipline that Islamic rituals offer have made me a better service member, and the ways the structure and discipline of the army make me a better Muslim. Indeed, when I first enlisted with the goal of becoming a better Muslim, I had no idea how much better I would eventually become, *al-hamdu lillâh*.

Note

1. Moral injury is the anguish one experiences when they are in a high-stakes situation, things go wrong, and the harm that results challenges one's most profound moral codes and capability to trust others or themselves. The result of moral injury is a spectrum of guilt, shame, isolation, psychic numbing, or depression that leads one toward maladaptive behaviors known as invisible wounds.

The Kinder Garden

Circles of Remembrance

KAMAU M. AYUBBI

So remember Me, and I shall remember you. Give thanks unto Me, and disbelieve not in Me.[1]

Anas ibn Malik reported: The Messenger of Allah ﷺ said, "When you pass by the meadows of Paradise, graze as you like." They said, "What are the meadows of Paradise?" The Prophet said, "Circles of remembrance."[2]

AS A MUSLIM HOSPITAL CHAPLAIN, I am no stranger to pain and suffering and, in contrast, the merciful gift of healing and spiritual realizations. Over the years, I have found ways of incorporating universal principles from the Qur'an and Prophetic way into my ministry to be compatible with and accessible to the needs of people from all walks of life. Over the years, I have held modest groups of meditation and remembrance under titles such as: "Finding

Kamau M. Ayubbi was born in Los Angeles in a family rooted in arts and social, cultural, and political activism. He found Islam during college, embracing the Naqshbandi Tarîqah Sufi path under direct supervision, education, and training from Shaykh Hisham Al Kabbani. He graduated from San Francisco State University with a BA in Visual Arts where he also found great passion in Holistic Health Studies. Kamau discovered chaplaincy while serving as assistant imam at Masjid Al Iman in Oakland, California. He completed his internship and residency and subsequently served as staff chaplain at Beaumont Hospital near Detroit for a total of nine years. Kamau joined University of Michigan Medicine in 2015, where he currently serves as staff chaplain. Kamau finds self-care through meditation, dhikr, and leading and engaging in devotional/reflective and artistic spaces. He is happily married and the father of four children.

Peace," "The Power of Peace," "15 Minutes of Peace," and recently, "The Kinder Garden of Meditation." These sessions have been attended by parents and their hospitalized children (as young as seven years old), adolescent and adult psychiatric patients receiving inpatient and outpatient treatment, nurses, social workers, and other members of the staff to find respite, relaxation, insight, and rejuvenation. Outside the hospital setting, especially since the pandemic, community partners—Muslim and not—with interest in the healing arts and contemplative spiritual and religious practices have also hosted such circles more explicitly expressive of Qur'an, hadith, and the wisdom of scholars and *awliyâ' Allâh* (saints of the Sufi traditions).

In this essay, I offer examples of and reflections upon the meditative practice developed and utilized under the title "The Kinder Garden of Meditation," using spiritual frameworks drawn from Islam that translate across religious and even nonreligious affiliations. In the hospital, participants join me for fifteen to thirty minutes of intentional relaxation and contemplation. As the soft, soothing notes of the *ney* (reed flute) play in the background, I invite participants into a guided visualization using the concepts of A-B-Cs, 1-2-3s, and primary colors to convey meanings that support wellness. Inspired by 'Ali ibn Abî Tâlib's teaching, "Speak to people only according to their level of knowledge,"[3] I formulated the simple and nostalgic idea of using the ABCs as related to awareness (*murâqabah*), breath (*nafas*), and compassion (*rahmah*). By highlighting these three concepts, we begin to identify ways of applying them in our lives to enjoy the benefits found therein. The following is an excerpt example script of guided imagery divided into three sections with some contextual commentary. In practice, I would convey something similar to this script in full for a ten to fifteen minute guided reflection.

A, B, C: Awareness, Breath, Compassion

Join me in gently engaging the three elements of awareness, breath, and compassion. By breathing in through the nostrils, the windpipe, and the lungs, we appreciate the tree of life within . . . the lungs that purify and energize the body with the breath. . . . We affirm the breath that rides upon the water in our body, within the subtle iron of our bloodstream, toward the heart. . . . We affirm the form of the heart, the movements of the heart, the energy of the heart . . . and the light of the heart. . . . That light carries deep within it the gift of compassion: forgiveness, love, empathy, connection, and understanding. This heart faithfully receives and distributes the gifts of compassion within the breath. It energizes itself receptively to our intentional remembrance before it radiates to infuse the brain with energy that flows through each element of the nervous system and our unique form.

We embrace the inner witnessing of the form (body) that we occupy, the mercy that infuses the bloodstream with balance, vitality, and wisdom. This attitude of compassion draws our awareness deeper to these fields of light that permeate and encompass every drop of blood individually . . . and further, the ocean of cells expressing complex communication and immeasurable harmony. Our invocation and awareness of forgiveness manifest as a healing balm, a means to perceive, process, and surrender the burdens we may have accumulated within our spiritual, emotional, and physical bodies back to the oceans of compassion . . . the expansion of love and appearances of multiple names and attributes that communicate through every fiber of our being. As we are grounded in the depth of sensation within the body, we can now intentionally raise our awareness to acknowledge the sky above, the blue dome, the expansive air, the clouds, the birds, the edge of the atmosphere that opens up within our awareness to the canopy of stars, our solar system, the oceans of beauty and harmony that connect the galaxies that mirror the orbits of life force through the bloodstream and vital organs.

1, 2, 3: Form, Meaning, and Spirit

By engaging awareness, breath, and compassion, we not only recognize the form of the body but also layers of meaning and the spirit of what takes place within us. We continue:

Within the heart's remembrance of the activities of our being, the faculty of contemplation is opened to include layers of heaven above. Where the atmosphere meets space, the heart's vision can affirm the presence of the stars, reflecting an even deeper and broader ocean of stars in which we are a drop of this beauty and unity. We may witness the world of light as active and harmonious, and we receive the blessing of that vision. Let the various orbits of our cells and the communication and the angelic power between them be affirmed.

This faculty of contemplation, once opened, allows us to leave the limited constructs of the self that often produce fight-or-flight responses within. After applying compassionate awareness to the body and mind, patients, families, and staff are given a chance to expand their awareness in the larger sense of the cosmos. After some time in this state, participants are invited back to the sensations of the body to integrate expansion, peace, and healing into their bodies. Through this conscious use of awareness, participants seem to connect with meanings shared.

Colors: Internal and External

Colors are an intrinsic part of the universe we live in. The yellowish sun is the brightest form of light in our physical universe, and our heart is similar in this way of being radiant in relationship to the other organs. The water in our body contains the red blood cells, which convey oxygen and energy through our entire interior body. White can be reflected in a sandy beach, the clouds, or the stars above. Green reminds of the embodiment of beautiful qualities in a garden, lush with trees, fruits, and flowers. Black can represent the vast mystery of deep space or the most hidden water within and beneath trees and forests. Colors convey meanings and allow us to have a focus for internal awareness and see the connections with the beauty within the universe. A concluding section of the meditation continues here:

Bring your awareness back into the sensations of the body and rest into the color of green, the color of the garden, the trees and plants, the vibrancy of life. Consider the roots reaching into the earth, the branches extending to the skies, the leaves, the plants, the blossoms, the rivers that flow through, and the water that infuses each aspect and color of the garden. Consider the harmony and communication within the garden. . . . What qualities and characters are embodied there and within your own body? Bounty, generosity? Steadfastness, vitality, balance? Deep within and beneath the garden is the movement of pure life . . . water that informs, sustains, and keeps supple. Indeed, love is the water of life.

Conclusion: Spreading Peace and Kindness

The following captures the sense in which we conclude the session to affirm a sense of connectedness to self through both the community present in the circle and a broader sense of connection that exists in the relationship we have to those who might be absent from us physically.

As we reflect on the depth of our inner self and the peace we may have experienced and cultivated within, we conclude by extending the intention of peace through our beings to those who have sat with us today. . . . We may extend peace to those we are connected to, those we love . . . from this place of intention we may acknowledge this potential of peace within the hearts of humanity, relating from this circle like a ripple on a lake. . . . To conclude, we gather our awareness to the core of our being, appreciating the moment . . . acknowledging that deep mystery of who we are in essence. . . . As we slowly open our eyes, we bring our awareness through the depth into that shared field of unity, through the water of our body . . . into the form of our being . . . back into the day with clarity, courage, or whatever intention would be helpful.

We conclude by acknowledging the layers of our being that we often forget in the busyness of daily life and gently integrating that back into an embodied intention. What I find satisfying is to see parents, staff, and young people open their eyes with a sense of peace and beauty in their faces, and a spirit of calm community among themselves. Partnering with unit hosts, there is often tea or cookies for participants to enjoy while socializing for a while. "I needed that," "I could feel the tension leave out of the bottoms of my feet," "That was so relaxing," are some of the comments we have heard from participants over the years. Gratefully, in partnership with members of the medical community, we have consistently been able to experience the "Kinder Garden Effect," spaces of blessed company in circles in which tranquility and insight are experienced. Since the pandemic began, educational video series and Zoom spaces have continued the sharing and practice. With a sense of intention and willingness, we cultivate compassionate awareness in community and find a taste of paradise in often highly stressful and technological spaces.

Notes

1. al-Baqarah/2:152.
2. al-Tirmidhî, *Sunan* 3510.
3. al-Bukhârî, *al-Jâmi' al-Sahîh* 127.

26

Mercy to Self

Preserving the Gift of Empathy in Life's Winters

TRICIA PETHIC

*"Plants and animals don't fight winter; they don't pretend it's not happening
and attempt to carry on living the same lives that they lived in summer.
They prepare. They adapt. They perform extraordinary acts of
metamorphosis to get them through. Winter is a time of withdrawing from
the world, maximizing scant resources, carrying out acts of brutal efficiency
and vanishing from sight; but that's where the transformation occurs.
Winter is not the death of the life cycle, but its crucible."*
—*Katherine May*[1]

I AM WRITING THIS IN WINTER, not long after the conclusion of 2020: the year of suffocation. People suffocated from COVID. Even nonsufferers felt suffocated behind masks. Then George Floyd suffocated. The one-two punch of COVID and George Floyd's death mentally thrust me back into two places I'd been trying to recover from: prisons and hospitals.

Tricia Pethic is a graduate of Hartford Seminary's Islamic Chaplaincy Program and holds an MA in Near Eastern Studies from the University of Arizona. She previously served at Albion Correctional Facility in New York and is founding director of Muslim Prisoner Project, a nonprofit that provides books to prisoners and Eid gifts to their children. Tricia enjoys surprising strangers that she is, in fact, "just a white girl from upstate New York," although her studies in genealogy have revealed much more. A member of the Association of Muslim Chaplains, she enjoys quiet time with her husband and not-so-quiet time with her two children.

I began the year as a "recovering" former prison chaplain. I'd ministered to people on the receiving end of handcuffs but also the ones who carried them. George Floyd's story reminded me of many inmates I'd counseled who had their personal demons but who would make valiant attempts to start anew. I also saw moral injury in Officer Derek Chauvin, the kind of cynicism I'd seen from many in law enforcement who had become accustomed to dealing with the worst of human nature—*Aw, he doesn't really need his mom. They're criminals/inmates; they're always putting on an act.*

If Floyd's death brought me back to the prisons, COVID brought me back to my hospital days, trekking out to hospitals within a three-hour radius to see humans in various states of death and dying as I met with their families to discuss organ donation. It was on this job that I suffered a nervous breakdown and began to reassess the emotional candle that I'd burned at both ends. My mind told me to prepare for the coming task, but my body told me it needed rest. I was expected to be empathetic and firing on all cylinders continuously, but as Gabor Maté points out, "when the body says no," there is no backtalk. It wins.[2]

I had left at 8:00 a.m., driven many hours, and absorbed three different family scenarios at three different hospitals. I was now supposed to show up at 2:00 a.m. to support a fourth family withdrawing their loved one's life support; the patient would then become an organ donor. But my meeting with them would not happen. In episodes that would return in milder forms for months, my whole body shook with fight-or-flight symptoms that started with my face flushing with heat, then chills. I agonized trying to bring my body into alignment with my mind, but it would not subside. I called my supervisor and told him I needed backup. I couldn't do it.

Hanging up the phone, I was racked with shame at being unable to do what I was paid to do, and physically burdened by the fight-or-flight response. I struggled for hours to fall asleep in my hotel room, miles from home. When I finally awoke a few hours later, I was tired but wired—it sounds strange, but anxiety sufferers know exactly what it's like. I later learned from Peter Levine's important work in somatic experiencing that these episodes were my body's primordial way of trying to discharge all the energy I had marshaled.[3] This finding would later comfort me, as well as remembering how the Prophet ﷺ would shake with chills upon receiving revelation. Under my blanket each evening, I would endure the waves and feel a sense of communion with him. I figured that just as his sensations would give way to revelation, mine too would give way to something.

But what?

It was time to minister to the one person I'd neglected: myself. I took up swimming. I lost thirty-five pounds. I became one of those "wellness" people. And then, just like that, COVID hit, and many of the healthy habits I had built were gone in the blink of an eye. The local swimming pool went silent and waveless. I couldn't see my therapist except through a Zoom call. On my recovery to-do list had been a commitment to spend less time on social media and more time with friends; suddenly social media was the only way to connect with friends.

To make matters worse, I was seven months into an experiment in parenting two young boys alone as we hoped my husband could transfer from his own corrections chaplaincy job to be closer to home. Alone with my two energetic boys, who needed more attention than I could give, I felt the slow simmer of anxiety threaten me daily; phenomena like "impending doom," "dissociation," and "paresthesia" would soon become part of my experience and my vocabulary. The artifice of self-care that I'd built to heal from the things I saw and heard in prisons and hospitals was gone. In the blink of an eye.

"O most Merciful, ever subsisting, in your mercy I seek refuge. Rectify all my affairs for me, and do not leave me to my own devices for the blink of an eye."

—Prayer of Prophet Muhammad ﷺ[4]

There were times I felt left to my own devices. Intellectually, I knew God was there. But when mental illness inserted itself, it was like a phone filter changing colorful photos to gloomy black and whites. The picture is still there, but something has wrapped itself around it. I realized that, thus far, my self-care had mostly concentrated on the physical. I'd not seen how artificial the separation of mind and body was, how much of my pride was wrapped up in my job such that I felt shame for needing help. I understood for the first time that when I overburden myself, the body has a way of literally stopping me by means of biological processes that I didn't even know existed. It's actually a marvel. In better moments, I am grateful to my body and the One who created it, for putting this stop sign in place . . . even though I want to tell my body, *The danger is gone. Can we cut this out now?*

Discovering my empathetic limits has been a religious experience, despite my body signaling to me occasional despair and hopelessness: two traits that I never had before as a person of faith. Yet I know that as created beings, we all have our limits. I am pleased to know where my limits are. My gift of compassionate presence is not something from my own self; it was given to me by the One in the same way someone may be gifted a skill on the basketball court or on computers. But I did not know how to nurture, preserve, and protect that gift of presence—housed as it is in a fragile human brain and heart.

But I do know now.

As I felt the structure of life give way to the gnawing passage of time and uncertainty about the virus, I understood what trauma therapist Bessel van der Kolk meant when he said that central to trauma is a sense of lacking control.[5] I began to watch van der Kolk clips the way people pop candy. His warm and wise elderly countenance comforted me. He understood me. My symptoms were not just worries I could wave off. I had trained my brain to be ready at a moment's notice to show up in traumatic circumstances, absorb emotions, and offer organ donation to the grief-stricken, the stakes of which were someone not getting a life-saving transplant. No pressure! I'd trained my brain to do this and now it was doing it—too well. I was primed for disaster around the corner. I was staring into a gaping maw. The word MAW came to me one day as I almost hallucinated with anxiety. I felt a big lifeless hole sucking me in.

"I don't think this is going to end," I said to my therapist, with a straight face. I'd given many a sermon to women inmates. I'd lifted many chins to the sky. I'd grasped many hands and offered hope. But there I was, deflated and hopeless. A pale shell of myself. Sincerely believing that COVID would never end. I think in some sense I meant the larger narrative: the sense that the planet itself is suffocating and we're not doing enough about it, and the apocalyptic signs my religion had warned us of. I was sober enough in thought to also remember the words of our Prophet Muhammad ﷺ: "If the end of times comes and you are planting a seed, finish planting it."[6] It was actualizing this message, and really knowing it in my heart and not just my mind, that came harder for me.

Many unhelpful inner voices arise when we begin to tread the path of recovery, particularly if we evolved (or so we thought!) from a postcolonial "identity Islam." In the latter mode, questions like "Who developed this cure or practice? Were they Muslim?!" crowd out the implications of the prophetic saying, "The word of wisdom is the lost property of the believer. Wherever he finds it, he is most deserving of it."[7]

When I opened myself up to the implications of this prophetic wisdom, I immersed myself unapologetically in whatever benefited me, whether it was yoga, breathwork, acupuncture, HRV biofeedback, talk therapy, grounding, pharmaceuticals, or herbs such as ashwagandha—all self-care practices I've explored in my journey.

It may not be obvious at first glance that Islam addresses self-care, with all the talk of "disciplining" and "breaking" the *nafs* (lower self). Yet

Prophet Muhammad 🕌 scolded a man for not balancing his zealous spiritual practice with his (and his wife's) bodily needs. God also informs us we will be embodied souls when in paradise; after withdrawing our souls from our bodies, there is a happy reunion of sorts, reminding me of the importance of mind-body connection. God also invokes our physical faculties as a meditative focal point.[8]

And then there was the time that the Prophet 🕌 himself was shy to assert boundaries until God Himself intervened on behalf of His "Chaplain of the desert" whose "clients" would come shouting for him at all hours at his "home office."[9] Like the Prophet, we need boundaries. Like that disciple, we need to listen to the needs of the body or our body will speak up for us. On Judgment Day, our body parts will speak up and testify concerning us, and so it was not such a stretch to read Peter Levine's work on somatic experiencing, rooted though it may be in evolutionary psychology. As a Muslim, my body will speak for me when I die, and it spoke to me both during my prison ministry and later as an organ donor family support person. Driving home from the prison one day, I felt my body seize up as if it anticipated a punch. I knew, of course, that mental anguish could manifest somatically. I'd seen it when I delivered my first death notification to an inmate. As soon as the terrible news escaped my lips that her four-year-old had died, she buckled in her chair as if receiving a blow to the abdomen.

Self-care is a preventative act that honors our gift of compassionate, empathetic presence. This self needs environments where it is not needed. It needs moments when there are no inputs, so that we might increase our creative and spiritual outputs. We cannot call others to the mantle of mercy if we have excluded ourselves from its warmth.

The herb ashwagandha has helped, as has limiting my news intake. As an empath, I now listen to and honor my physical self. I enjoy embodied activities like yoga, which draws me away from my churning thoughts and toward my body. Deep breathing was foundational in my recovery and even enriched my practice of *salât* (ritual prayer). Without consciously trying, I began to alternate inhales and exhales between the different prayer postures. This was not an attempt to change the prayer or graft a foreign practice onto it: it was literally what I needed to do to calm my autonomic nervous system enough to make my way through the prayer. We are alive because God breathed into Adam His *rûh*.[10] When our spirits constrict due to hardship, our bodies often constrict, and along with it, this life-giving breath as well.

Even drawing boundaries for myself has taken on a spiritual essence. Admitting that I can't counsel as much as I'd like, or absorb every story I see, or that I need to turn off the news, is a blow to my *nafs* (ego/lower-self). Like a pain-addled performer whose days are numbered, I've had to ask myself who I am without my art form. "You'll do it again," the shrink tells me. I say, again with a straight face, "I don't know. This person—me—is so needy. It'll be a while."

I think of inmates I counseled who wouldn't recognize this fragile version of me. "*What's wrong, chappie?*" I hear them say. I see their green uniforms, tattooed hands, worn eyes that have seen too much. And I also see their humanity and their concern for me. I feel shame and yet I remember telling them never to feel ashamed when you need help. And I think of hospital families who trusted me to support them, how they cried and supported one another— and sometimes me. I remember a brief stint as a hospital chaplain and being dispatched to a husband still crying over his wife's dead body in the hospital bed. There I was, a total stranger, head-scarved, and obviously not the usual chaplain. I offered a prayer of comfort to the family, even though I'd never seen a dead body and wasn't even sure this was death. When the husband learned it was my first day on the job, he called to his son, "Hey, Bobby! Get over here! It's her first day! Let's have her say another prayer with us so she can get practice!" They then thanked me and gestured me toward the bereavement tray of cookies and juice. To thank me. For praying with them.

I think of that man often. He allowed his tragedy to be my "practice." He let me into his intimate world of grief. He believed in me. And so, I must believe in me too. The suffocated remind me that I can still breathe, and I must. Deeply.

Notes

1. Katherine May, *Wintering: The Power of Rest and Retreat in Difficult Times* (Riverhead Books, 2020).

2. Gabor Maté, *When the Body Says No: The Cost of Hidden Stress* (Knopf, 2003).

3. Peter A. Levine with Ann Frederick, *Waking the Tiger: Healing Trauma* (North Atlantic Books, 1997).

4. al-Nasâ'î, al-Hâkim, and others.

5. Bessel van der Kolk, *The Body Keeps the Score: Brain, Mind, and Body in the Healing of Trauma* (Penguin, 2014).

6. Ahmad ibn Hanbal, *Musnad* 12902.

7. al-Tirmidhî, *Sunan* 2687.

8. Tâ Hâ/20:78.

9. al Hujurât/49:4.

10. al-Hijr/15:29.

27

What I Learn from the Prophet ﷺ About Death and Dying

SOHAIB N. SULTAN

SINCE THE BEGINNING of April 2020, my family and I have been grappling with my diagnosis of Stage IV cholangiocarcinoma, which is a very rare, aggressive, and incurable cancer. When we were given the diagnosis, I asked the doctor "How much time do I have?" "Typically, one or two years," he replied. I want to say at the very beginning, because I know that a lot of my beloveds are listening, that I have full faith, as do you, that matters of life and death are entirely in the hands of our most merciful and wise Lord. Therefore, we do not take anyone's diagnosis or prognosis as gospel, but rather a doctor's best estimation trying to prepare someone for life and end-of-life. So I have not given up. But I have entered into a very different mode of living, in which

---

Sohaib N. Sultan (August 26, 1980—April 16, 2021) was the first full-time Muslim life coordinator and chaplain at Princeton University. A graduate of Hartford Seminary's Islamic Chaplaincy Program with one unit of Clinical Pastoral Education (CPE), his research and academic interests were in Islamic spirituality and psychology, as well as the development of practical skills in religious leadership. He was a well-known author and speaker who traveled all around the United States, the Middle East, and Europe to promote mutual respect and understanding. Sohaib was a member of the Association of Muslim Chaplains and lived in Hamilton, New Jersey, with his wife and constant companion, Arshe Ahmed, and their young daughter. He loved being near water, watching soccer, and spending time with family.

On January 15, 2021, Chaplain Sohaib N. Sultan delivered the following address for CelebrateMercy as part of their Friday Gems series. This transcription has been abridged with permission for publication.

I am actively preparing for death, I am preparing for the grave. I see myself as someone who already has one foot in the grave, and as someone who regularly sees dreams in which I am told that the time is near.

As I have been reflecting upon and grappling with the reality of my mortality, I have become increasingly appreciative and grateful to Allah ﷻ that He sent to me, and to all of us as Muslims, a guide in the Prophet Muhammad ﷺ who not only teaches us how to live but also teaches us how to die. And the reason that I'm so grateful for that is because death is a universal, inevitable reality—*every soul will taste death*.[1] There is no living being that does not have a finite beginning and a finite end to their earthly and worldly existence.

If we place the Prophet ﷺ in the discourse of the philosophers, we would say that he is, undoubtedly, the most brilliant existential philosopher in human history—a philosopher who not only believes that death is both inevitable and imminent but also that death gives life meaning. It is death that pushes us to ask some of the most important and serious questions about life: Why was I born? What is my purpose? What is my value? What should I do with this very limited time I have on earth? I learned about death from the Prophet ﷺ that contemplating death's reality, inevitability, and imminence is essential to the spiritual path and to the journey to Allah ﷻ because only when we come to terms with our mortality, do we start to ask the questions that lead us to living the most purposeful life. This is why when the Prophet ﷺ would come upon people engaged in frivolous speech or actions, he would say to them, "Remember frequently the destroyer of pleasure," and by that he meant death, because it removes from a person this notion that we are just created for entertainment. We were not created except to worship and serve Allah ﷻ and to cultivate the earth.[2]

The Prophet ﷺ taught us that we should live life as if we are on a journey, that our time in the world is like when a traveler stops under a tree to seek some shade and refresh themselves before continuing on their journey. Thus, our soul had a life before it came into the world and it has a long way to go after it departs the world. This world is just a temporary stop where we take shade and refresh ourselves. How do we refresh ourselves? Through faith and good deeds. Our life's purpose is to cultivate faith in our hearts, to beautify our character, and to do righteous deeds so that we return to Allah ﷻ with *qalbun salîm*, a purified, peaceful, and tranquil heart—that is what this entire affair is all about.

The Prophet ﷺ teaches us that contemplating death is one of the most important things we can do on our journey to Allah ﷻ and that contemplating it is not morbid, but instead it should strengthen our faith and motivate us to do good. One of my favorite stories from the life of *Rasûl Allâh* ﷺ that teaches us about death is when he was told that his infant son, Ibrâhîm (*radiyallâh 'anhu*), was gasping for his last breaths. Remember, at this point, the Prophet ﷺ had already buried five of his children with his own hands—a man who had gone through immense loss in his life, and now this baby that had brought him such joy toward the end of his own life, and that had brought such joy to the Medinan community, was also now dying. So he takes his baby, Ibrâhîm (*radiyallâh 'anhu*), into his arms and starts to weep. Tears, flowing down his face, wet his beard. As he is sobbing, one of the Companions asks him, "What is this O *Rasûl Allâh*? Are you not content with God's decree?" In that moment, the Prophet ﷺ says, to those around him, that these tears are *rahmah* (mercy) and they are an indication of a soft heart, that one feels sadness over the departure of their loved one. He continues, "Verily, the eyes shed tears, and the heart is grieved, but we will not say anything except what is pleasing to our Lord. We are saddened by your departure, O Ibrâhîm."[3] One of the most profound aspects of this hadith is that the Prophet ﷺ is teaching us how to marry grief with contentment. Because oftentimes, people think that expressing grief means that you are discontent with the decree of God, and that if you are content with the decree of God it means you should not be aggrieved. But here, the Prophet ﷺ is teaching us through his own personal example that the two can be married together and are not contradictory. You feel grief because of the softness of your heart and you feel sorrow at being separated from your loved one. This is the Prophet ﷺ who knew with faith, which is beyond the faith of any other human, that he would soon be reunited with his beloved in the afterlife and yet the departure and separation in this life from his beloved was so intense that it caused him to sob. Despite this pain, he says, "We will not say anything except what is pleasing to our Lord," meaning that we will be content with the decree of Allah ﷻ.

When I received my diagnosis, I was so grateful that my parents and teachers had taught me these lessons. After the diagnosis, all my wife and I could say was *al-hamdu lillâh*; Allah gave us such a beautiful life. There is nothing that I ever wanted from life that my Lord did not give me. Nothing. And on top of that, my Lord gave me things that I can never express enough gratitude for. If I just think about my daughter, Radiyya, and if I were to spend the rest of my life in *sujûd* (prostration) for that gift, it would not be enough to express my gratitude—this is the generosity of my Lord. But there are moments where I feel sad: to leave my daughter, my parents, my wife, my sister, my nephew, my niece, my friends, and the work that I love, but *al-hamdu lillâh*, I have *ridâ* (contentment). These are the teachings of our Prophet ﷺ.

The Prophet ﷺ also taught us that it is important not to go to extremes when we grieve. He taught his Companions not to be among those who beat their chests, rip their clothes, and wail loudly, but instead try to be moderate in your grief. He teaches us how to mourn with dignity so that those who are dying can leave peacefully, because those who die can hear certain things by the permission of Allah.

I am also really grateful for how the Prophet ﷺ solves one of the great dilemmas we face as we approach the end of our lives and we feel, perhaps, we should give away all our money in charity. It is anxiety about appearing before Allah ﷻ with a deficiency or an inadequacy in our charitable giving. So there's a story, from the authentic Hadith tradition, that I want to share about a great Companion of the Prophet ﷺ named Sa'd (*radiyallâh 'anhu*) who reported:

> The Prophet ﷺ visited me while I was ill in Mecca. I said, "I have some wealth. May I donate all of it?" The Prophet ﷺ said, "No." I said, "Half of it?" The Prophet ﷺ said, "No." I said, "A third of it?" The Prophet ﷺ said, "Yes, a third, but this is still too much. That you leave your inheritors wealthy is better than leaving them dependent, begging for what people have. Whatever you spend on them is charity for you, even the morsel you feed to your wife."[4]

I am grateful that it *seems* that Allah ﷻ has not decreed a sudden death for me, and so I have some time to prepare, which includes arranging my family affairs. The Prophet ﷺ advises and teaches us to have a will prepared to make sure you are taking care of your family so if death comes upon you slowly or suddenly, they do not become impoverished. Prepare for death not only for your soul but also for your family's worldly affairs; this has brought me great comfort as I arrange my family's affairs before leaving this world.

Related to this is a great hadith, with a very weak chain [of transmission], but the meaning of which is very true. When the Prophet ﷺ felt death approaching, he wanted to address his community so he took one of his relatives and stood in front of the people to say:

> O people! Your rights upon me have drawn near upon me, so whoever's back I have whipped, here now is my back, so let him take his revenge! Whoever's honor I have smeared, here now is my honor, so let him take his revenge! Whoever's wealth I have taken, here now is my wealth, so let him take his revenge. . . . I hereby declare it: let not a single one of you fear the slightest resentment from the Messenger of Allah, for resentment is neither my nature nor my engagement. I hereby declare it: the most beloved of you all to me is he who takes his rights from me, thereby freeing me to meet Allah with stillness in my soul.

When I first announced my illness and difficult prognosis to the community that I serve, one of the things I said in my letter was: if I owe anyone anything, just tell me now. If there's anything I ever did to hurt you, if there's anything I ever did to make you feel bad, anything at all—just tell me now so that I can meet my Lord peacefully. This is part of what *qalbun salîm* means, having a heart that is empty of everything other than Allah. Start to ask people for forgiveness, even if you have no sense that death is near you. Start to clear your debts. Start to rectify your affairs with people that you are in conflict with because you do not want to take these things to your grave and to Allah.

I also want to share some lessons that I learned from reading the *Shamâ'il* [noble characteristics] about the Prophet's ﷺ final hours before he returned to his Lord ﷻ. I was deeply struck by how enormously painful death was for the Prophet ﷺ. His family bore witness to this as they took care of him in his final days. They said they had never seen another human sweat and suffer in such debilitating pain before. We call this *sakarât al-mawt*, the pangs of death as the soul is being separated from the body. This really struck me because we often think that if somebody is righteous and beloved to Allah, that Allah will make their death very easy, very painless, and will take their soul very peacefully. But the death of *Rasûl Allâh* ﷺ teaches us that, in fact, a sign of God may be that He puts you through immense suffering before you die, that He is purifying you and elevating you through the pangs of death.[5]

In that moment of great anguish as the Prophet ﷺ is experiencing the pangs of death, his daughter, Fatima (*radiyallâh 'anhâ*) starts to weep and says, "Great hardship has come upon my father!" because she was so saddened by the suffering of the Prophet ﷺ. Deeply concerned for how his daughter was feeling, he said to her, "After this day, your father will feel no more pain." He wanted her to know that he would soon be in a state of great joy in communion with his Lord ﷻ. Thus, the Prophet ﷺ taught us that, for the Believer, death is not something to be saddened by, but rather, death is freedom and great joy because it is your soul finally returning to your beloved Lord, Most High. This is why in Surah Al-Ahzâb, Allah ﷻ says that the Prophet ﷺ is a role model, "for the people who yearn and long for Allah."[6] If you yearn for Allah, then the Prophet ﷺ is your role model because he was always yearning for, longing for, and wanting to be with Allah. When he saw that death was upon him, he was happy because he knew from that moment on, he would not be distracted by anything of the world, that his soul would spend eternity with Allah and those whom Allah loves. This was the spirit about death which he cultivated in his Companions. When Bilal (*radiyallâh 'anhu*) was on his deathbed, his wife started crying and exclaiming, "This is a day of great grief!" But Bilal (*radiyallâh 'anhu*) replied, "No, this is a day of great joy. Today I meet my *habîb*, my beloved Mustafa, Muhammad ﷺ!" For the one who longs for Allah, death is not sorrowful. It is great joy.

Lastly, for those who bury their loved ones, how do they honor those who pass away? The Prophet ﷺ taught us to make *dua* [supplication] for the deceased to stay connected to them and to give charity on their behalf to benefit their soul. Just as importantly, he also taught us to take care of all of the people who were beloved to the deceased. Look at the way the Prophet ﷺ treated and took care of the friends and relatives of his beloved wife, Khadîjah (*radiyallâh 'anhâ*), after she died as a way of honoring her! So I always tell my friends that as long as I am alive, all my needs are taken care of and I do not expect anything from you. But after I die, I expect you to take care of my family and to be like a father figure to my daughter, Radiyya. I know that they will be there for my family because a believing and loving community is there for each other, not only during life but also after death. God bless you all. Inshallah, I hope you have taken something beneficial from this and that you keep me in your *duas*, as I keep you in mine.

Notes

1. Âl 'Imrân/3:185.

2. Hadiths refer to sleep as the sister of death: https://abuaminaelias.com /dailyhadithonline/2016/03/24/people-jannah-not-sleep-die/.

3. al-Bukhârî, *al-Jâmi' al-Sahîh* 1241: https://abuaminaelias.com/dailyhadith online/2020/02/20/death-of-prophets-son-ibrahim/.

4. al-Bukhârî, *al-Jâmi' al-Sahîh* 5039.

5. While not in his original address, the author later offered this clarification, "Thankfully, scholars of the Sacred Law from the earliest period determined, based on their study of the Muhammadan Way, that among the maxims of the *sharî'ah* is to alleviate suffering and to remove hardship. When pain can be lightened, it is Allah's Mercy. When pain cannot be lightened, there is also Allah's Mercy. As such, based on this Prophetic understanding, I have personally taken every medicine recommended by my doctors to lighten the pain when possible."

6. al-Ahzâb/33:21.

28

Lasting Grief in Hospice

Reflections of a Shi'a Muslim Chaplain

SAMEER ALI

MY THEOLOGY OF GRIEF emanates from Sh'ia Muslim theology, originating in the Qur'an, in the Sunnah (traditions) of the Prophet Muhammad ﷺ, and in the commands, silences, and prohibitions found in the reports from the Twelve Imams and *al-Ma'sûmûn* (the Fourteen Infallibles). The effect of this deep spiritual affiliation with these sacred beings, their teachings, and subsequently their suffering and martyrdoms is that it brings forth tears and softens the heart, guides the believer to the path of salvation and true belief and action, and absolves sins. The central element of this theology of grief is the retelling of the martyrdom of Imam al-Husayn and his children and companions. The goal of the believer is to commemorate them and to hold that grief for them as a source of grief greater than grief for our loved ones. This grief is vertical, originating with Adam, continuing with the subsequent prophets, and finding its final manifestation within Islam. It must be discovered and revisited time and time again throughout the spiritual markings of sacred time throughout the week and the year.

Sameer Ali currently serves as a hospice chaplain in Milwaukee, Wisconsin, and at Marquette University. Sameer appreciates visiting patients in the many different hospice settings, including inpatient and in their homes, and serving on the Professional Consultation Committee for a local Clinical Pastoral Education (CPE) site. He holds an MA in Religious Studies from Stanford University, has completed four CPE units, and is board certified through the Spiritual Care Association. His cultural home is South Asia, and he enjoys reading, fishing, traveling, and learning new languages. Sameer is an imam and 'alim in the Shi'a Muslim community.

In the grief for al-Husayn, the grief for family or loved ones remains and is enveloped by *al-ʿazâ'* (mourning). All other griefs are set aside, and a consoling aphorism says, "There is no grief like the grief for al-Husayn, and all other losses are small compared to the loss of al-Husayn." Each year, I witness Muslims from around the world recite eulogies, poems, sermons, and expressions of sadness as they recall the tragedy of Karbala, and I journey with them, bound by this emotional devotion despite the barriers of language. This grief is incomparable to anything else, as it cannot be measured or weighed against any loss; a hadith narration claims, "The grief for al-Husayn remains [lit] in the heart of the believer and can never be extinguished,"[1] which is to say it is the most illuminated sadness in the life of a believer.

Where does my theology of grief lead me as a hospice chaplain? I have had the honor of accompanying patients and their families as they journey through the cycle of hospice care, which consists of the initial palliative consult, the decision to abandon curative methods, the often nervous first encounter with hospice and comfort care, the gradual acceptance of the terminal diagnosis, death, and the eventual emotional process of mourning and meaning-making. This is the *horizontal* manifestation of another grief, which is experienced by humankind on earth. It is not the same as *al-ʿazâ'*, but it is another marker of the experience of the believer inhabiting a finite world where there is suffering, injury, and death. My upbringing and theology as a Shiʿa Muslim and my connection to the mourning process for Imam al-Husayn informs the ways in which I perceive every part of the hospice journey. This central commemoration of *al-ʿazâ'* gives the spiritual opening of the heart (*al-fuʾâd*) the ability to decipher, sense, and be present with grief when it presents itself in the horizontal plane where I subsist as a clinician and a believer.

I think of hospice as having four stations. During the **first station**, the patient and family recognize that seeking a cure is no longer possible or they are not further interested in such a search, and they then begin to emotionally reckon with abandoning hospital visits, testing, and curative measures. A hospice agency provides comfort measures in a person's home, a special facility, or in some hospitals. An interdisciplinary team supports the family and the patient, including nurses, social workers, chaplains, as well as music, pet, and massage therapists. This embrace of hospice support causes a shift in the emotional posturing of the patient and family and provides an opportunity for the chaplain to explore and reflect with them and identify that which is important to them.

I was told by her nurse that June, in her seventies and recently admitted with terminal cancer, would not say more than a word during the nurse's hourlies. Not one word. I entered her room, and June turned her head away and looked outside at the bird feeders on the patio below. I introduced myself and then stood silently; June looked at me and looked away again. There were no birds on the feeders. June did not dismiss me right away, so I decided to sit across from her. I began with the mundane, talking about the schedule of the groundskeeper and when he comes to fill the bird feeders. A faint smile crossed June's face, but she continued to avoid looking at me. I sat for fifteen minutes and, between providing nonverbal presence and talking about the everyday, I did not get one word from June. As I stood up to leave, she looked at me, followed me with her eyes, and smiled.

Initially, June had appeared agitated with the nurses. When the nurse had first called me, she requested I try to instill a sense of calm and peace with June and help them to understand how she was feeling. June was a tough patient to visit: she consistently had a flat affect and only gave occasional, gruff one-word answers. She gradually became more expressive during visits, though still short: "I like music," once. Another time, "Maybe prayer will work, I don't know." Upon my fifth visit, she took a photo of two lovely cats from her handbag and passed it to me saying, "I wish this could improve a little, I want to be home with my two cats." Suddenly, I could make tangible what she had been longing for and grieving. She reiterated that she wanted to "get better" to be with her cats "until I am called to go home."

June understood that she was dying. She did not debate or argue with her oncologist, and she accepted the comfort medications prescribed by the hospice doctor. But she was not pleasant with the nurses; they bore the brunt of her grief. June wanted to get better *just enough* to be home with her cats. A sense of sadness and loss enveloped me on the drive home that day, and I thought about how important and deep the companionship between June and her cats was. I witnessed how lonely she was, despite the efforts of the nurses, staff, music therapists, and social workers to make her feel at home. For June, a cure meant even just a temporary reprieve from the hospital for a short visit home to be with her cats. This small insight she trusted me with led us to arrange a pet therapist visit with two cats. Sadly, June died before I could discern if it helped bring her peace.

What I name as *a station in the cycle* of hospice care begins with the initial realization of the terminal nature of the illness. This is where June was when we met, and as is common, she—like most patients—experienced sadness and an impending sense of loss, while patients' families often experience anticipatory grief. The patient may gradually come to terms with the medical diagnosis and may also be tired of all the interventions aimed at a cure. They have already made the journey across the first station of abandoning curative measures, but this stationing may not be a smooth one. Desires to find cures, as well as expressions of resentment, anger, confusion, or the absence of acceptance may lead a patient or family to abandon hospice and return to the hospital in an attempt to seek treatment.

The **second station** is coming to terms with the nature of hospice. During this station, the patient and family's central focus is in the body and the realization that comfort measures can be difficult to adjust to and to find stability in, as the physical condition of the patient continues to deteriorate. Patients often emotionally seek to give up control of their bodies and embrace or reject the medications and measures available for their comfort care.

At my inpatient unit, Jeff, a seventy-four-year-old patient, presented with renal failure. He had been on dialysis for five years, and twice a week his wife would drive him to the hospital, taking three to four hours for each visit. After Jeff arrived on hospice, the first thing he said during my initial assessment visit was, "It's nice. There are no big machines with loud sounds. I will go in peace." He expressed his relief at the absence of constant medical interventions which had become bothersome to him since, in his words, "there was no point to it all."

The process through which humankind realizes this moment of impending departure is a moment of emotional turns and turmoil. Through our conversation, I saw that Jeff now realized he'd felt a sense of safety in his earlier routine—the schedule with his twice a week dialysis trips, his diet. He'd not thought ahead to its termination and felt discombobulated with its abrupt end. Realizing that he wasn't bound by his regular schedule and that he was free to eat as he pleased brought about some joy as well for Jeff and his wife. My response when I witnessed this shift was *relief*. I was happy to see that Jeff was not upset or angry but pleasantly accepting of his diagnosis and open to interventions of comfort.

A **third station** in the cycle is a plateau of emotional expression that explores closure, examines unfinished business, brings family members together around the event of impending death and departure. Key elements of this phase are legacy consideration, family dynamics and relationships, and finding space for spiritual upliftment and emotional closure. This is the most intense period of emotional processing for the patient and the family as they have the opportunity to fully come to terms with what lies ahead, including the patient's mortality, family systems, financial considerations, as well as funeral and memorial planning. If a patient lingers at this station, they examine larger, existential questions and make meaning from their experience.

Daisy, a seventy-eight-year-old cancer patient, spent a few months at this reflective station. She took up knitting again, an old hobby of hers, asking her son for large amounts of wool and yarn, and industriously commenced knitting baby hats, socks, and sweaters. For three months, she vigorously made these items and sent them to the children's hospital for newborns. Each time I visited, I saw large piles of clothing items in various colors on her desk. I explored what this gesture meant to her, and Daisy told me, "I want to make these clothes for the newborns. I want them to be warm and safe when I am gone." Daisy desired to extend her presence in this world through these items to those she would never meet but who would benefit from her generosity and kindness. Daisy felt joy in her activities and would smile and sing as she knitted. One Sunday, she stopped eating, drinking, knitting, and then passed peacefully in my presence on a sunny Tuesday afternoon.

As a Muslim, I witnessed that Daisy desired a legacy of *khayr* (good in the world) and that her theomorphic nature, her *fitrah*, was expressive in calling her to do good. Prophet Muhammad ﷺ said, "When a person dies, the angels ask about what they have brought with them and the people ask about what they have left behind."[2] This expression of legacy was evident with Daisy as she knit clothes for the newborns that she might be remembered. She was diligent, joyful, and present during her knitting, and her energy and enthusiasm were admirable and infectious. She expressed her strong Lutheran faith and mentioned the importance of kindness and sacrifice as her work demonstrated her belief in these values.

At times, I witness the essence and the core reality of a person manifest during a hospice stay. Gary was an avid outdoorsman and hunter in his sixties, admitted to hospice with a brain tumor. Raised in a family of hunters, he'd practically lived outdoors, according to his wife. The tumor left him with partial mobility, and one of his hands no longer functioned. Over several months, I had the opportunity to provide the couple pastoral care. One morning, I found him looking out the window. He lamented to me, "I wish I were a free turkey, roaming around the woods." After that, on sunny days, we took our visits outside, him leading in his wheelchair identifying trees as we passed and birds from their songs. I observed that the most consistent activity in Gary's life defined him—his *dhât* (essence) was imbued with the act of hunting and his connection to the outdoors. Out on the patio, surrounded by trees and sunlight, Gary was an astute outdoorsman and could recognize the sounds of birds, the types of trees, and would give me endless tips about hunting and fishing. I witnessed his authentic self express itself with such joy and unhindered enthusiasm and thought to myself, *What is at my own core? What would I be excited about if I was in his shoes?* Gary's deep desire was to be out in nature, and his funeral wishes changed over the course of his stay: his initial plan to be buried changed to the desire to be cremated to scatter his ashes over a small parcel of land he hunted on.

The **third station** ends with death. During this time, it is common for a person's breathing to become shallow and interspersed with a sound known as the death rattle, made by terminal secretions. This sound, often difficult for family to hear, always brings me to the Qur'anic verse, "when it [the soul] reaches the throat, while you are looking on,"[3] a witness to the process of death. This verse addresses the persons observing death and reminds them of their position as witnesses to the process which is in the *qudrah* (power) of God. Humankind is helpless, in awe, present, and unable to fully perceive the reality of death as we "see not."[4]

Sometimes family members are unable to bear witness to the dying, even if mentally prepared for it. I remember TC, a middle-aged man, who had flown in to be present for his mother's passing. TC had consistently talked about the process of death and dying and had expressed that his belief was different from that of his very devout Catholic mother. Raised Catholic, he had moved away after his experience as a social worker led him to find that "religion did not always make sense." We had many conversations about the nature of dying as he explored his beliefs. TC and I were present in the room when his mother began to die, and after a short, silent observation of her labored breaths and the death rattle, TC turned toward me and started talking. He began to talk of mundane, everyday things; I was confused, our six weeks of conversations had been sober and speculative. I realized slowly that TC did not want to watch his mother die and I was the distraction for him. I turned my attention to the mundane topics and stayed with him, while also watching his mother breathe her last. When the nurse entered shortly thereafter, TC turned to her and asked, "Is she gone?" Receiving her confirmation, TC silently looked out the window. TC *knew* his mother would pass, but he *could not watch* her pass. His mind made the journey before the heart was ready for it.

After death, the **fourth and final station** is grief and mourning in the hearts of the family members, close friends, and hospice staff. The family members hold on to the cooling embers of the event of death and passing and carry with them the memories and defining events and turns of their own relationship with the deceased. Sadness, grief, relief, curiosity, and loneliness converge for the bereaved in different ways and through various sense-scapes in the emotional aftermath. Immediately after a loved one passes, sadness and a sense of loss usually follow closely. After an initial expression of grief, the bereaved can feel a sense of relief that the patient is no longer suffering, as the soul is no longer inhibited by the body. Then come the emotions and memories, which will last for a longer period of time.

There is certainly a marked difference between al-'azâ' and grief in hospice, and I am aware that both are different in origin and in cause; the former is part of the existential nature of îmân (faith) and the latter a part of life on earth, but with its own language, importance, and process, so *how do I see them connected?* I find that my own personal experience with grief when I have lost loved ones, or my emotional proximity to others and reflection of loss for them, is heightened by my knowledge and experience of al-'azâ'. They are intertwined, connected, and marked in complex ways, which is sometimes hard to express but understood and experienced by the heart, one almost a shadow of the other.

Jessica, a middle-aged Christian I'd accompanied through her mother Brenda's hospice journey, requested my presence at the funeral. I joined a crowded hall of tearful faces and grieving hearts, as Brenda had a large family and many church friends. The pastor, who had a long-standing relationship with the family, opened with words of welcome and a eulogy with Bible passages before inviting me forward. I shared from what I'd learned in my visits with Brenda and her family, reciting a poem on mourning, and encouraging the attending crowd to be aware of the process of grief to honor the memories they held of Brenda.

After meeting some of the mourners and speaking with them, I realized that both the pastoral presence of the pastor and my invitation to grief were effective on the audience in their own way. Scripture and poetry played different roles in claiming space in the process of mourning and remembrance for the audience. I had recited "Safe in their Alabaster Chambers" by Emily Dickinson, and it recalled ways in which the deceased are safe and sound in death and stay static in their peace as the world continues to change dynamically around them.

For me, as a Shi'a Muslim, an 'âlim, and a hospice chaplain, my own personal grief and that of those I accompany through the stations of hospice are wrapped up in that of Karbala. The loss of a family member, the memory of mourning and grieving, the sadness that I receive from my encounter with patients, is present with me. But I find the most cumulative, overwhelming, perfect, and emancipating time is mourning for al-Husayn. The evergreen banner of al-'azâ' and mourning is unraveling itself for me whenever I witness sadness, grief, and loss. Simultaneously, I witness that God has guided me to be present for others and to journey alongside them when they make their way in a world where there is loss, injury, and death.

Notes

1. *Jâmi Ahâdîth al-Shî'ah,* vol 2.
2. *Mîzân al-Hikmah.*
3. al-Wâqi'ah/56:83–84.
4. al-Wâqi'ah/56:85.

An Islamic Theology of Pastoral Care

RABIA TERRI HARRIS

MY MOTHER HAD ALZHEIMER'S. My grandmother before her had Alzheimer's. The possibility of my own entry into that state is therefore always before me. The clear awareness of such a possibility has a number of consequences. Some of them are theological. I don't believe that a theology of pastoral care can be separated from a theology of identity. To whom, to what, are we attempting to offer care? If we don't know that—or at least, if we don't have a good working approach to that question—then how can we offer care at all?

The reality of Alzheimer's poses a major challenge to many theories of identity. Having spent a lot of time with my mother and grandmother, and many other dementia patients since, I find it absurd to claim that such people have lost their identity. They have lost their histories with their memories, but they have not lost themselves: they remain present. Merely recognizing that fact in

Rabia Terri Harris is a speaker, writer, editor, activist, community chaplain, and founder of the Muslim Peace Fellowship. The first president of the Association of Muslim Chaplains, she also cofounded Community of Living Traditions, a multireligious community of practice fostering faith-rooted approaches to peace, justice, and care of the earth. The child of a Jewish father and a Christian mother, Rabia received forty years of Islamic spiritual education through the Halveti-Jerrahi Tariqa. She holds a BA in Religion from Princeton University, an MA in Middle Eastern Languages and Cultures from Columbia University, and a graduate certificate in Islamic Chaplaincy from Hartford Seminary. She has worked in hospice (adult and pediatric) and completed seven units of Clinical Pastoral Education (CPE). Rabia refreshes herself through gardening.

a personal encounter can be a significant pastoral intervention with dementia patients. But the fact itself has implications that travel far beyond the realm of care for the very old. For how is it that our *sense* of identity, in earlier life, gets so caught up in events and relationships that may later vanish without a trace?

I have been educated by the Halveti-Jerrahi Sufi *tarîqah*, a religious order that finds its place within the larger Turkish Sunni discourse. In that tradition, we are taught that there is great virtue in the constant recollection of death. One difficulty with this practice in Western society today is that, among Westerners, death is often institutionally sequestered. The fortunate are therefore easily able to repress its reality. But once Alzheimer's enters a family, it introduces a reality that is very hard to repress.

A fundamental Sufi teaching states, "Whoever knows herself, knows her Lord"—or her Sustainer, as we might better translate *Rabb*, that central Islamic term. There is an experienceable Something beyond us that somehow sustains us, a Something that all of us encounter at one time or another, and that many of us have found a way to acknowledge, at least from time to time. It is our continuing connection with this Sustainer in every circumstance, conscious or unconscious, that truly benefits and heals us, whether we are aware of it or not. But most often, we are unaware of it, and that lack of awareness has consequences. For it is the absence of conscious connection to our Sustainer that produces our psychic pain. To relieve our psychic pain, it is necessary to rediscover our Sustainer. And to rediscover our Sustainer, it is necessary to know ourselves anew.

God exists inside and outside history. We too exist inside history and outside history. To care for ourselves and others inside our complex developing stories, we must call upon essential human presence, which is independent of all the stories we tell. Once essential human presence is engaged, God may be recognized anywhere. As a chaplain, I am devoted to the honoring and engagement of essential human presence.

All Islamic theology begins with the affirmation of the unity of God, or *tawhîd*. According to Ibn 'Arabî,[1] God in God's wholeness is mirrored in only two places: in the universe in its entirety, and in the human being. Following this vision, the basic affirmation requires of us two additional affirmations. Along with taking our stand upon the unity of God, Muslims ought also to stand for the unity of creation and the unity of the person.

If creation and the person are, in their essence, mirrors of the divine, and the divine is one, a key element of spiritual and pastoral practice necessarily follows. I must cultivate the attitude that whoever faces me, faces me in God.

In daily living, preexisting unity translates into the sense of connection. *Tawhîd* suggests that human connections do not need to be created. They need to be discovered. There is never a gap to bridge. There is only the movement from the unknown to the known. I may or may not be privileged to uncover the meaning of my encounter with the person who faces me. But the relationship already exists whether I grasp its meaning or not.

Very often we experience not unity but fragmentation. We feel not connected but isolated. Pastoral care addresses itself to this sometimes terrifying experience. Sufi teachers refer to that experience as the *pain of separation*. Though people in crisis feel it most acutely, the pain of separation is a chronic condition. If *wahdah*, the Unity, is a reality, we must ask ourselves how the pain of separation can exist.

There are two major approaches to this question. One is the conversation about sin. Though very relevant in its own sphere, it does not concern us here, for from a Muslim point of view, the conversation about sin does not properly address *existential* pain. Theologically, one of the major ways that Islam differs from Christianity is in its dismissal of the notion of original sin. The Qur'an tells us that Adam was forgiven. Humanity, therefore, cannot be bearing the punishment for his act.

Muslim metaphysicians take another tack. We ask ourselves, "What is it that the creation gives to the Creator?" It is axiomatic that God is self-sufficient and needs nothing. Yet God must *want* something from us: otherwise, we would not exist. To establish what that might be, the Sufis turn to a famous saying, often classified as a Hadith Qudsi, or non-Qur'anic divine utterance, in which God declares, "I was a hidden treasure, and I longed to be known, so I created the universe." Thus, we find that the whole business of existence is to come to know God. Yet it is also axiomatic that God already knows God. What makes our knowing valuable?

Ibn 'Arabî teaches that the existence of creatures allows the establishment of myriad distinct points of view, each of which offers a unique contemplation of God, a unique perspective. It is the eccentricities of our adaptations that define us, both as individuals and as species. The distinctiveness of each creature is the sum total of its limitations—the degree to which it cannot be anything else, through which it carves out its own niche in the field of unbounded possibility. What the finite offers the infinite, therefore, is precisely the opportunity of limitation. But limitation hurts. We have enormous nostalgia for unbounded possibility. Rumi famously summons the voice of the reed flute, the sound of the human condition, in the opening lines of his great *Mathnawî*:

Listen to the reed, how it tells a tale, complaining of separations—
Saying, "Ever since I was parted from the reed-bed, my lament has
  caused man and woman to moan . . .
Everyone who is left far from his source wishes back the time when he
  was united with it."[2]

The point of this haunting image is that the reed has been cut from the reed-bed *for the sake of the beauty of its sound*. The reed's pain is the unavoidable side effect of its fulfilling the function for which it is dearly loved. Our pain *is* our personhood. It comes from the core of human dignity. It is not a mistake to be fixed; it is the price of a high destiny. Our pain delineates our service to God. And God is grateful.

It is not possible to remove any pain, small or great, until its time is over, but it is possible to remove the terror surrounding pain. That terror derives from the sense of being trapped and alone. But we are never trapped: no matter how difficult our position, we are always in some stage of a process leading onward. And we are never alone: God is always present. These two reminders are the most important communications that a chaplain can make. But words are never enough. In order for anything to happen, sufferers cannot merely hear these facts. They must feel them.

When I reflect upon my own best experiences as a recipient of pastoral care, I find that two things have helped. One is that the person who engages me recognizes my suffering and takes it seriously. And the other is that he or she sees beyond it. When both these qualities are combined in a single encounter, the result is relief. When I taste my own relief, I remember God.

What does it mean to remember God? It means to be conscious, for an instant, of total love and total freedom, not as far away, but as wholly present: inalienable, in fact. The initial flash of awareness may go almost unnoticed, but its result is always a flooding of peace—the relief itself—which is so longed-for that gratitude is spontaneous. And with the upwelling of gratitude, God is named in the heart. "Are not hearts at peace in the remembrance of God?"[3] All this may last no more than a moment, but it is a moment with consequences. For a moment of peace means a moment of disengagement from relentless interior pressures, and from neutral it is possible for our hearts and minds to switch gears. After my situation is recognized by a compassionate listener, I frequently find that it changes—if not in its outlines, then in my attitude toward it. I am less afraid and less resentful, and that makes a world of difference.

When I am the provider of pastoral care, therefore, I keep these goals in mind. One of the greatest gifts people can give to one another, I believe, is the opportunity to disengage from our persistent painful stories. Our stories are much more manageable when we realize that they, too, shall pass.

Existential pain is noble. Ordinary pain is rarely so.

God says in the Qur'an, "For truly with hardship comes ease! Truly with hardship comes ease!"[4] The statement is repeated, perhaps because it is far from obvious. The ultimate cure for our pain is in the pain itself, in God's honoring what we suffer. But it is pointless, sometimes detrimental, and often spectacularly arrogant to preach the incomprehensible to the brokenhearted. We each must discover God's presence for ourselves, in our own time, and in our own way. Divine love is immense and does not fit into cozy and comfortable sentiments. It is only through losing old illusions that we can encounter new realities.

Rarely will people come to you and say, "I am suffering from existential pain." Nor will they say, "I have had a moment's sublime rest from the human condition." Instead, our joys and sorrows are tied to very specific things, from the trivial ("I lost the game!" "I won the match!") to the profound ("My child has died." "My grandchild has been born."). Rumi's flute sings:

> In every company I uttered my wailful notes, I consorted with the
>   unhappy and with them that rejoice,
> Everyone became my friend from his own opinion; none sought out
>   my secrets from within me.[5]

As God respects the particularity of the creature, so we as chaplains must respect the particularity of the client. This often means "keeping the secrets" of healing. But what sometimes cannot be said can nonetheless be shown— that God's mercy is always present with even the deepest wound. It is our business as chaplains to manifest that mercy, to make ourselves available to serve it. I see two dimensions to our service, which I call *honoring the work of suffering* and *access to light*.

Honoring the Work of Suffering

God says in the Qur'an, "Truly We created man in the most beautiful stature, then We cast him to the lowest of the low."[6] I take "the lowest of the low" to mean the most perilous position that any species can occupy in this universe, the existential position where it is easiest to lose track of God. When things are going well, we are generally oblivious to where we are. But people in crisis know keenly that they are in the darkest of holes.

God also says, "We have indeed honored the Children of Adam, and We carry them over land and sea."[7] Our honoring, then, is not diminished by our lowering, for it accompanies us in our dispersal through all the many conditions of life. In fact, our honoring is in our lowering, for God says, "Truly We offered the Trust unto the heavens and the earth and the mountains, but they refused to bear it, and were wary of it—yet man bore it."[8] What a tremendously difficult task we have undertaken! And in this life, we are almost always unconscious of having undertaken it.

The chaplain's first job, therefore, is to honor the difficulty of the work of the patient. That work is very specific, tied to a particular condition and a particular pain. We need to bring our honoring to *that* condition and *that* pain: if we aim to serve mercy, we can neither turn away nor allow the precise point of suffering to be obscured by generalities. We need to bear witness, along with the patient, to just how tough the situation is. But at the same time, we need to bear witness to its dignity, something the patient frequently cannot do.

One Clinical Pastoral Education supervisor-in-training heard the value of honoring the work of suffering reflected back in the clearest of terms after assisting a student chaplain following the death of his father. "I knew if I could get to my supervisor, everything would be all right," he told his peers. "My supervisor is like a rock!" Of course, the supervisor was deeply gratified. However, where the solidity of the connection actually lay was in the firm pastoral practice of assigning dignity to the student's grief. Later, this student chaplain was able to do that himself, and consequently he grew through his loss.

Access to Light

God says of God in the Qur'an, "He it is Who blesses you, as do His angels, that He may bring you out of darkness into light."[9] God also says, "God is the Light of the heavens and the earth."[10] So when we talk of light, we are speaking simultaneously of the awareness of God and of the nature of God. One elegant way to understand this is to say that God is present in the awareness of God.

Of course, God is present everywhere—but when we become aware of God, God presents as a transforming blessing. *Every time we become aware of God, our state changes.* And subject to God's will, human beings always have the possibility of this awareness. We always have the possibility of transformation.

The particular conditions that bind us may be overwhelmingly complicated and immovably constraining. Yet the seed of freedom never leaves us. It is this that makes the human being a special creation. God said to the angels, "I breathed into him [the human being] of My spirit, [so] fall down before him prostrating."[11] The Angel of Chaplaincy prostrates itself before the humanity of each patient, because within each patient the spirit of God awaits.

The second task of the chaplain, therefore, is to assist the patient in rediscovering his or her intrinsic spiritual light. I have referred to this shift earlier as "remembering God." And I have referred to that through which remembrance is possible as "the essential human presence." The chaplain's second task is therefore gently to summon the patient back to his or her own essential presence. And the most effective method I have found for accessing this presence is *to look at each patient as beautiful.*

Probably the most dramatic and moving demonstration I have had of the usefulness of this method occurred when I was serving in a hospital extended care unit. One of the patients was a very angry, acid-tongued older woman who was recovering from the amputation of a lower leg due to diabetes. She had refused rehab for weeks. Every day I took a few minutes to talk to her, admiring the power of the personality that was expressed through such bitterness, and refusing to be put off as she tried to put everyone off. One day, seemingly out of nowhere, she told me tremulously that she had changed her mind and wanted to learn to walk again. I encouraged her to inform the physical therapist, who was thrilled. Afterward, when we were talking, this patient burst into tears. "This is because of you!" she said. "You never gave up on me, even when I was evil, and I was pretty evil. Because of you, I have found Jesus!"

What an odd and awkward moment that was for me, and how profoundly touching. The two of us never actually talked about religion. Despite my covering my head, it never occurred to her that I might be Muslim. The vocabulary she had for what had happened to her was not the vocabulary I use, but it didn't matter. God makes use of whatever is around for the work of God. Light is always light.

Whoever we are, our peculiar shortcomings in attention and comprehension will directly affect the mirror we can offer to our clients. Consequently, I take it to be a central responsibility of my role as a chaplain to be constantly working on my current set of shortcomings. Yet for *limitation to reflect limitation* is also a valid mirror: it reveals to both parties their share in the universal servanthood.

There is no need for a chaplain to be a saint. There is a pressing need for a chaplain to stay awake. And the demand for consciousness that chaplaincy makes upon us is one of the great gifts that our clients give us. For the quest of light is the work of God, and chaplains aspire to be servants of God. As we support our clients, so they support us. We are all engaged in the same business.

No Muslim enterprise endures that does not recognize the leader of the caravan. So I here bear witness that whatever I undertake as a chaplain, or will ever undertake, is through the spirit and example of Muhammad ﷺ, the Beloved of Allah, the Healer of Hearts, who was sent as "a mercy to the worlds"—all of them. To that greatest of mirrors, I humbly dedicate this essay and this work. The benefit comes from Allah, and the errors are mine.

Notes

1. For a thorough scholarly introduction to the teachings of Ibn 'Arabî, see William C. Chittick, *The Sufi Path of Knowledge: Ibn al-'Arabi's Metaphysics of Imagination* (State University of New York Press, 1989).

2. *The Mathnawî of Jalâlu'ddin Rúmí*, Translation of Books I and II, ed. and tr. R. A. Nicholson (Gibb Memorial Trust, 1982), 5.

3. al-Ra'd/13:28.

4. al-Sharh/94:5–6.

5. *The Mathnawî of Jalâlu'ddin Rúmí*, 5.

6. al-Tîn/95:4–6.

7. al-Isrâ'/17:70.

8. al-Ahzâb/33:72.

9. al-Ahzâb/33:43.

10. al-Nûr/24:35.

11. al-Hijr/15:29, Sâd/38:72.

30

Skipping Stones

AZLEENA SALLEH AZHAR

WHEN I WAS six years old, my grandmother fell ill, and my father, who was completing his doctorate overseas at the time, packed up our things in a panic. While it was a sudden, unexpected death, we reached her bedside in time to say our farewells. There was closure and an understanding that she had lived a full and meaningful life. My father would tell stories of her as my brothers and I sat by her grave, embraced by the heady fragrance of frangipani blossoms. To my young self, that was a gentle parting, how death is supposed to be and the deceased are supposed to be remembered.

Decades later, as a chaplain in the hospital's pediatric cardiac intensive care unit (PCICU), I learned that death there was rarely gentle. When death

Azleena Salleh Azhar came to the United States from Malaysia to Carnegie Mellon University for a BS in Information and Decision Systems. After years of working in the tech industry, she obtained a graduate certificate in Islamic Chaplaincy from Hartford Seminary, doing her field education at Duke University, and one Clinical Pastoral Education (CPE) unit at a large research hospital where she currently serves on the Pastoral Advisory Committee. She is involved with spiritual care and mental health for refugees, Muslim women, and families of children with special needs in her community. She founded Hope Sisters, a safe and nonjudgmental support group for Muslim women, and is a founding member of a pro bono referral program for accessible mental health care. Azleena is a member of the Association of Muslim Chaplains and is pursuing an MSW from the University of North Carolina at Chapel Hill. She finds peace and joy in nature, her husband, their three boys, and three cats.

knocked on the door, the cavalry was armed and ready to fight it off tooth and nail. Parents were forced to choose between doing all they could to keep their child alive and allowing them a peaceful death. Death was something evil to deceive and taunt. The stakes were so much higher because the child was an *amânah* (trust) from God, and parents were their *walî* (protector). Allowing them to die without a fight seemed to mean they had failed to be their protector, that they allowed their child to be wrongfully stolen from them.

In some cases, the families sacrificed so much for their child's health, traversing oceans, learning languages, and crossing cultural barriers. A select few came under the auspices of their government, a seemingly benevolent body, investing in the health of its citizens. The stakes for these children to fight at the edge of beckoning death and get better were much higher. The tools they received to fight death were provided, but in that pact, the families lost their agency to determine which tools to use and what the terms of the fight were.

One tragic story that embodies this example is the case of Asma. Not only were her final moments of life torturous, but her death was traumatic for everyone that her life touched—for her mother at her bedside, her family thousands of miles away, and her care team in the hospital. It was a death everyone who knew her remembered for many months to come—burdened by its harshness and unnecessary suffering.

I remember the first time I met Asma. Whenever I am informed there is a Muslim family in the unit, I do my best to pay a visit as soon as possible. On this particular spring day, wearing the blue booties all visitors had to wear and with my hands thoroughly sanitized, I made my way to the nurses' desk. I checked in to make sure it was okay to visit, and then knocked on the door next to a sign scrawled in bright red marker that said, "Ladies may enter. Men, please stay outside." A female voice said, "Come in." A little girl with short black curls was sitting up in bed, holding a pencil tightly in her right hand. A notebook and a blob of red Play-Doh were on the tray table. On the bedside sat a lady I recognized as one of the hospital's teaching staff. She smiled at me. Asma, too busy with her Play-Doh to notice me, brought the pencil down, not onto the notebook but into the big red mound. She let out squeals of glee and her round eyes sparkled with excitement as she poked deep, perfect holes. I was quickly drawn to her mischievous grin and her vibrant joy.

From the corner of my eye, I noticed a young woman sitting on the sofa bed next to the window, wearing a black abaya robe, with henna-dyed hair tied up in a bun. She looked up inquisitively as if wondering who this hijabi was who walked in the room—a rare sight in this Southern hospital. I approached her and said *salâm*. She returned my greeting and said she was Umm Asma— literally "Asma's mother." I introduced myself as a chaplain. She seemed puzzled but did not say anything. She asked me something in Arabic and I apologized that I couldn't speak the language. I figured I would have to explain what I was there for, particularly since chaplains are not common in Muslim countries. Most Muslims I encountered did not know what a chaplain's role was, even more so for female Muslim chaplains because we don't fit into the typical peg holes. I told Umm Asma that I was an advisor, hoping it would help her understand. The irony is not lost on me now, because I realize that I ended up learning more from this small girl and her mother than they did from me.

As I got to know the family, I learned that Asma's cards were stacked against her the moment she was born. The rare genetic disorder she had made her susceptible to continuous infections, which resulted in her spending much of her young days going back and forth to hospitals. The moment her parents heard of their government's program that would sponsor her treatment in America, they jumped at the opportunity. It didn't matter to them that they didn't speak the language and their support system would be thousands of miles away. Her parents were willing to do anything to give their youngest child hope for a normal life. Without this treatment, Asma's prognosis was very bleak—a higher probability of cancer and higher mortality rate; and if she did survive, she would be destined to a life fighting infection after infection.

Her mother was from an upper-middle-class family in the Arabian Gulf. She had left a life of comfort, shielded from the unpleasant chores of life. Before she knew it, she found herself here in the United States, where she had to do her own shopping, find her own transportation, and learn how to navigate the intricacies of independent Western life. No longer did she have her husband and family to shelter her from the outside world. Umm Asma often felt like a fish out of water, frustrated with the language and cultural barriers. Despite these challenges, she was grateful to be in this strange land. The government's assistance opened up a whole world of possibilities. She would face all the discomfort necessary as long as her daughter had a chance at a long, healthy life.

Little Asma quickly became the heart of the pediatric cardiac intensive care unit (PCICU). Her lilting giggles sounded like little wind chimes fluttering in the wind. If her door was open, her laughter would float down the hall intriguing other families and visitors, like moths to a flame.

Two months after my first visit, Asma showed me her courage beads. The last few times I had dropped in, she had been preoccupied with procedures and I didn't get to see her. On this day, she looked paler than usual and her breathing was ragged.

She held up her beads to me as I approached.

"*Jameel*?" she asked. *Aren't they beautiful?*

The courage beads were like little trophies for the children in the ward, a reminder of their bravery for each procedure or obstacle they overcame. She loved the brightly colored glass beads and delighted in choosing new colors and shapes from the art basket the unit teacher brought with her. She hung the strand up on her bed tray, within sight and easy reach.

I sat on her bedside and we counted each one together. Her eyes lit up and she fondled each bead like it was a precious gem. Her wonder was infectious to the staff who cared for her. But I couldn't help thinking in the back of my head that there were no beads for the ultimate sacrifices she had made, to which no other child in the PCICU—or the hospital for that matter—could claim. The sacrifice of coming thousands of miles to a foreign country, living in the hospital seeing no other family than her mother for months on end; being constantly hassled by a steady stream of medical personnel who poked and prodded and asked questions in a foreign tongue—only for another team to come shortly after with the same incomprehensible questions. Lather. Rinse. Repeat. No bracelet of beads would compensate for her losing her childhood.

One summer day, I came by and found Asma protesting loudly and kicking in bed. Her chain of courage beads had grown. She had also lost a lot of weight, causing her hospital bracelet to slip off her wrist. She was gaunt, and her curly locks had started falling out. Her bright brown eyes were filled with tears. Umm Asma had told her that it was time for physical therapy, which she detested. It meant pushing herself more than she wanted to in places that hurt.

Umm Asma looked away as I entered, visibly frustrated and embarrassed. I knew she wouldn't say one word of complaint to me—she never did. But I could see the weariness etched on her face as Asma continued her long outburst. Being a mother, I knew that feeling of frustrated exhaustion too well. My mind raced to what I could take from my bag of tricks. I fumbled in my pocket and felt something. I took out a little green and white box and shook it. It rattled. Asma continued her wailing but glanced curiously out of the corner of her eye. I knew better than to give food directly to a patient, and handed the box to Umm Asma.

"This is candy. It's called jelly beans."

Asma's curiosity peaked and her protests simmered down. Umm Asma breathed a sigh of relief as calm descended. She mumbled something to Asma and quickly rushed to ask the nurse if jelly beans were okay.

After that, Asma knew that if she went for physical therapy, she could have her choice of jelly beans. Never in her five years of life had she ever eaten a jelly bean until she came to America. Now she couldn't get enough of them. She delighted in finding new flavors every time, and winced at something unexpected like cappuccino or licorice. She had a mental list of her favorite flavors, which included cherry and marshmallow. She even saved the speckled green ones for her grandpa across the ocean, who loved watermelon.

One day, a small, dark-haired man dropped by Asma's room. He wore blue-rimmed glasses and a white coat that swallowed his narrow frame and almost swept the floor. He was the pediatric palliative care expert. His wiry stature belied his larger-than-life reputation. He was usually flanked by medical students eager to observe him in action. This time, though, there were no students, just a medical interpreter.

Things had taken a turn for the worse, and Asma's body was rejecting the latest stem cell transplant. It necessitated him to have The Conversation with Umm Asma. As her chaplain, I had been asked to join them to "bridge the cultural gap." Not being Arab, I felt like an impostor, as it seemed the interpreter was culturally better equipped. But in spite of the language barrier, I had come to know and love the family. I knew I had to be there, if only to provide moral and spiritual support.

"It's the merciful way," the palliative doctor said of the DNR (do not resuscitate) order. He placed the paperwork on the tray, urging Umm Asma to sign it. "CPR is painful and unnecessary torture," he said, looking sympathetically at Asma's pale sleeping figure. "If you don't sign, and your little one stops breathing . . . or her heart stops beating . . . they will do CPR. The agony of chest compressions will cause more pain than even the anesthesia and the respirator can alleviate." The interpreter translated her words to Umm Asma in quick fluent Arabic that rolled off her tongue.

"Think about it," the doctor said, straightening up. "Ask yourself what a beautiful death would look like. What does your religion say about death?" He glanced over at me as if expecting an answer.

Umm Asma's forehead creased, processing what the doctor was saying. The transplant specialist had told her that there were other options, a series of steps they could take, albeit increasing in risk. Yet the team had seemed hopeful—and she had faith that Asma was a fighter. They had *not* said that Asma was dying. She asked a series of questions through the interpreter. "Are you saying there isn't hope anymore?" "Why else would you consider not resuscitating my baby?" "And if there isn't hope, why don't you send us home?"

The doctor did not have easy answers that day. He left after Umm Asma signed the DNR but not before tears were shed. Umm Asma looked to me for support. I read her the first verse that came to mind: "And when thou art resolved, trust in God; truly God loves those who trust."[1]

In later conversations, I came to understand the cultural factors that added to Umm Asma's confusion that day. If she were back home, she would not be burdened with difficult decisions and having paperwork in legal jargon to sign. Back home, she would have only sweet Asma to attend to. These other matters her husband and father would handle, as making difficult decisions was traditionally the burden and responsibility of the menfolk. And the heartbreaking medical decisions were entrusted to the doctor, not the family. It was simple to a fault. If the doctor back home said, "Take the patient home, feed them whatever they want and make them comfortable," it meant that the patient was dying and this was the will of God. In America, if the doctor said, "We have to take the patient off life support," the family would also trust the doctor's judgment. This too, would be the will of God.

Asma was moved to the pediatric intensive care unit (PICU) in the fall. In the PCICU, her window would have been bathed by the bright red and orange hues from the maple trees outside. But not in the PICU. All the other ICUs in the hospital were windowless, timeless capsules, with no sense of day or night.

The call from the embassy came a few weeks after Umm Asma had signed the DNR. The embassy informed the director of global patient services that it was their mandate that as long as the patient was under their sponsorship, they would have to pursue remedial treatment. Asma's father, who was back home, called the family liaison the minute the embassy opened the next day and spoke to him, *pleading* for an exception that would allow his child to die peacefully without futile medical intervention. The family had made their peace with the DNR and prepared themselves. But his pleas did not budge the official; in fact, it only made him more adamant. The embassy had already invested in many months of treatment. As long as the patient was on American soil, they had to exhaust every possible avenue. That was their policy. "Giving up" was not an option.

Umm Asma had no choice but to rescind the DNR or assume all of the medical costs.

Wealth and children are the adornment of the life of this world, but that which endures—righteous deeds—are better in reward with thy Lord, and better [as a source of] hope.[2]

I visited Umm Asma shortly before her daughter's passing. The ominous silence of the PICU greeted me as I entered, broken only by the incessant beeping of the monitors and whirring of machines that kept Asma's frail organs functioning. The quick steps of the nursing staff and the murmur of conversation broke the monotony. It seemed like a lifetime had passed since I had joined her and the palliative care doctor.

Umm Asma was witness to Asma's dying days like a captive spectator watching a tragedy playing out on stage—unable to intervene and yet unable to walk out of the theater. Asma's drained little body was too weak from having fought for almost a year.

The day I visited, Umm Asma had Qur'an recitation playing on the bedside player, its soothing melody embracing the room like a blanket. As I approached, she looked up from her prayer book with weary eyes. Self-conscious, she tried to smooth out her black abaya, crumpled from the sleepless nights in the bedside chair. Her gray headscarf was stained with tears. Her sunken face and red eyes told the story of her grief.

In her halting English, she told me she remembered the palliative care doctor's words about making death beautiful. Her mind tormented her with thoughts of what a peaceful ending would have been if the embassy had allowed it. Would she have been able to see Asma's smile once more, and let her choose her last courage bead? Would Asma have been able to say goodbye to her grandpa and grandma? All these regrets consumed Umm Asma, and ultimately, this choice she was given—which she originally did not want to make—was stolen from her.

She started crying, and I struggled to respond. How I yearned to alleviate her pain and comfort her with some profound insight, to tell her that God had a greater plan and that heaven was waiting for Asma. However, I knew in the back of my mind that those words would be of little comfort when faced with unimaginable loss. I could hear the reassuring words of my CPE supervisor, "Why the need for words of wisdom? This is the worst time of their life. Nothing you say can change that."

With that weight lifted from me to speak, I reached out and embraced Umm Asma—absorbing her quiet sobbing, feeling the heaviness of the past year weighing on her trembling body, and imagining her roller coaster of hurt and hope. We sat together in silence, accompanied by the perpetual whirring of Asma's ventilator.

———◆———

Asma's last moments were surrounded by blurred figures in blue and white rushing about the room during a code, her mother squeezed out of the room, teary-eyed. Umm Asma was unwilling to see the crushing jolts on her baby's frame as they did CPR, reluctant to hear the sounds of the AED paddles being charged up and to see her limp body jump as it was shocked. Sobbing, she walked away with nowhere to go . . . the soft refrains of Surah al-Mulk still playing softly behind her.

———◆———

Some think of life and death as absolute, independent realities—as we pass through a door from one realm to another, we close the door behind us. I look upon them as two worlds with a porous edge. While we move from one domain to the next, we still leave fragments of our life in the world we left behind. The young lives that leave us are like skipping stones—leaving ripples in a pond that slowly fade toward the shore. Some stones skip more than others, teasing their loved ones who try to catch them. Like the stones, these young lives skim the surface of eternity for a brief moment, then are engulfed by the water, leaving behind ripples in the pond to caress those who loved them—daring them to forget they existed, as they hold on to treasured memories of their short lives.

The care teams who were like family to Asma—the doctors, nurses, teachers, and interpreters in the PCICU where she spent many months, and the staff of the PICU where she spent her final days—were shaken and devastated by Asma's passing. It wasn't often that a pediatric patient so ill did not have a DNR. "Do no harm" was part of their code of ethics.

Asma's colorful finger paintings were still up in the PCICU hallway—drawings of sunny days and little stick figures, a reminder of a life worlds away. The chaplain's office created a memory board for Asma—a small memorial of a little girl who had stolen our hearts with her cheeky grin and squeals of delight. The staff filled it with their last farewells, highlighted by red hearts and little angels. At the next staff meeting, the unit chaplain led a moment of silence to commemorate Asma—helping the team process their grief and find closure in the tragic loss of her life.

———◆———

Umm Asma was not around to see the memory board or the goodbyes for Asma. She had flown home the very next day, overwhelmed by grief. In the outside pocket of her purse was a small box of speckled green jelly beans and a bracelet of brightly colored glass beads.

> *"Goodbyes are only for those who love with their eyes. Because for those who love with heart and soul there is no such thing as separation. Death has nothing to do with going away. The sun sets. The moon sets. But they are not gone."*

—Rumi

Notes

1. Âl ʿImrân/3:159.
2. al-Kahf/18:46.

Ziyara Spiritual Care

International Effort for Spiritual Support and Human Connection

KAMAL ABU-SHAMSIEH, WITH SAKINAH ALHABSHI
AND TAQWA SURAPATI

Background

IN SPRING 1972, I wandered through the dark covered *sûq* (market) in Hebron, also known as Al-Khalil, named after Prophet Ibrâhîm. I was only

---

Dr. Kamal Abu-Shamsieh is assistant professor of Practical Theology and director of the Interreligious Chaplaincy Program at the Graduate Theological Union. The founder and codirector of Ziyara Muslim Spiritual Care, he has extensive international experience as a trainer for spiritual care providers and has served since 2012 as a relief chaplain at Stanford Hospital and Clinics. A graduate of Hartford Seminary's Islamic Chaplaincy Program, he completed four units of Clinical Pastoral Eduation (CPE), a PhD in Practical Theology and Islamic Studies (with a focus on chaplaincy) at the Graduate Theological Union, and a certificate in Palliative Care Chaplaincy from California State University. Kamal is a founding member of the Association of Muslim Chaplains. He was born in Palestine and currently lives in California with his wife and their three sons.

Sakinah Alhabshi was born and raised in the coastal town of Kuantan, Malaysia. She attended Northwestern University for undergraduate studies in engineering, and later continued her education with an advanced diploma in Islamic Studies at Arees University, Malaysia, alongside other classes in traditional Islamic sciences. Sakinah completed six units of CPE. She is currently a chaplain at Stanford Health Care, a candidate at the Graduate Theological Union for an MA in Islamic Studies and the Interreligious Chaplaincy program, and on the board of Ziyara Spiritual Care. Sakinah finds rest and rejuvenation in nature, especially near large bodies of water, and enjoys cooking for others and cloud-gazing.

Taqwa Surapati's biographical information appears with her own essay in chapter 19.

---

five years old and trying to find my way to the *Haram Ibrâhîmi* (Mosque of the Tomb of the Patriarch). "On your mark! Get set . . ." I said as I calmed myself while wiping my tears. Why wouldn't I cry? I was the youngest of seven siblings, and today was the funeral of my eldest sister, Najah. All I wanted was to see her and say goodbye. The alleys became darker, and I felt lost. I traced my footsteps back and decided to walk to the cemetery, hoping to have a glimpse of my sister before the burial. There were two adjacent cemeteries, 500 feet apart, and my luck led me to the wrong cemetery on that heavy day. Tired and sad, I walked between the graves looking for my sister. Eventually, I returned to my grandfather's home, where no one had even noticed I was gone. My family lived in Ramallah, and instead of the original plan to attend my uncle's wedding today, we had a funeral.

Najah was like a second mother to me. She would often bring me treats on her way back from school, or she would give me money and ask me to go to the nearby store to buy treats for both of us. However, in the weeks and months that followed her death, no one talked to me about what happened. I heard she died of food poisoning, so I thought I bought the expired food that ultimately killed her. I carried the pain and guilt for forty-four years until I was trained as an end-of-life chaplain and dared to talk about it with my mother. I was attending a conference in South Africa when my brother Hani called to inform me that our mother had suffered a stroke. I changed my itinerary, flew to Jordan, crossed the West Bank borders, and visited my parents. My recovering mother and I sat on the veranda, enjoying the warmth of a sunny autumn day while sipping tea with sage. I finally gathered the courage to ask the question that had been brewing inside me for decades: "Tell me about Najah." My mother was visibly uncomfortable and tried to deflect the question. Eventually, she started sharing how she lost her teenage daughter. Then she said, "On the day before she died, you and I traveled to Hebron. Your sister and father were supposed to follow us the next day." I interrupted and said I was with my sister in Ramallah, but my mother insisted I had been with her.

This assurance of my mother lifted the burden of an inaccurate memory I carried for decades. I broke down in tears and shared with my mother my experience of going to the wrong cemetery on the day of the funeral. My grief-stricken mother blamed herself for neglecting to care for her youngest. She sobbed, and we hugged.

The personal and painful experience I experienced was not unique. Families rarely talk about death, especially with children. People grieve alone and silently. The compound impact of losing my sister and carrying the pain alone for so long prompted me to create space for families to talk about end-of-life. This gave birth to the establishment of Ziyara Spiritual Care, a nonprofit organization, to provide spiritual care and train professionals in end-of-life care worldwide.

Models of Islamic spiritual care have existed throughout history as both a professional service and as part of our community over the generations. During the reign of Caliph ʿUmar ibn al-Khattâb, a *waqf* (endowment) was created to offer spiritual care to patients and the wayfarer. These services offered solace to patients through "chaplain" visits to chant *dhikr* and recite Qurʾan; having a melodic voice was a requirement for these spiritual providers. Also, the two night-shift "chaplains" would stand behind a curtain where a patient could hear but not see them, and spread words of motivation and news that this patient was recovering well and would go home soon. My goal for Ziyara Spiritual Care involved continuing this Islamic tradition of visiting the sick, with a focus on specialty training of formal assessment and intentional intervention.

The Global Journey

In January 2013, the Federation of Islamic Medical Association (FIMA) organized an international conference on spiritual care in Riyadh, Saudi Arabia. Muslim chaplains from England, Africa, and the United States and FIMA physicians from more than forty-two countries including the United States joined hundreds of Saudi *murshid*s (religious guides) in discussion, unearthing a lack of knowledge and some tension among physicians regarding the role and function of chaplains. I met with physicians from Malaysia, Pakistan, and South Africa, among others, who were eager to learn from a U.S.-trained chaplain to introduce professional spiritual care to their communities. Little did I realize that I would return to Saudi Arabia under the banner of Ziyara two years later to train their *murshid*s. Two weeks after this conference, Dr. Ishak Masud invited me to visit Malaysia for a spiritual care conference in June 2013. This invitation ignited an international interest that was unmatched.

Ziyara's international presence began with a number of annual and semi-annual visits to Malaysia and Indonesia between 2013 and 2020. Invitations to organize spiritual care training globally took Ziyara to Pakistan (2014 and 2018), South Africa (2013), Oman (2017), Saudi Arabia (2013, 2014, 2015, 2019), Jordan (2016 and 2017), Germany (2017), Abu-Dhabi (2015 and 2017), and Turkey (2018 and 2019). The spiritual care training ranged from offering a few presentations on connecting spiritual care and chaplaincy to Islamic normative texts and introducing spiritual care concepts such as mercy, empathy, compassion, and service leadership, to holding intensive multi-day seminars and clinical practice.

Ziyara in Malaysia

Malaysian healthcare providers welcomed spiritual care as they understand well the interconnectivity of the mind, body, and soul in healing; spiritual soul care was the missing piece in the care for patients. Dr. Ishak, a physician trained in Australia and England, was aware of the work of chaplains in Western healthcare contexts. He launched a campaign for *Hospital Mesra Ibadah*, a worship-friendly initiative, and encouraged the Malaysian Ministry of Health to hire dozens of *ustâdhs* (religious guides) to offer spiritual care in Malaysian hospitals. However, the *ustâdhs* were not trained in clinical settings and limited the scope of spiritual care services to teaching patients how to pray or offering supplications. In fact, nurses were required to wake up patients to perform the daily prayers on time, especially *Fajr* (morning) prayer, and record in the medical records and notify the *ustâdh* if someone wasn't waking up. Dr. Ishak felt combining Ziyara's Islamic foundation of care with the North American approach to spiritual care would offer a more skillful and intentional patient-centered presence at the bedside. He offered Ziyara a ten-minute slot at a national healthcare conference to speak on spiritual care. Those ten minutes led to twenty, and then thirty, and eventually opened the door for invitations to speak at hospitals across Kuala Lumpur in subsequent years. Ziyara engaged with physicians, nurses, counselors, chaplains, hospital administrators, and Ministry of Health representatives.

Ziyara considered its efforts in Malaysia a pilot for introducing spiritual care globally. In 2015, Ziyara introduced spiritual care clinical rounds where Malaysian chaplains visited patients in different clinical settings. Hospital Sungai Buloh hosted Ziyara for a two-day intensive seminar. In 2016, University Malaya Medical Center hosted a three-day intensive seminar that included twenty-four-hour on-call chaplaincy training over the seminar, the first of its kind in any Muslim-majority country.

Students were taught to chart spiritual care notes and work alongside other interdisciplinary care team members. In clinical rounds, four groups of students consisting of two men and two women chaplains participated in supervised visits to patients. In the initial stages of training, chaplains stood in the middle of the room and talked to patients while standing, somewhat awkwardly. They offered generic prayers, and the visit lacked the intimacy of deep listening, compassionate comforting, or active presence. Ziyara demonstrated how to visit and where to sit, use of physical touch appropriate for their cultural context, questions to ask or not ask, spiritual assessment, and responding to spiritual care needs. The deeper connection resonated for both the patients and the student-chaplains. However, after several follow-up visits to Malaysia, I realized the student-chaplains were not consistent in applying the given skills. Ziyara needed a paradigm shift! One idea was to recruit qualified Malaysian chaplains to come to the United States to study and train. Another idea was unprecedented—to offer a complete course in Clinical Pastoral Education (CPE) in Malaysia.

Ziyara achieved its first goal in March 2018 by recruiting Sakinah Alhabshi. Sakinah understood the Malaysian context, a multicultural country with a diverse ethnic and religious population, of which approximately 60 percent are Muslim, 20 percent Buddhist, 10 percent Christian, and 6 percent Hindu. Sakinah, a former corporate oil and gas consultant, had left her career to focus on her formal Islamic education, volunteer work with disaster relief and hospice, as well as to spend more time with her parents, especially following her father's dementia diagnosis. The more she connected spiritual care to her personal life, it became clear that professional chaplaincy was the perfect path that aligned with her passion and interest. Sakinah proved instrumental in setting up Ziyara's engagement with the Malaysian Ministry of Health, alongside the National Palliative Care Taskforce, as well as with multiple universities and teaching hospitals in Malaysia. Her father and grandfather's unfortunate deaths later in 2018 led her to apply to CPE residency programs in the United States. Sakinah eventually chose Stanford Health Care in California, where she continued beyond her residency into a fellowship, alongside her graduate studies at the Graduate Theological Union in Berkeley.

Clinical Pastoral Education in Malaysia

In parallel, the next significant phase for Ziyara was the Malaysian Minister of Health acknowledging the need to step up professional training and certification of spiritual care providers in healthcare institutions. Through a mini-grant from the Association for Clinical Pastoral Education (ACPE), Ziyara partnered with the Clinical Pastoral Education of Central California (CPECC), Universiti Teknologi Mara in Kuala Lumpur, and the International Islamic University Malaysia to launch the first international ACPE-accredited spiritual care training in Malaysia.

Dr. Diana Katiman, a palliative care physician in Malaysia, assembled a task force and started reaching out to medical institutions to train their staff. In California, Ziyara recruited Rev. Rod Seeger, a retired chaplain supervisor, to lead a half-unit of intensive CPE. The six-week program brought together six men and six women physicians, nurses, chaplains, and counselors from six hospitals. The half-unit CPE ran from February through April 2020, just as the COVID-19 global pandemic began. The CPE students and supervisor met in person for the first half of the program and conducted the reflection sessions virtually for the remaining half of the program.

The Ziyara program was the first clinical chaplaincy training in a Muslim-majority country and the second of its kind in the Asia Pacific region. Malaysian Christian faith leaders historically received clinical training through the Association of Hong Kong Hospital Christian Chaplaincy Ministry. The limited number of ACPE educators who are competent in Islam, culturally and religiously, the limited financial resources, and the nuances of navigating religious diversity in Malaysia were among the challenges that Ziyara encountered in this half-unit CPE program, yet the intention to continue has remained.

The involvement of Ziyara in Malaysia included a simultaneous engagement in neighboring Indonesia. With the help of Dr. Ishak, Ziyara connected with the Indonesian Muslim Medical Association. Ziyara traveled to Makassar, Bandung, Jakarta, and Banda Aceh to introduce spiritual care in healthcare settings. In a workshop on end-of-life in Jakarta, the audience was asked, "Would you consider the experience of a practicing Muslim who was incommunicative and unable to recite *shahâdah* (attestation of faith)[1] prior to dying, a good death?" The audience's unanimous response that it couldn't be a good death was astonishing. Imagine the disappointment of the bereaved family to learn that not only did their loved one die but that the experience wasn't a good ending. It became apparent there was a need to partner with religious clerics to reexamine some religious texts that lead to widespread misunderstanding on how to achieve *husn al-khâtimah* (a good ending). Ziyara turned to the National Shariah Board of Indonesia and the National Fatwa Commission to endorse its end-of-life model.

In Indonesia, Ziyara needed local links to bridge cultural and linguistic gaps. In 2018, Ziyara recruited Chaplain Taqwa Surapati to its board. Born and educated in Indonesia, Taqwa, who lives in California, began her spiritual care journey as a volunteer, then a co-coordinator for the Muslim Spiritual Care group at Stanford Health Care, before becoming a professional chaplain in 2012. The training of professional chaplains in the United States consists of completing a graduate degree in chaplaincy and a master's degree in religious studies. Taqwa earned an Islamic chaplaincy certificate from Hartford Seminary and completed a master's degree in Islamic studies at the Graduate Theological Union, in addition to five units of CPE. In December 2018, Taqwa,

Sakinah, and I traveled to Indonesia to introduce the Ziyara vision for spiritual care and end-of-life care to the Shariah Board of Indonesia and Majelis Ulama Indonesia. In the end, Indonesia's highest clerical body issued a letter of endorsement certifying Ziyara to train Indonesians in Islamic hospitals across the country. This momentous step gave Ziyara the long-awaited national and international recognition to lead global Islamic chaplaincy.

Bridging the Gap in Indonesia

The visit to Indonesia by the Ziyara team helped create a local advisory committee that consisted of chaplains and physicians. Indonesia is the fourth most populous country, with 272 million people, 87 percent of whom identify as Sunni Muslims. There is a lot of emphasis on studying, living, and practicing Islam in Indonesia. Yet, for specialized care for patients, the focus of spiritual care was on legal-physical-practical matters. How does one perform ablution and pray while sick? What does one say when supplicating in Arabic? There was less emphasis on the heart's emotional and spiritual issues, such as how one connects with God in times of hardship. Caring for the heart was needed with as much local nuance as possible.

The challenge of teaching spiritual care for Muslims in Indonesia is both familiar and foreign. Its familiarity stems from being part of the Indonesian Islamic tradition to visit the sick; however, when spiritual care encompasses one's heart to care for others' hearts, and processing difficult emotions like grief, shame, and anger, suddenly it becomes foreign. Culturally, loss and grief remain private and unspoken. The introduction of spiritual care skills to care for self and others complemented traditional Islamic roles that teach how to perform ablution, prayers, or supplicate when hospitalized.

In December 2018, Ziyara and the Indonesia Islamic Medical Association organized two seminars in Jakarta hospitals. The Ziyara team delivered three-day seminars, each with a full schedule of lectures, role-plays, and active interactions giving an overview of providing spiritual care, patient visits, and integrating with the hospital operational structures. Taqwa, Sakinah, and I accompanied chaplains and demonstrated real-time visits to patients in their hospital rooms, and invited patients to share their feedback with participants.

Taqwa finally had the opportunity to lead workshops in her native language, Bahasa Indonesia. Following the lecture part of the workshops, pediatric and adult patients were being brought into the lecture hall (with their consent), and Taqwa conducted spiritual care visits onstage with them. She demonstrated the dynamics of care to the patients and their loved ones in front of hospital administrations, doctors, nursing staff, and chaplains. In all conversations, she provided presence, asked guided questions, demonstrated spiritual care assessment methods on what is essential for the patients, and explored their worries and hopes. It was very touching to care for Indonesian patients in a way she never had before. Many of them also were touched by the encounters, shedding tears as they told Taqwa their stories.

On the last day, one of the seminar participants asked Taqwa a question, which made her heart jump with both surprise and fear. He asked if she used some aspects of "black magic" in doing spiritual care, seeing how everybody who entered into conversation was moved to tears. She brushed off the comment while emphasizing that she *"mengerahkan seluruh jiwa raga saya"*—utilized all her being and spirit for presence—during those encounters. Bringing this into context, the word "spiritual" has multiple connotations that extend to matters beyond the "seen" world into the realm of the unseen. There are shamans (*dukun, orang pintar*) who may extort money from unsuspecting people facing illness and desperation. This misunderstanding was an important example to the Ziyara team that all training outside of the American context needs to be even more attentive to the local cultural context and engage with chaplains who speak the language, know the cultural background, and can establish trust and connection.

Ziyara in Saudi Arabia

Spiritual care in Saudi Arabia is in its infancy stages. There are hundreds of men and women working as *murshids* (religious guides) in different chaplaincy settings with having religious knowledge being the only requirement. None of the *murshids* had chaplaincy training in clinical settings prior to their encounter with Ziyara. The Saudi Ministries of Health and Defense invited Ziyara to three international conferences to lead spiritual care workshops in Saudi Arabia in Jazan, Riyadh, and Jeddah. Ziyara conducted three-day seminars and accompanied a small group of *murshids* into practical clinical visits in Jazan, Jeddah, Taif, and Riyadh. The Saudi context meant Ziyara needed to conduct the workshops and training in Arabic. Hundreds of Saudi *murshids* attended these seminars. Ziyara called on the conference organizers to include female Saudi *murshids* in the program and clinical rounds. The request was approved and led to having separate rounds for men and women, but it was the first of its kind for female *murshids* in Saudi Arabia. Each visit included coordination with nurses as gatekeepers of patients, and debriefing following each encounter. Like Malaysia and Indonesia, Saudi Arabia's future success depends on a follow-up to support *murshids* as they seek to deepen and apply the chaplaincy skills they acquired.

Ziyara's Model for Spiritual Care

Ziyara prioritizes developing partnerships with palliative care teams in the countries we venture into, as both the patients and clinicians are receptive to this pioneering work. Currently, Ziyara is working with the palliative care physicians affiliated with the Eastern Mediterranean Regional Office of the World Health Organization to advance spiritual care among the palliative care teams in Arab countries.

Ziyara bases its spiritual care model after the example of Prophet Muhammad ﷺ, and specifically his end-of-life experience. Ziyara understands that Prophet Muhammad's mission was mercy for all creation, all humankind, regardless of their faith or practice. The creation of Allah deserves spiritual care that is respectful of religious and ethnic diversity and that honors their dignity and unique needs. As such, we look forward to continuing this journey of supporting healthcare institutions to develop trained chaplains in support of this basic human-soul right.

Chaplaincy helped me recognize that every death experience is different. I am grateful I was able to help my family in Palestine make end-of-life decisions. The communication I had with my siblings led to arranging palliative care for our mother at home until her death in August 2017. Also, in 2020, I listened as my youngest brother, Raed, who was battling an aggressive form of B-cell lymphoma, shared his wishes not to have additional surgeries or intrusive interventions in the last weeks of life. On the day he died, our family honored his wishes and didn't transfer him to the intensive care unit. Instead, my family gathered around his bed, prayed, and comforted each other. This personal and professional journey of vulnerable souls that meet in the comfort of God's closeness and bountiful mercy creates human connections of love among caregivers and patients alike.

Note

1. Muslims encourage the actively dying to recite part of the *shahâdah* ("There is only one God"), if alert and oriented. If they are unable, the family may recite the *shahâdah* for them.

Epilogue

We Are Not Competitors, We Are Companions

SOHAIB N. SULTAN

MY BELOVED BROTHERS and sisters, as I sit down to write this epilogue, I do so with the expectation of only having a few more months to live. Therefore, I address you from this very distinct perspective.

Beloveds, since this epilogue is also a farewell, I want to emphasize something that I now see more clearly with one foot in the grave, which is that the inner work that we Muslim chaplains must commit ourselves to—the work of refining the heart and soul—is just as fundamental, if not more fundamental, to the success of Islamic chaplaincy in North America as any sort of outward work that we put together. It is only by working together as individuals *and* as a community of chaplains that we can focus on developing hearts of *ikhlâs* (sincerity) and hearts of *mahabbah* (love) for Allah ﷻ, His Messenger ﷺ, the *ummah* (community), and one another.

Sincerity and love, motivated by this inner work, are the pathways of the prophets who accomplished so much in their legacies. They radiated this deep sincerity and love despite the obstacles, trials, and tribulations that they faced. Therefore, as a community of chaplains who strive to follow the Prophetic Way, we must work together to make *tarbiyah*—spiritual and ethical training of the chaplains—a necessary part of everything that we do and offer.

As such, my beloveds, I submit to you this very basic yet essential idea: We are not competitors, we are companions in this journey of serving Allah ﷻ, the Messenger ﷺ, the *ummah*, and humanity at large. This profession of Islamic chaplaincy is not like other professions where people compete for the highest positions, the best paying jobs, the most honorific titles, and the most prestigious awards. Rather, we must aspire to be *awliyâ'* (protecting friends) to one another in the way that the Qur'an so beautifully describes:

> And the believing men and the believing women are protecting friends [*awliyâ'*] of one another, enjoining right and correcting wrong, performing the prayer, giving the alms, and obeying God and His Messenger. They are those upon whom God will have Mercy. Truly God is Mighty, Wise. God has promised the believing men and the believing women Gardens with rivers running below, to abide therein, and goodly dwellings in the Gardens of Eden. And Contentment from God is greater; that is the great triumph![1]

So, we protect each other, we counsel each other, and we are sincere in the *nasîhah* (good advice) that we offer each other. Your success is deeply tied to my success, and my success is deeply tied to your success, and our collective success is deeply tied to the success of the *ummah* of the Prophet ﷺ. Therefore, our spirit of togetherness must be of deep sisterhood and brotherhood and of truly loving for each other what we love for ourselves.

Our goal for Islamic chaplaincy in North America must not be limited to the life of this world. Rather, our aspiration must be to be together in the highest places of Paradise, drinking from the hand of our noble Messenger Muhammad ﷺ a drink from the river of *al-Kawthar* that will quench our thirst forever. Our goal must be to gaze upon our Guardian-Lord with contentment and for our Guardian-Lord to gaze upon us with contentment forever.

We are not competitors. We are companions. We are lovers for the sake of Allah ﷻ. We are tied together not by our profession but by our faith. We are tied together not by our distinct titles but by our most beautiful title—we are *Muslimîn*, we are submitters to the will of Allah. At the end of the day, if our priority is not submitting to God, then I fear that our work may become the work of the ego, and the work of the ego is ultimately the work of *Shaytân*. God reminds us in the Qur'an that some of the leaders of faith communities unjustly consumed the wealth of the people, and in doing so, turned people away from the path of God. God willing, a commitment to *tarbiyah* will protect us from following in those ways. We seek God's protection and mercy, for Allah is our *Walî* (Protector).

So, what must we do then? We must focus on the spiritual and ethical development of the chaplains. We must prioritize the development of our hearts and our characters for our own sake and standing before God, yes, but also for the sake of those we seek sincerely to serve.

Therefore, my advice to the community of Muslim chaplains in North America is that we should identify a sagacious group of experienced teachers of diverse backgrounds who serve as models and mentors to all the chaplains. These mentors, who can be considered the chaplains' chaplain, should be freely available to the community of chaplains to offer counsel, classes, and cultivation of character. The mentors can play an active and engaging role in weekend retreats where chaplains have an opportunity to look inward and to develop the right spiritual tools to strengthen themselves for the road ahead.

Speaking of retreats, I strongly encourage the community of chaplains to organize for themselves at least one spirituality retreat every year where the focus is on (re)connecting with Allah ﷻ and the way of the Noble Messenger ﷺ and, just as importantly, with each other. Developing a strong culture of *suhbah* (companionship) where we learn to trust each other and to see the best in each other, despite our differences and different approaches, will be key to realizing the idea and ideal that we are not competitors, we are companions. If we are to be individually and collectively successful, then we must rely on each other for advice and mentorship. The overall culture of autonomy disrupts the cohesiveness of the field of Islamic chaplaincy; rather, we ought to seek a culture of fellowship organized by key common principles. This is not to take agency away from the individual chaplains nor to deprive us of one of our greatest gifts, which is creativity. The goal of creating a culture of *suhbah* is to be able to have important and sensitive conversations about our field while holding good opinions about each other and the gifts we individually have to offer.

So, beloveds, in conclusion, if it is true, by God's decree, that I am among the first of you to pass from this world into the Hereafter, I will be praying for you from the *barzakh* and cheering you on.[2] And please know that I will eagerly await your goodly company when the time of reunification is decreed. I will be waiting on the other side of the ocean to greet you at the place where the angels sing *salâmun alaykum* upon the Believers.[3] For now, I leave you with the prophetic greeting: *as-salâmu ʿalaykum wa-rahmatullâhi wa-barakâtuhu.*

Chaplain Imam Sohaib Sultan
March 10, 2021

Notes

1. al-Tawbah/9:71–72, author's translation.
2. The liminal state where souls dwell before the final judgment. The isthmus between the *dunyâ* (the temporal world) and the *âkhirah* (the everlasting reality).
3. al-Nahl/16:32.

ACKNOWLEDGMENTS

"Whoever does not thank people has not thanked Allah."
—*Prophetic Hadith, Sunan Abī Dāwūd 4811*

AS FOUR CHAPLAINS without previous publishing experience, this book would not have been possible without the enthusiastic and generous support of many along the way. Our deepest gratitude is extended to Dr. Lucinda Mosher and Dr. Cheryl Giles, who graciously shared their experiences. Similarly, Dr. Carrie York Al-Karam, editor of *Islamically Integrated Psychotherapy*, was tremendously supportive, especially her reminders that sometimes on the publishing journey, it is important to fast and pray *istkihârah* to ensure that you remain on the *sirâtal-mustaqîm*. Dr. Ingrid Mattson also provided support and encouragement for the project, and Dr. Timur Yuskaev's early conceptual help was most beneficial. We deeply appreciate Dr. Seyyed Hossein Nasr for the complimentary use of *The Study Quran* for translation purposes.

Dear colleagues and friends of ours and of our authors have supported the book in many ways, including reading our essays in advance and providing helpful feedback. In this regard, our editorial team feels especially grateful to Chaplains Khurram Ahmed, Shareda Hosein, Ibrahim J. Long, Leenah Safi, Seher Siddiqee, and our beloved Sohaib Sultan. We are also grateful to the friends who have been in conversation with us along the way, particularly Dr. Nancy Khalil, Dr. Kameelah Mu'Min Rashad, Munir Shaikh, Dr. Shawkat Toorawa, and our spouses and families—without their generosity in supporting us with childcare, cooking, and companionship, editing this book would not have been possible.

While this project was not an undertaking of the Association of Muslim Chaplains (AMC), it would not have been possible without AMC. AMC was invaluable for connecting with contributors, but additionally much of the depth present in these essays is the result of the fellowship that AMC has fostered among members, allowing them to explore, test, and refine their practical theologies over the past decade.

We thank our authors: your willingness to collaborate with us as we tried to tell the story of Islamic chaplaincy through your essays has been a blessing. Please forgive us for our shortcomings.

We thank the teams at Templeton Press and Westchester Publishing Services for providing a generous platform. Your patience, support, and collective wisdom throughout this process cannot be overstated by this humbled and grateful editorial team.

Most importantly, God, our Sustainer, makes what feels like the impossible possible through His Grace and Limitless Generosity. All praise and thanks are due to Him, The Compassionate, The Merciful. *Al-hamdu lillâh.*

INDEX